W9-BBF-344

DATE DUE

Tennessee Folk Culture

Tennessee

Folk Culture

An Annotated Bibliography
by Eleanor E. Goehring

THE UNIVERSITY OF TENNESSEE PRESS

KNOXVILLE

**Library of Congress Cataloging in Publica-
tion Data**

Goehring, Eleanor, 1904–
   Tennessee folk culture.

   Includes index.
   1. Folklore—Tennessee—Bibliography.
2. Tennessee—Social life and customs—Bibliography.
I. Title.
Z5984.U6G63 [GR110.T4]   016.390′09768
81–16036   ISBN 0–87049–344–2   AACR2

TO THE MEMORY OF *Norbert F. Riedl* WHO SUGGESTED THIS PROJECT

Contents

Foreword *by Herbert Halpert*

Not only folklorists and Tennesseans, but all students of American life will welcome this excellent, annotated bibliography of Tennessee folk culture. It is impressive for its breadth of concept, the range of topics covered, and the sheer bulk and variety of published sources included.

Yet the term "folk culture" in the title may be misleading and may require some explanation. Anyone who expects primarily a bibliography of folklore will see from the table of contents that while folkloristic topics are indeed covered in depth in the latter half of this work, they are treated in fewer than ten of its 24 sections. If on the other hand the reader is *au courant* with the jargon currently fashionable in American folklore circles, he will look in vain in this bibliography for such modish terms as "folklife," "folklore and folklife," "folklife research," or "folklife studies."

All of these terms derive from the Swedish words, *Volksliv* and *Volkslivsforskning*. The latter refers to the academic discipline of folklife research, which originated in Sweden in 1909. It is the Scandinavian form of the discipline that has become the popular scholarly bandwagon, first in most of the British Isles, including Northern Ireland, and within the last 25 years or so in the United States as well.

The word *Volksliv* was consciously modelled on the German word *Volkskunde*. Although the word itself dates from the beginning of the nineteenth century, *Volkskunde* as a study began somewhat later; but it has been pursued vigorously in German-speaking countries since then.

In his learned article on "Volkskunde" in Volume 1 of the *International Dictionary of Regional European Ethnology and Folklore*,[1] Åke Hultkrantz says that the word was created in 1806-1808, and he also notes that the term "was apparently the model for the English term *folklore* created by [W.J.] Thoms in 1846." (I might interject here that Thoms himself does not mention this.) The active use of *Volkskunde* as the term for the scientific discipline began in the middle of the century. Hultkrantz remarks that "The definitions of *Volkskunde* are legion" and classifies them under eight types, of which the first is, "*Volkskunde* investigates *folk culture.*"

It is this Germanic discipline of *Volkskunde*, rather than its Scandinavian parallel, *Volkslivsforskning*, that influenced the thinking of the late Norbert F. Riedl, an anthropologist at the University of Tennessee. His interest in *Volkskunde* is set forth clearly in all three[2] of his major articles. Indeed the word itself appears in the title of the paper he first read to his fellow anthropologists at the annual meeting of the American Anthropological Association in December 1964, and then published in the June 1965 issue of the *Tennessee Folklore Society Bulletin*: "Folklore vs. 'Volkskunde': A Plea for More Concern with the Study of American Folk Culture on the Part of Anthropologists."

I shall not discuss in detail Riedl's excellent articles; they deserve analysis by someone thoroughly familiar with studies in the field of *Volkskunde*. This bibliography, however, as its compiler, Eleanor E. Goehring, points out in her

Preface, was part of Riedl's overall vision in "A Plan for the Organization of the Folk Culture of Tennessee." (I shall use the abbreviation, "A Plan," when I cite this article.) She also credits Dr. Riedl with his active, helpful advice on its contents. I assume that an essential part of this advice was to help decide on the subject headings for the different sections. In order to evaluate properly the goals of the bibliography, I shall either quote or refer to a few of Riedl's own statements, though without citing page numbers.

Riedl translates *Volkskunde* as "folk culture research," rather than "folklife research." Although he explains briefly what he means by "folk culture" in all of his articles, I shall cite only the shorter of the two definitions he gives in "A Plan":

> "Folk culture" has been defined in its broadest form as unconscious, unreflective, traditional behavior, the main constituents being: settlement patterns, housing, clothing, speech, folk art, games, tales, song, dance, and [a] wide range of customary behavior in general.

With this definition we have a better idea of what "folk culture" means to Riedl, and particularly what it means in the title of this bibliography.

While this definition establishes some of the principles underlying this bibliography, it is only partly helpful when we look at the comprehensive list of topics given in the table of contents. Most of them are in the definition, from Settlement Patterns to the folkloristic headings. But I, for one, cannot see how such topics as Ethnic Groups, History, Transportation, Travel, and Education derive from the definition. I can only suggest that while Dr. Riedl may have selected some of them from European *Volkskunde* studies, others probably came from his realization that historical conditions in America differed so widely from European ones that these topics were needed to catch the full American cultural record. I would certainly agree that all are essential subjects for a comprehensive record of Tennessee culture. Most of the broad topics in the bibliography would be equally important for any other state that undertakes a survey of its own published record of folk culture or folklife.

One final observation essential for a full appreciation of this bibliography is a comment Riedl makes in his third paper, published in the *Journal of American Folklore*. Speaking of some of the valuable if uncoordinated work of scholars in various disciplines and of "dedicated lay people," he remarks:

> It has often been done out of personal interest and initiative, without help from research institutions and with little chance of finding other than local, or often obscure, outlets for publication. Anyone who has tried to locate such work, or has accidentally stumbled upon it, will agree that this is no exaggeration. One of the first tasks which an organized attempt at the study of American material folk culture will have to undertake will be the finding, screening, and compiling of such contributions from their varied sources.

One needs only to change "American material folk culture" to "all aspects of Tennessee folk culture," to have an excellent description of some of the difficulties involved in the task Miss Goehring undertook.

It is clear that Dr. Riedl regarded this bibliography as a major component of the study of Tennessee folk culture. Just as he wanted the Tennessee survey to serve as a model for other state surveys, so he undoubtedly hoped Eleanor Goehring's bibliography could be used as a pattern for other states to follow. I am going to comment on this work from that perspective, not systematically, yet not quite at random for I have been involved with folklore and regional bibliographies for years. Indeed, I have tried my own hand at a couple of them and used others in a slightly mad attempt to build up a personal English-language library of folk culture; and I have developed some strong convictions on bibliographical matters.

To me a good bibliography must include full bibliographical details, especially what is actually printed on the book's title page, give the number of pages, and preferably be annotated. Often I've searched for years for a promising title found in some unannotated bibliography only to end up with either a trivial pamphlet, or a large book whose contents give the lie to the title. If the book's author uses a pseudonym, most libraries will catalog it under his real name; only the superior library will also list it under the pseudonym. Bookstores that alphabetize by author will usually have it under the pseudonym. The annotation should also mention how the book is illustrated: maps, photos, old prints, local drawings, etc. This is especially important in a folk culture/folklife bibliography. On practically all of these points Miss Goehring gets high marks.

One of the problems faced in undertaking the folk culture bibliography of a state was suggested by Riedl's "A Plan" in his comment that "cultural behavior does not stop at political boundaries." To put it another way, any state as large as Tennessee, which extends from the mountains in the east to the Mississippi River on the west, includes various cultural regions. East Tennessee shares its geography, history, and culture with the other Southern Appalachian states from West Virginia and western Virginia down to northern Georgia, while Tennessee west of the Cumberland River differs completely from the east in all three respects: geography, history, and culture.

These cultural differences were brought home to me years ago when I taught in a college in the Jackson Purchase area of west Kentucky, in a town which, but for the accident of a jog in the state line, would have been in western Tennessee. My folklore students had to read two classic folk-belief collections: Newbell N. Puckett's *Folk Beliefs of the Southern Negro* and Vance Randolph's *Ozark Superstitions*. Most of my West Tennessee students felt at home with Puckett's material but found Randolph completely foreign. My few students from the eastern mountain country had exactly the reverse reaction to these books. Obviously the mountain cultures, Appalachian and Ozark, were related historically, while the settlers of West Tennessee had originally come from the non-mountain South, the area in which Puckett's material was collected, and had bypassed the mountains in their westward migration.

The state is divided, as usual, into its three major regions or Grand Divisions—East, Middle, and West Tennessee—and these are indicated on a map which also clearly outlines and names all of the counties in the state. Such a map is invaluable because county references are so frequent in the literature.

This tripartite cultural division of the state is reflected in the substantial section on History, in which general references are given first, while others are listed in their proper places under East, Middle, and West Tennessee. Such a division is not followed in the section on Settlement Patterns because it has a rather small group of references and also because the titles of most of the works listed name the regions covered quite precisely. I might add that the annotations of books in the History section clearly indicate whether the book is primarily formal history, or if it also includes anecdotes and other material of interest to the folk culture student.

Not surprisingly, the section on Ethnic Groups has subsections on most though not all of the British Isles. In addition to the Scotch-Irish, Irish, and Welsh, there are listings for the German and Swiss, and for Jewish people, as well as for that interesting mixed-blood group, the Melungeons. It is worth observing that several other states have similar mixed-blood enclaves. I find the absence of any writing on the Blacks in Tennessee curious since West Tennessee has a substantial Black population whose folklore is listed in later sections of the book.

That there is no subsection for articles specifically on the English is rather amusing. It is a good example of what is called the ethnocentric predicament: the dominant English felt no need to study themselves. Eleanor Goehring carefully points out, however, in a useful headnote that books in the History section frequently mention the English settlers, and that two standard general books also have discussions of the English in the area. In the same headnote we are told that while the American Indian is not treated specifically in the bibliography, there is much information on Indian and white settler contact, again in books in the section on history, as well as in four other books, which she names, found in other sections.

This use of headnotes to call attention to particular problems and to give references to books in other sections that are pertinent to the topic of the section being presented is an excellent device for integrating the bibliography. If my checking is correct, the compiler has headnotes for six chapters. In a few other sections she gives similar cross references at the end of the section.

A problem faced by the compiler of any bibliography is that some works treat a number of different topics almost equally well. Each title could fit quite appropriately under several different sections, but to repeat each of them might lead to a multi-volume bibliography, which is undesirable. In this book most of such works have been given a single, permanent home. As I have just mentioned, a partial solution has been the liberal use of cross references to books in other sections. A second way of handling this problem is to have a good index, and I look forward to examining the index when this bibliography is published.

A third device, also occasionally adopted here, has been to group such plural reference works either in a complete section by themselves (there are two General sections), or when they belong under one topic, in a subsection labelled "General." The section on Buildings is a good example. Here there are subsections on four major categories, such as Dwellings, Farm and Utility Buildings. These four are preceded by a General subsection, which, as the headnote points out includes the multi-topic volumes. But the compiler also includes a variety of minor topics that would not fit under the other subsections, ranging from pioneer construction and historic sites to the building of riverboats, ferries, and tunnels.

There are only a couple of other points that I shall make when I comment on the folklore sections of the bibliography. I am too unfamiliar with the basic literature of many of the other topics handled in the bibliography, some in quite short sections, to feel competent to evaluate them. Certainly the compiler has found a wealth of references in a variety of unexpected sources. What I will say about these sections is that the annotations got me fascinated in topics very far from my normal interests.

In the quite substantial section on Religion, where I have some knowledge of the literature, the compiler has done an excellent job in presenting the wide range of materials available from frontier camp meetings to snake-handling cults. The section is particularly full on the autobiographies of itinerant ministers, of whom Peter Cartwright is the best known. These autobiographies are valuable sources for life on the frontier, and many of them are rich in anecdote. Histories of the various denominations and of particular churches are also given. Here, as in the other sections of the bibliography, the compiler has located, read, and annotated many doctoral dissertations and master's theses. These are a valuable supplement to the printed literature.

Turning now to folklore: most people are aware that Tennessee is rich in folklore and that much has been published, especially on Tennessee folksongs. Far too many have the stereotype that Tennessee folklore is found only in the mountain country. No one would deny that the mountain people have rich traditions, but what this bibliography amply demonstrates is that Middle and West Tennessee are equally rich. Much of the credit for the collecting and publishing of folklore from all of Tennessee must be given to the members of the Tennessee Folklore Society. The quarterly *Bulletin of the Tennessee Folklore Society* has appeared regularly since 1935 and is still flourishing. The only state folklore society with an older publishing tradition is Texas, whose annual volumes have appeared regularly since 1923.

Although I see the logic of having a separate section on Speech, it is annoying to have other unrelated topics between it and the Folklore sections since proverbs have long been accepted as part of folklore. The first subsection, Speech, includes all aspects of regional language, lists of dialect terms, etc. Then follow Proverbs and Proverbial Sayings, a very small section on Personal Names, and lastly, Place Names. In addition to a wealth of articles and monographs, these subsections include most of the by-now classic American references: H.L. Mencken's *American Language*; works by Archer Taylor and B.J. Whiting under Proverbs; and the books of Henry Gannett, George E. Shankle, and George R. Stewart under Place Names.

On checking the various Folklore sections, again we find most of the major American indexes and organized compilations. For Beliefs and Superstitions, we have Fanny D. Bergen, Wayland D. Hand, and Newbell Niles Puckett. The very long section on Music, Song, and Dance is especially full of the great names: H.M. Belden and A.P. Hudson, B.H. Bronson, T.P. Coffin, G.M. Laws, Jr., H.W. Odum with G.B. Johnson, and N.I. White, all under Ballads and Songs; Dorothy Horne and George Pullen Jackson for Religious Songs; Archie Green, George Korson, and Odum and Johnson, under Work Songs; with D.K. Wilgus under Surveys and Performers. Continuing further, Paul G. Brewster shows up under Customs, and again in Games and Toys; Archer Taylor, Henry C. Bolton, and Thomas W. Talley are listed under Riddles and Rhymes; and E.W. Baughman under Folk Narratives.

I have given this lengthy catalog of authors' names to emphasize an important point. While the "classic" works by these authors may have been included chiefly because they have some Tennessee references, their presence also serves other worthwhile purposes. For the general reader who is not a folklore specialist but may be interested in some special subject, it is helpful to learn what the standard works are in a specific area. But these works also provide the scholarly context in which we can view the folklore collecting done in the state. Norbert F. Riedl wanted a full survey of Tennessee folk culture in the hope that eventually other similar state surveys might make broad comparative studies possible. It is worth observing that at least in many genres of folklore such studies are already possible because of the basic scholarly works cited above.

From the length of the specific Folklore sections, one can get an approximate idea of which folklore genres have had most attention in past years. Proverbs, Riddles and Rhymes, and Games and Toys have attracted fewest Tennessee collectors, and that handful has done most of the work. Superstitions and Beliefs, Customs, Medicine and Home Remedies, and Legends (listed under Folk Narratives) are rather more popular and roughly on a par in the number of collections. Of course, such estimates are crude and might change if one added material from the Folklore-General section and from the major earlier section, General Sources. As one might have guessed from knowing that songs and ballads have been the major focus of American folklorists for nearly a century, the combined song subsections under Music, Song, and Dance, make that section the largest of the Folklore ones. Three of the Music subsections are smaller: Dances and Singing Games, Musical Instruments, and Surveys and Performers. The last is particularly interesting since it includes works on hillbilly/country music. After all, folk tradition continues to operate even under changed circumstances.

Once again the compiler must be applauded for the breadth of sources she has covered: articles in obscure journals as well as the standard ones, theses, all the standard books—it is astonishing how many major folksong collectors have worked in Tennessee—and many less known ones, like the useful pamphlets of the Cooperative Recreation Service. Tennesseans have published much, though apart from articles in the *Tennessee Folklore Society Bulletin*, many good books deserve to be better known: Justus for her fine collection of children's lore; the folksong and play-party song collections of the McDowells; the three major older books by Bell, Ingram, and Miller, all three reprinted, on that fascinating poltergeist miscalled The Bell Witch; and in the final section of the book, Humor and Folk Tales, the almost unknown anecdote collections by Robert Love Taylor, once governor of Tennessee, and by Bert Vincent, who was a Knoxville newspaper columnist.

I have saved for last the longest and most miscellaneous section of the bibliography, section IV, General Sources. This is the part of the bibliography that best shows the great variety of sources the student of folk culture must examine ranging, as the compiler's headnote observes, "from scholarly surveys . . . to personal reminiscences of life as it was." Each of the 130-odd books in this section takes up too many aspects of folk culture to fit into any one subject division; but it is this comprehensiveness that makes them so important. Of these books six are among my favorites and are among the truly great books on southern culture. I shall try to show why I think so.

Two of the finest American books on social history are Harriette Arnow's *Seedtime on the Cumberland* and her *Flowering of the Cumberland*. I think Arnow is a fine novelist, and these two books show the novelist's eye for selecting significant documented details, along with the novelist's skill in organizing and presenting a vivid picture of what life was like in pioneer days.

John C. Campbell was an outsider who lived in the Southern mountains for twenty-five years. In his *The Southern Highlander and His Homeland*, he combines history, geography, and statistics with full quotations from personal interviews to give us a scholarly yet sympathetic picture of mountain people and their life that would be hard to match. He also includes some fine photographs.

Another outlander, Horace Kephart, was an outdoorsman (he wrote a standard book on camping and woodcraft), who lived, hiked, and hunted on the North Carolina side of the mountains. His book, *Our Southern Highlanders*, shows his gift for listening to the speech and observing the culture of the people among whom he lived.

One of the greatest books on pioneer life that I have ever read is F.D. Srygley's book of reminiscences, *Seventy Years in Dixie*. The compiler's annotation of the volume shows the great range of topics on which it gives excellent details, illustrated by awkward but vivid drawings. It is also rich in humorous anecdotes that convey better than sober descriptions the character of life in those days.

The annotation of Emma Bell Miles' *The Spirit of the Mountains* gives the essential facts about what the book covers. She was a Tennessee mountain woman with the ability to present her own culture beautifully. I have treasured my copy of the book for over 35 years, and it is everyone's good fortune that it has been reprinted by the University of Tennessee Press.

I could easily pick out another 30 fine books from this list, books that are excellent and worthy of discussion; but a Foreword is not a book-review column. Let me add a complaint. Dr. Riedl felt important but obscure books should be compiled for the record. Eleanor Goehring has done this admirably. But how does one get hold of some of these locally-published books? My American bookseller found half a dozen of them for me, but came up with no results on ten others. Ironically, she could not locate one that I wanted urgently to help me write this introduction: the volume of essays honoring the memory of Norbert F. Riedl!

When Dr. Riedl persuaded Eleanor Goehring to undertake this bibliography of Tennessee folk culture, I am sure neither of them thought it would take more than 15 years to complete it. But the result is before us and it is a fine one. This bibliography will serve Tennessee for years and is a model that other states might well seek to emulate. Miss Goehring has dedicated it to the memory of Norbert F. Riedl. No one could wish for a finer monument.[3]

Memorial University of Newfoundland
St. John's, Newfoundland, Canada

NOTES

[1]See Åke Hultkrantz, *General Ethnological Concepts* (Copenhagen, 1960), 243–47. Other pertinent articles in that volume are those on Culture, Folk Culture, Folklife, Folklife Research, Folklore, and Regional Ethnology. See also Don Yoder, "The Folklife Studies Movement," *Pennsylvania Folklife*, 13 (1963), 43–56. For a more recent treatment of certain aspects, see Alexander Fenton, "The Scope of Regional Ethnology," *Folk Life*, 11 (1973), 5–14.

[2]See Norbert F. Riedl, "Folklore vs. 'Volkskunde': A Plea for More Concern with the Study of American Folk Culture on the Part of Anthropologists," *Tennessee Folklore Society Bulletin*, 31 (1965), 47–53; Riedl, "A Plan for the Organization of a Statewide Survey of the Folk Culture of Tennessee," *Tennessee Folklore Society Bulletin*, 32 (1966), 67–75; Riedl, "Folklore and the Study of Material Aspects of Folk Culture," *Journal of American Folklore*, 79 (1966), 557–63.

[3]I am indebted to my colleague, G.M. Story, for a critical reading of most of this Foreword.

Preface

This compilation of Tennessee folk culture materials began with the request of Norbert F. Riedl, the late associate professor of anthropology at the University of Tennessee, Knoxville, for such a bibliography. Professor Riedl was intensely interested in encouraging the study of folk culture and folklore in Tennessee and in Southern Appalachia. In his "Plan for the Organization of a Statewide Survey of the Folk Culture of Tennessee" (*Tennessee Folklore Society Bulletin*, XXXII, 1966), he proposed "to compile and synthesize the existing knowledge pertaining to Tennessee folk culture" as one of the basic approaches to his plan. The listing of existing information is the phase of his proposal that I am undertaking in this publication. Before his untimely death, Professor Riedl was generous and helpful with his assistance and advice in determining the contents of this volume.

An effort has been made to assemble as comprehensive a bibliography as possible, covering many aspects of folk culture. In the interest of getting this task completed, I have concentrated on printed materials; also included are many dissertations and theses and some student papers, all available in libraries. Excluded, for the most part, are newspaper articles, regional novels, festival handbooks, museum and restoration projects, and recordings, films, and video tapes—all of which are excellent sources of information.

The following catalogs, indexes, and bibliographies have been checked through 1974: *Subject Index to the National Union Catalog, Catalog of the White Collection* at the Cleveland Public Library, *Vertical File Service Catalog, Social Sciences and Humanities Index, Readers Guide, Index Medicus, Art Index, Music Index, Writings in American History, MLA International Bibliography*, Dundes' *Folklore Theses*, and numerous thesis lists and subject bibliographies. Beyond the basic cutoff date of 1974, a general search continued to uncover items that have been added to this compilation. With very few exceptions, I have examined each item in this bibliography. Quotations in the annotations are taken from the publications themselves.

At various stages in the search, visits have been made to the Berea College Library in Berea, Kentucky; Appalachian State University Library in Boone, North Carolina; Western Kentucky State University Library in Bowling Green; Fisk University, Vanderbilt University, and George Peabody College Libraries in Nashville; the Lawson McGhee Library and the University of Tennessee Libraries in Knoxville. Their courtesies are appreciated. I have corresponded with reference librarians in the Tennessee state universities and in Indiana University, who assisted in the search for theses, and to them I express my thanks.

Some may regret that works on the American Indian have not been included. Much of this material can already be found in Murdock's *Ethnographic Bibliography of North America*, in Haywood's *Bibliography of North American Folklore*, in Sam B. Smith's *Tennessee History, A Bibliography*, and in numerous Tennessee histories and other sources which are listed in Bibliography (Section I). Relations of the Indians with the early settlers are mentioned, however, in a number of titles in this compilation.

Readers may find other areas that do not seem adequately treated. Perhaps later this bibliography can be updated and these areas filled in. Although my search has gone on for about fifteen years, there is still work to be done. This compilation is unique in its coverage at this time, and it is my hope that it will be useful to scholars at all levels and to all who are interested in the subject.

I wish to express my sincere appreciation to many people, named and unnamed, for their assistance in the compilation of this bibliography. To Ann Mitchell and Robert Bassett in the Reference Department, to John Dobson in Special Collections, and to Flossie Wise and Margaret Humphries in Interlibrary Services, all of the University of Tennessee Library, Knoxville.

To Katherine Montague of the Memphis Public Library.

To Marian Shaaban of the Indiana University Library.

To the late Louis T. Iglehart, former director, and Carol Orr, director, of the University of Tennessee Press for their interest and encouragement.

To Lynwood Montell, Charles Wolfe, Ralph Hyde, Linda White, and Kenneth Goldstein for their comments and suggestions.

To Herbert Halpert for his suggestions and for writing the Foreword to this bibliography.

To Linda Lawkins for her careful typing and attention to bibliographical detail.

To Winifred Simmons for all of the work that she has done in searching and checking—and for her wonderful support.

Eleanor E. Goehring

September 1980

I. Bibliography

This current compilation repeats much of the information found in the entries given below. These titles, however, also give a wider coverage, reaching into adjacent geographic areas or into fields such as newspaper articles, regional novels, recordings, and films, which are touched very lightly, if at all, in this volume.

Excellent bibliographies may also be found among subsequent listings such as Ethnic Groups (Section II), M. Slonina, *German Speaking Peoples in Tennessee*; or General Sources (IV), T. G. Clark, *Rampaging Frontier*; or Religion (XIV), C.A. Johnson, *Frontier Camp Meeting*; and others.

Abstracts of Folklore Studies. 13 vols. Austin: Published for American Folklore Society by Univ. of Texas Press, 1963-75.
Helpful abstracts of articles in about 40 international periodicals, listed alphabetically by periodical titles, with an annual index.

Appalachian Bibliography. 3 vols. Morgantown: West Virginia Univ. Library, 1975.
A good annotated bibliography, alphabetized by detailed subjects, which incorporates entries found also in Robert F. Munn's bibliography listed below.

Boggs, Ralph Steele. "Folklore Bibliography." *Southern Folklore Quarterly*, 1938-73 (appeared annually).
A useful bibliography. Compiled by Ralph Steele Boggs, covering the years 1937-59; Americo Paredes, 1960-63; Merle E. Simmons, 1964-72.

Brenni, Vito J. *American English: A Bibliography*. Philadelphia: Univ. of Pennsylvania Press, 1964. 221p.
A good bibliography, partially annotated, with listings by region and state.

Brewton, John E. "Scholarship in Tennessee Folklore." *Tennessee Folklore Society Bulletin*, XX (Dec. 1954), 91-97.
Tells of courses in folklore in Tennessee colleges; faculty research in the field of Tennessee folklore; theses, dissertations, and other contributions to Tennessee folklore scholarship, with a list of masters' theses and Ph.D. dissertations on American folklore.

Center for Southern Folklore. *American Folklore Films and Videotapes: An Index*. Memphis: Center for Southern Folklore, 1976. 338p.
Contains over 1800 titles, and consists of a subject listing, film and video annotations, location of special collections, and title listings and addresses of distributors.

Clark, Thomas D. ed., *Travels in the Old South: A Bibliography*. 3 vols. Norman: Univ. of Oklahoma Press, 1956–59.
Compiled by 12 southern historians, these volumes list over 1,000 travel books covering the years 1527 to 1860. Annotations give the area of the travel accounts and an evaluation of their importance.

———— ed. *Travels in the South: A Bibliography*. 2 vols. Univ. of Oklahoma Press, 1962.
Covers 1865–1955, and includes a number of books on Tennessee.

Coffin, Tristram P. *An Analytical Index to the Journal of American Folklore*, Vols. 1–67, 68, 69, 70. Philadelphia: American Folklore Society, 1958. 384p. (Publications of the American Folklore Society, Bibliographical and Special Series, Vol. VII.)

"Current Bibliography and Discography." *Ethnomusicology*, 1953–.
International bibliography published in three numbers annually. Includes dissertations since Volume XI, 1967.

DeCaro, F.A., and W.K. McNeil, comps. "American Proverb Literature: A Bibliography." *Folklore Forum,* (Dec. 1970), 1–81. (Bibliographic and Special Series, No. 6.)
Annotated.

Dundes, Alan. *Folklore Theses and Dissertations in the United States.* Austin: Univ. of Texas Press, 1976. 610p. (Publications of the American Folklore Society, Bibliographical and Special Series, Vol. 27.)
Arranged by year from 1860 through 1968, with indexes by subjects, authors, and institutions.

Emerson, O.B., and Marion C. Michael, eds. *Southern Literary Culture: A Bibliography of Masters' and Doctors' Theses.* Rev. and enlarged ed. University: Univ. of Alabama Press, 1979. 400p.
Ballads, Folklore, Music, and the Folk Tradition, pp. 226–38.

Harvey, Frank, comp. "Guide to the Folk Culture Material in the Library and Herbarium-Archives of the Great Smoky Mountains National Park Sugarlands Visitor Center." 1972. 43p. Student paper, Riedl Collection, University of Tennessee Library, Knoxville.

Haywood, Charles. *A Bibliography of North American Folklore and Folksong.* 2 vols. 2nd ed. New York: Dover, 1961.
Bibliography on Tennessee, I, 274–77.

Henry, Mellinger Edward. *A Bibliography for the Study of American Folk-Songs With Many Titles of Folk-Songs (And Titles That Have to Do With Folk-Songs) From Other Lands.* London: Mitre Press, 1937. 142p.
"There are listed, besides recent books of folksongs, many reviews and magazine and newspaper articles, all of which should help to make the bibliography of some value to the student."

Illinois Historical Records Survey. *American Imprints Inventory No. 32: A Check List of Tennessee Imprints* *1793–1840.* Chicago: Illinois Historical Records Survey, 1942. Rpt. New York: Kraus Reprint, 1964. 285p.
"Includes holdings of libraries all over the country as well as those in Tennessee." Has a general index.

Jaffe, Harry Joe. "American Negro Folklore: A Check List of Scarce Items." *Southern Folklore Quarterly,* XXXVI (March 1971), 68–70.
Items from Elizabeth Lay Green's "The Negro in Contemporary American Literature," *University of North Carolina Extension Bulletin,* 7 (June 1928), 86–88: Herskovits' *The Myth of the Negro Past;* Dorson's *American Negro Folktales;* Puckett's *Folk Beliefs of the Southern Negro;* "with several items uncovered independently."

Kesner, Richard M. "A Bibliographic Survey of Dissertations Dealing with Appalachia." *Appalachian Journal,* VI (Summer 1979), 277–308.
There are 512 citations, arranged by subject.

Kolasa, Kathryn Marianne. "Food and the Southeastern United States." 1972. 28p. Student paper, Riedl Collection, Univ. of Tennessee Library, Knoxville.
A good annotated bibliography.

Lomax, Alan, and Sidney Robertson Cowell. *American Folk Song and Folk Lore: A Regional Bibliography.* New York: Progressive Education Association, 1942. 59p. (P.E.A. Service Center Pamphlet No. 8.)
A good annotated bibliography.

Luttrell, Laura E., and Pollyanna Creekmore, comps. *Writings on Tennessee Counties.* Nashville: Tennessee Historical Commission, 1944. 50p. Rpt. from *Tennessee Historical Quarterly,* II (Sept. 1943), 257–79; II (Dec. 1943), 336–61; III (March 1944), 81–83.
Lists available material in printed or typewritten form, pertaining to the counties, with certain specified exceptions.

McMillan, James B. *Annotated Bibliography of Southern American English.*

Coral Gables, Fl.: Univ. of Miami Press, 1971. 173p.
> Contains a number of items applicable to Tennessee.

MLA International Bibliography of Books and Articles on the Modern Languages and Literatures. New York: Modern Language Association of America, 1921-.
> The folklore section, expanded in 1970, gives a wide coverage, including material culture.

Munn, Robert F. *The Southern Appalachians: A Bibliography and Guide to Studies*. Morgantown: West Virginia Univ. Library, 1961. 106p.
> Entries have been incorporated in *Appalachian Bibliography*, 1975.

Murdock, George Peter, and Timothy O'Leary. *Ethnographic Bibliography of North America*. 4th ed. 5 vols. New Haven: Human Relation Area Files Press, 1975. (Behavior Science Bibliographies Series.)
> This title has not been checked for this compilation, but it is a good source for materials on the American Indian.

Pochmann, Henry A., comp., and Arthur R. Schultz, ed. *Bibliography of German Culture in America to 1940*. Madison: Univ. of Wisconsin Press, 1953. 483p.
> Contains about a dozen references to Germans in Tennessee.

Ross, Charlotte T., ed. *Bibliography of Southern Appalachia: A Publication of The Appalachian Consortium, Inc.* Boone, N.C.: Appalachian Consortium Press, 1976. 235: 16p.
> Includes books and monographs only.

Scott, Patricia Bell. "Black Folklore in Tennessee: A Working Bibliography." *Tennessee Folklore Society Bulletin*, XLIV (Sept. 1978), 130–33.
> " . . . an attempt has been made to compile a 'working bibliography', the purpose of which is to serve as a starting point for persons interested in Black folklore of Tennessee."

Sealock, Richard B., and Pauline A. Seely. *Bibliography of Place-Name Literature, United States and Canada*. 2nd ed. Chicago: American Library Assoc. 1967. 352p. Updated in *Names*, XVIII (Dec. 1970), 208–22; XX (Dec. 1972), 240–65; XXII (Dec. 1974), 150–64.

Simmons, Merle E. *Folklore Bibliography for 1973*. Bloomington: Indiana Univ., 1975. 175p. (Indiana University Folklore Institute, Monograph Series, Vol. XXVIII.)
> Annotated.

Sioussat, St. George L., ed. "A Preliminary Report Upon the Archives of Tennessee." *Annual Report of the American Historical Association for the Year 1906*. Washington, D.C.: Government Printing Office, 1908. Pp. 197–238.
> A good source of information on early official records.

Smith, Sam B., and Luke H. Banker. *Tennessee History, A Bibliography*. Knoxville: Univ. of Tennessee Press, 1974. 498p.
> A comprehensive bibliography, with an especially helpful listing of Tennessee county histories.

Szwed, John F., Roger D. Abrahams, et al. *Afro-American Folk Culture: An Annotated Bibliography of Materials from North, Central and South America and the West Indies*. 2 vols. Philadelphia: Institute for Study of Human Issues, 1978. (Publications of the American Folklore Society, Bibliographical and Special Series, vols. 31–32.)
> The volumes contain 27 Tennessee references but were received too late to be checked for inclusion in this bibliography.

Tennessee Folklore Society. *Index to the Tennessee Folklore Society Bulletin*. Vols. I-XXXVIII, 1935–72. Murfreesboro: Published by the Society with assistance from Middle Tennessee State University, 1973. 121p.
> Indexed by titles of articles, topics, au-

thors of articles and reviews, authors of books reviewed, records reviewed, and items not indexed elsewhere.

Tennessee Historical Records Survey. *Check List of Tennessee Imprints, 1841–1850.* Nashville: Tennessee Historical Records Survey, 1941. 138p. Rpt. New York: Kraus Reprint, 1964.

"All reported titles, irrespective of locations, are listed." Has a general subject index.

———. *List of Tennessee Imprints, 1793–1840, in Tennessee Libraries.* Nashville: Tennessee Historical Records Survey, 1941. 97p.

"This list consists of 469 entries representing the holdings of 34 separately maintained libraries and 12 private collections." The listing is chronological, with a general index.

Tennessee State Library and Archives, Reference Department. *Writings on Tennessee Counties Available on Interlibrary Loan from the TSLA State Library Division.* Nashville: Tennessee State Library and Archives, 1971. 47p.

Loans are made through library requests only.

United States, Library of Congress. Archive of American Folk Song. *Check-List of Recorded Songs in the English Language in the Archive of American Folk Song to July, 1940.* Alphabetical list with geographical index. Washington, D.C.: Library of Congress, Division of Music, 1942. 3 v. in 1. rpt. New York: Arno Press, 1971.

Checklist for Tennessee, pp. 108–12.

II. Ethnic Groups

Although no effort has been made to include a section on the American Indians, information on their contact with the settlers is given in many of the books listed in History (Section V); and in such books as Arnow's *Seedtime on the Cumberland* and Hale's *Backward Trail*, in General Sources (Section IV). Mahoney's *Cherokee Physician* and Vogel's *American Indian Medicine*, in Medicine (Section XIX), tell of the influence of the Indian in this field.

No specific articles on the English are listed, but the histories (Section V) frequently mention them among the early settlers. Grant's *The Conquest of a Continent* (Section II) and Roosevelt's chapter on "The Spread of the English-Speaking People" in volume one of his *Winning of the West* (Section V) give interesting discussions relative to the English in this area.

General

Grant, Madison. *The Conquest of a Continent: or The Expansion of Races in America.* Rev. ed. New York: Scribner's, 1934. 395p.

"This book is an effort to trace the arrival in the United States of the various elements, both racial and national, constituting its population, and to follow their subsequent spread as well as to make an estimate of their respective numbers."

Hesseltine, W.B. "Tennessee's Invitation to Carpet-Baggers." *East Tennessee Historical Society Publications*, No. 4 (Jan. 1932), 102–15.

The immigration of labor into Tennessee after the Civil War. Includes information about ethnic groups.

Knox, John Ballenger. *The People of Tennessee; A Study of Population Trends*. Knoxville: Univ. of Tennessee Press, 1949. 191p.

The first chapters deal briefly with national origins and racial distribution.

Smith, Earl Jennings. "The Free, Foreign-Born Population of Nashville in the 1850's." Unpubl. Master's thesis, Vanderbilt Univ., 1968. 265p.

"Ireland, Germany, Scotland, and France, in that order were the countries which furnished the most immigrants to Nashville in both 1850 and 1860." Intermarriage, occupations, and literacy are discussed; and lists of names, with place of birth, are given for the 1850 census and 1860 census.

Tracy, Sterling. "The Immigrant Population of Memphis." *West Tennessee Historical Society Papers*, IV (1950), 72–82.

Irish, Germans, English, and Scots and their contributions to the community. "The proportion of the foreign-born to the native white population in Memphis was far greater in 1860 than it was before or since."

United States, Bureau of the Census. *A Century of Population Growth, From the First Census of the United States to the Twelfth, 1790–1900*. Washington, D.C.: Government Printing Office, 1909. 303p.

Gives some population characteristics of Tennessee.

Weeks, Stephen B. "Tennessee: A Discussion on the Sources of Its Population and the Lines of Immigration." *Tennessee Historical Magazine*, II (Dec. 1916), 245–53.

A statistical view of Tennessee population, 1790—1910; original home states, 1850-1910; nationality, 1790; routes traveled by people.

German and Swiss

Allred, Charles E., et al. *How the Swiss Farmers Operate on the Cumberland Plateau*. Knoxville: Dept. of Agricultural Economics and Rural Sociology, Univ. of Agricultural Experiment Station, 1937. 30p. (Monograph No. 33.)

A study of conditions in 1935 "of a group of sixteen farms operated by Swiss farmers near Gruetli, Grundy County, Tennessee."

Buffat, Alfred, and Mrs. Eliza (Bolli) Buffat. "*Reminiscences . . . *Spring Place, Knox County, Tennessee, 1908." 72p. Typed copy in McClung Collection, Lawson McGhee Library, Knoxville.

Reminiscences of Alfred Buffat give an interesting account of a Swiss family who moved to Knoxville in 1849; tells of their way of living, farming, religion, schools, burial, etc.

———— . "Diary of Eliza Buffat (nee Bolli). Spring Place, Knox County, Tennessee; Some events of My Childhood days and Incidents of My Life During the Civil War." Typed copy made by Barbara A. McClung, 1918. Bound with Alfred Buffat's "Reminiscences" (above).

Cooper, Hobart Schofield. "German and Swiss Colonization in Morgan County, Tennessee." Unpubl. Master's thesis, Univ. of Tennessee, Knoxville, 1925. 123p.

History of the settlement, taken largely from manuscript sources and interviews. A good account of the people, their land acquisition, and development of industrial and community life.

Faust, Albert Bernhardt. *The German Element in the United States*. 2 vols. Boston: Houghton Mifflin, 1909.

Volume I contains a chapter on "The German Element in Kentucky and Tennessee" in frontier days.

Fries, Adelaide Lisetta, ed. "Report of the Brethren Abraham Steiner and Friedrich Christian Von Schweinitz of their Journey to the Cherokee Nation and in the Cumberland Settlements in the State of Tennessee from 28th October to 28th December, 1799." *North Carolina Historical Review*, XXI (Oct. 1944), 330–75.

A translation of the diary kept by Abraham Steiner "is of value for the contemporary information it gives as to roads, conditions under which the white settlers lived, and the situation and customs of the Indians." Frequent mention is made of German settlers with whom the travelers stayed.

Hahn, Phyllis Elizabeth. "German Settlers in Nashville, Tennessee." Unpubl. Master's thesis, Vanderbilt Univ., 1935. 132p.

History and biography, giving information on the "part the Germans formed of that ethnic composite which became the population of Nashville, Tennessee, and its immediate environs."

Jackson, Frances Helen. "The German Swiss Settlement at Gruetli, Tennessee." Unpubl. Master's thesis, Vanderbilt Univ., 1933. 70p.

Describes the community life of settlers; agricultural pursuits; devotion to school, church, music, and woodcarving.

Kollmorgen, Walter M. *The German-Swiss in Franklin County, Tennessee: A Study of the Significance of Cultural Considerations in Farming Enterprises.* Washington, D.C.: U.S. Dept. of Agriculture, Bureau of Agricultural Economics, 1940. 113p.

"The agricultural practices of the German-Swiss and of the control groups in Franklin County sustain the belief that cultural backgrounds are extremely significant in farming enterprises."

——— . "Observations on Cultural Islands in Terms of Tennessee Agriculture." *East Tennessee Historical Society Publications*, No. 16 (1944), 65–78.

"Agriculture is definitely tied in with culture and has a basis in tradition and folklore." A consideration of the German-Swiss and Pennsylvania German cultural-agricultural islands in Tennessee and their contribution to Tennessee agriculture.

——— . "A Reconnaissance of Some Cultural-Agricultural Islands in the South." *Economic Geography*, XVII (Oct. 1941), 409–30.

The effect of immigrants of different nationalities on farming methods in Tennes-

see: Germans in Wartburg; Poles in Deer Lodge; Germans and Swiss in Gruetli; Germans in Lawrenceburg.

——— . "Agricultural-Cultural Islands in the South–Part II." *Economic Geography,* XIX (April 1943), 109–17.

(See description above.)

Macpherson, Joseph Tant, Jr. "Nashville's German Element—1850–1870." Unpubl. Master's thesis, Vanderbilt Univ., 1957. 133p.

Particularly useful for information about occupations, secular and religious organizations, and lists of German heads of families in 1850, 1860, and 1870.

Montgomery, James E. "Three Appalachian Communities: Cultural Differentials as They Affect Levels of Living and Population Pressure." Unpubl. Master's thesis, Vanderbilt Univ., 1944. 236p.

Comparison of the Swiss Colony at Gruetli with two other settlements, "to discover whether and to what extent cultural differentials are correlated with levels of living when natural resources are held constant."

——— . "Three Southern Appalachian Communities; An Analysis of Cultural Variables." *Rural Sociology*, XIV (June 1949), 138–48.

Data "developed in the study of three small rural communities in Eastern Tennessee": Browntown, Gruetli, and Bird's. Cross-comparisons of cultural variables in 1943 are shown in charts containing general characteristics, economic behavior, family and kinship behavior, outside contacts, other community folk designs, and integrating and disintegrating forces.

Neskaug, Selmer Reinhart. "Agricultural and Social Aspects of Swiss Settlement in Grundy County, Tennessee." Unpubl. Master's thesis, Univ. of Tennessee, Knoxville, 1936. 184p.

Characteristics of Swiss agriculture in Grundy County: layout of farms, soil resources, fruit and vegetable crops, and livestock. Includes a brief history of the social and religious aspects of the settlement.

O'Connell, Richard B., trans. "Report About and From America, Given from First-hand Observation in the Years 1848 and 1849 and Published for Emigrants" by J.G. Häcker from Chemnitz. *MVC Bulletin,* No. 3 (Fall 1970), 5–74; No. 4 (Spring 1971), 85–118.

Translation of a document originally intended to persuade Germans to settle in Morgan County, near Wartburg, where a German community had been established. "A large part of Häcker's *Report* is devoted to an astonishingly detailed description of the proposed settlement," including projected expenses and income over a seven-year period. Also describes the way of living, farming, and housing of Tennesseans in Morgan County.

Rauchle, Robert. "Biographical Sketches of Prominent Germans in Memphis, Tennessee in the Nineteenth Century." *West Tennessee Historical Society Papers,* XXII (1968), 73–85.

Contains 34 brief biographical sketches, noting contributions to the community.

———. "The Germantown Near Milan, Tennessee." *West Tennessee Historical Society Papers,* XX (1966), 61–76.

An account of German families in and near Milan: their way of life, customs, and contributions to the community.

———. "Social and Cultural Contributions of the German Population in Memphis, Tennessee, 1848-1880." Unpubl. Master's thesis, Univ. of Tennessee, Knoxville, 1964. 101p.

Native customs and traditions perpetuated by German organizations and societies.

Slonina, Maria. "German-Speaking Peoples in Tennessee From Colonial Times to World War I: An Introduction and Bibliography." Unpubl. Master's thesis, Univ. of Tennessee, Knoxville, 1973. 156p.

A good history, with a 66-page bibliography.

Stone, Grace. "Tennessee; Social and Economic." Rpt. from Jan., April, and July issues of *Sewanee Review,* 1938. 44p.

Includes an account of the Swiss colonists in Grundy County.

"Tennessee's Swiss Colony: Fine Cheese and Wine Were Gruetli's Pride." *Tennessee Magazine,* XVII (May 1974), 10–11.

A brief history, and account of the traditional way of living.

White, John Bowman. "The German Christian in Tennessee and Western North Carolina Prior to 1800." Unpubl. Bachelor of Divinity thesis, Vanderbilt Univ., 1932. 103p.

Tells the personal characteristics of German settlers, who were scrupulously practical, good workers, and good farmers: points out anti-war, anti-slavery, anti-alcohol, pro-work, pro-education attitudes.

Wust, Klaus G. *Wartburg: Dream and Reality of the New Germany in Tennessee.* Baltimore: Society for the History of the Germans in Maryland, 1963. 25p.

History of the German settlement and the people who created it.

Irish

Flanagan, James Joseph. "The Irish Element in Nashville, 1810–1890; An Introductory Survey." Unpubl. Master's thesis, Vanderbilt Univ., 1951. 107p.

The number of Irish immigrants, their economic status, occupations, business and industrial leaders, political and military activities, and development of their Catholic churches. (There is nothing about their customs or way of life or influences on folk culture.)

Stanton, William. "The Irish of Memphis." *West Tennessee Historical Society Papers,* VI (1952), 87–118.

Names and contributions of individuals to the city's progress.

Scotch-Irish

Highsaw, Mary Wagner. "A History of Zion Community in Maury County,

1806–1860." *Tennessee Historical Quarterly*, V (March, June, Sept. 1946), 3–34; 11–140; 222–33. (See also Wagner, Mary Church.)

> An account of early Scotch-Irish settlers: church buildings, customs, discipline, education and schools, merchants and merchandising, status and life of slaves, landholdings, and the professions.

McCook, Henry C. "Scotch-Irish Women Pioneers." *The Scotch-Irish in America. Proceedings and Addresses of the Eighth Congress, at Harrisburg, Pa., June 4–7, 1896.* Nashville: Barbee and Smith, Agents, 1897. Pp. 83–94.

> Describes the way of living of Scotch-Irish pioneer women. (There is no mention of Tennessee.)

Park, James. "Pioneer Scotch-Irish Ministers and Teachers in East Tennessee." *The Scotch-Irish in America, Proceedings and Addresses of the Ninth Congress, at Knoxville, Tennessee, June 7–10, 1900.* Nashville: Barbee and Smith, Agents, 1900. Pp. 130–41.

> Five biographical sketches, with mention of numerous individuals who worked as ministers and teachers.

Temple, Oliver. "The Scotch-Irish in East Tennessee." *The Scotch-Irish in America, Proceedings and Addresses of the Third Congress, at Louisville, Kentucky, May 17–19, 1891.* Nashville: Publishing House of the Methodist Episcopal Church, South, 1891. Pp. 160–81.

> "History of Scotch-Irish from their original home in Scotland down to our own times." Gives a brief account of contributions to life in East Tennessee.

Wagner, Mary Church. "The Settlement of Zion Community in Maury County, Tennessee, 1806–1860." Unpubl. Master's thesis, Vanderbilt Univ., 1945. 125p.

> Settlement of the Scotch-Irish Presbyterian community of Zion, and the effect of church discipline.

Jewish

Frank, Fedora S. *Five Families and Eight Young Men, Nashville and Her Jewry 1850–1861.* Nashville: Tennessee Book Co., 1962. 184p.

> The development of the Jewish community in Nashville.

Tennessee Historical Records Survey. *Inventory of the Church and Synagogue Archives of Tennessee. Jewish Congregations.* Nashville: Tennessee Historical Records Survey, 1941. 55p.

> Historical introduction to Jewish settlements, with a brief history of each congregation and the identification and location of records.

Melungeons

Ball, Bonnie S. "America's Mysterious Race." *Read; Pick of the Month's Best Reading*, XVI (May 1944), 64–67.

> The story of the Melungeons.

――――. *The Melungeons (Their Origin and Kin).* Haysie, Va., c1969. 71p.

> A collection of information from various sources about the history and customs of the Melungeons.

――――. "A Vanishing Race." *Mountain Life and Work*, XXXVI (Summer 1960), 39–42. Rpt. Ross County (Ohio) Historical Society, 1960.

> A sketch on the Melungeons.

――――. "Who Are the Melungeons?" *The Southern Literary Messenger*, III (June 1945), 5–7.

> A brief review of the characteristics, customs, and legendary origins of "America's mysterious race."

Barr, Phyllis Cox. "The Melungeons of Newman's Ridge." Unpubl. Master's thesis, East Tennessee State Univ., 1965. 40p.

> A brief history, something about social conditions today, folktales, beliefs, customs, and list of medicinal herbs.

Berry, Brewton. *Almost White.* New York: Macmillan, 1963. 212p.

An inclusive review of the various theories and publications concerning the origin of the Melungeons; tells of their way of living, legends, and customs—such as burial customs, which "were also common practice in many other rural communities in years past."

Bible, Jean Patterson. *Melungeons Yesterday and Today.* Rogersville: East Tennessee Printing Co., 1975. 125p.

The Melungeons are included in this study of Americans of mixed blood.

Burks, Jacqueline Daniel. "The Treatment of the Melungeon in General Literature and Belletristic Works." Unpubl. Master's thesis, Tennessee Technological Univ., 1972. 112p.

Considers accounts of the origins of the Melungeons and of their folk life and customs as pictured in Stuart's *Daughter of the Legend,* Haun's *The Hawk's Done Gone,* Aswell's *God Bless the Devil,* and Hunter's *Walk Toward the Sunset.*

Burnett, Swan M. "A Note on the Melungeons." *American Anthropologist,* II (Oct. 1889), 347–49.

A brief history and description of characteristics.

Davis, Louise. "The Mystery of the Melungeons." *Tennessee Valley Historical Review,* I (Spring 1972), 22–29. Rpt. from *Nashville Tennessean Magazine,* Sept. 22 and 29, 1963.

Some observations on the history of the people and accounts of living descendants in Hancock County; has several photographs.

Dromgoole, Will Allen. "The Malungeon Tree and Its Four Branches." *The Arena,* III (May 1891), 745–51.

Relates the Melungeon people to four nationalities: Indian, English, Portuguese, and African.

———. "The Malungeons." *The Arena,* III (March 1891), 470–79.

The people—some of their personal characteristics and living conditions, as described by the author, who visited them. Contains speculation as to the Melungeons' racial origin.

Dunlap, A.R., and C.A. Weslager. "Trends in the Naming of Tri-Racial Mixed-Blood Groups in the Eastern United States." *American Speech,* XXII (April 1947), 81–87.

Mention is made of the Melungeons.

Gilbert, William Harlen, Jr. "Memorandum Concerning the Characteristics of the Larger Mixed-Blood Racial Islands of the Eastern United States." *Social Forces,* XXIV (May 1946), 438–47.

The location and social and economic characteristics of the Melungeons of the Southern Appalachians, pp. 443–45.

Ivey, Saundra Keyes. "Aunt Mahala Mullins in Folklore, Fakelore, and Literature." *Tennessee Folklore Society Bulletin,* XLI (March 1975), 1–8.

Discusses various accounts about Aunt Mahala, a Melungeon, and calls attention to inaccuracies.

———. "Oral, Printed and Popular Culture Traditions Related to the Melungeons of Hancock County, Tennessee." Diss. Indiana Univ., 1976. 529p. (Copy in Univ. of Tennessee Knoxville.)

A careful study of sources "from the travel literature of the 17th, 18th and early 19th centuries to the newspaper and magazine feature articles of more recent vintage," with personal interviews and a consideration of the "complex activities associated with 'Walk Toward the Sunset.'"

McMillan, Hamilton. *Sir Walter Raleigh's Lost Colony.* Rev. ed. Raleigh, N.C.: Edwards and Bros., 1907. 46p.

Concerns the Croatan Indians in the area of Robeson County, North Carolina. "Formerly these Indians called themselves 'Melungeans' and some of their old people still adhere to that name."

"The Melungeons." *Tennessee Conservationist,* XXV (Aug. 1959), 18–19. Rpt. *Tennessee Conservationist,* XXXIII (Aug. 1967), 12–13.

Discusses the possible origins of the Melungeons.

Nielson, Alfred Melville. "A Study of Certain 'Racial Islands' in the Eastern United States." Unpubl. Master's thesis, Ohio State Univ. 1947. 154p.

A study of 13 groups, including "Melungeons—located in Tennessee, Kentucky, southern West Virginia, and mountain regions of Virginia," using available written data to consider such phases as geographical isolation, physical features, beliefs as to origin, economic level. Good bibliography.

Pollitzer, William S. "The Physical Anthropology and Genetics of Marginal People of the Southeastern United States." *American Anthropologist,* LXXIV (June 1972), 719–34.

Includes the Melungeons.

Price, Edward T. "The East Tennessee Melungeons: Mixed-Blood Strain." *Annals of the Association of American Geographers,* XXXIX (March 1949), 68–69.

Abstract of a paper presented at the annual meeting in Madison, Wisc., Dec. 27–30, 1948.

——— . "The Melungeons: A Mixed-Blood Strain of the Southern Appalachians." *Geographical Review,* XLI (April 1951), 256–71.

The distribution, history, and derivation of the Melungeons, with maps and illustrations.

Price, Henry. *Melungeons, The Vanishing Colony of Newman's Ridge.* Sneedville, Tenn.: Hancock County Drama Association, 1971. 26p. (Originally presented before the American Studies Association of Kentucky and Tennessee in March 1966.)

A good account of the theories of origin, historical background, and way of life of the Melungeons. (The bibliography contains references to newspaper articles and court reports, but these are not included in this bibliography.)

Shepherd, Lewis. "Romantic Account of the Celebrated 'Melungeon' Case." *Watson's Magazine,* XVII (May 1913), 34–40.

An "interesting reminiscence by Judge Lewis Shepherd of his early success as a lawyer" in which he defended a Melungeon girl in a case based on her being a Melungeon rather than a person of Negro blood.

Werner, Diana. "The Melungeons: An Interstitial Racial Category of the Southern Appalachians." Unpubl. Master's thesis, Univ. of Georgia, 1973. 98p.

"This thesis is not a firsthand ethnographic study. . . . It is fundamentally an analysis of the position of Melungeons in Southern mountain society."

Willis, Thurston L. "The Melungeons of Eastern Tennessee." *The Chesopian,* IX (Feb., April, June 1971), 2–8. (Adapted from *Abstracts in Anthropology,* III [1972].)

"The various theories and arguments concerning the racial stock, national origin and former abode of these people are discussed at some length, but no definite conclusions are reached."

Worden, William L. "Sons of the Legend." *Saturday Evening Post,* CCXX (Oct. 18, 1947), 28–29, 128, 130, 133.

A good general account of the Melungeons of Newman's Ridge, with some pictures and references to other studies.

Welsh

Richards, D.J. *History of the Welsh in Tennessee, 1867 to 1873–75.* 12p. Printed, n.p. (Intended to be read St. David's Day, March 1, 1925.)

The Welsh colony of Knoxville and vicinity.

Shepperson, Wilbur S. *Samuel Roberts, A Welsh Colonizer in Civil War Tennessee.* Knoxville: Univ. of Tennessee Press, 1961. 169p.

Gives an account of Samuel Roberts' unsuccessful efforts to establish a permanent settlement of Welshmen in Scott County.

——— . "A Welsh Settlement in Scott County, Tennessee." *Tennessee Historical Quarterly,* XVIII (June 1959), 162–68.

"The brochure, 'Welsh Settlement in Tennessee' herein reproduced in full, is unique in that it represents one of the few attempts at Welsh cooperative settlement in the United States." The settlement was deserted after the Civil War.

III. Settlement Patterns

Amick, H.C. "The Great Valley of East Tennessee." *Economic Geography*, X (Jan. 1934), 35–52.

Background information on aspects that could be a factor in settlement patterns: topography, structure, climate, forest, wild life, inhabitants, agriculture, livestock, minerals, etc.

Bacon, Hollis Phillip, II. "The Historical Geography of Ante-Bellum Nashville." Unpubl. Ed.D. diss., George Peabody College for Teachers, 1955. 266p.

Treats the geographic influence on the settlement pattern in Nashville, stating that "Nashville had its origin, not as a result of the gathering together of various families that had emigrated individually into a land, but as the result of a definite plan for settlement at a particular location." Includes a discussion of agriculture, especially corn and cotton; development of various industries; transportation.

————. "Some Problems of Adjustment to Nashville's Site and Situation, 1780–1860." *Tennessee Historical Quarterly*, XV (Dec. 1956), 322–29.

Natural advantage of the site: high bluff giving command of the river, heavily timbered bluff, large salt spring, possible communication with other settlements, water supply from freely flowing spring. Transportation an important consideration in the city's development.

Browning, Tivis Jefferson, Jr. "The Historical Settlement Pattern of the Tellico Region." Unpubl. Master's thesis, Univ. of Tennessee, Knoxville, 1970. 119p.

Treats the settlement patterns, life style, and industry of the area from the time of Indian predominance to the present, concluding, "the agricultural life style, a conservative attitude, and a desire to maintain the status quo has persisted up to the present, and has begun to be broken only recently."

Burns, Inez. "Settlement and Early History of the Coves of Blount County, Tennessee." *East Tennessee Historical Society Publications*, No. 24 (1952), 44–67.

History of Tuckaleechee Cove, Cades Cove, Miller Cove, and Happy Valley settlements. Gives names of settlers; location of grist mills, saw mills, forges; and information on churches.

DesChamps, Margaret Burr. "Pioneer Life in the Cumberland Country." Unpubl. Master's thesis, Vanderbilt Univ., 1946. 81p.

Chapter I covers the land settlement.

Dobson, Jerome E. "Cultural Factors in the Hamlet Settlements of Northeast Tennessee." 1973. 10p. Student paper, Riedl Collection, Univ. of Tennessee Library, Knoxville.

The location and types of buildings.

Glenn, L.C. "Physiographic Influences in the Development of Tennessee." *Resources of Tennessee*, V (April 1915), 44–64. Nashville: State Geological Survey.

The purpose of the paper is not "to describe in detail the physiographic features of the state, but rather to set forth these features only in sufficient detail to show their relationship to man's activities." Gives routes of settlers and settlement patterns.

Miller, Laura Kate. "Geographic Influences in the Growth of Nashville." Unpubl. Master's thesis, George Peabody College for Teachers, 1923. 102p.

Considers the effect of such features as the Cumberland River, the bluffs, the highlands, and salt springs on the settlement; transportation by roads and river; and the effect of climate and soils on livestock and crops. Also the development of industries: the "hominy pounder," flour milling, lumber manufactures, and steel and iron.

Owsley, Frank L. "The Pattern of Migration and Settlement on the Southern Frontier." *Journal of Southern History*, XI (May 1945), 147–76.

Discusses the pattern of migration and settlement on public lands in the Southern states. Chiefly concerns herdsmen and agriculturalists.

Pearsall, Marion. "Some Frontier Origins of Southern Appalachian Culture." *Kentucky Folklore Record*, VIII (April-June 1962), 41–45.

Settlement patterns which favored the emergence of a distinctive cultural form.

Smith, J. Larry. "The Rural Settlement Patterns of the Little Tennessee Area: A Study in Cultural Geography." n.d. 35p. Student paper, Riedl Collection, Univ. of Tennessee Library, Knoxville.

"To describe and analyze the evolution of functions, the form of ground patterns (i.e.

roads and buildings) and field patterns associated with the rural communities in the vicinity of the Little Tennessee Valley."

Webb, George E. "The Settlement Pattern on the Cumberland Plateau in Tennessee." *Journal of the Tennessee Academy of Science*, XXXV (Jan. 1960), 24–30.

Land use due to topographic, geologic, and soil conditions has produced neighborhoods of sparse population, with no urban characteristics. Focal points at crossroads, centering around school, church, and store.

Webb, George Willis. "Resources of the Cumberland Plateau As Exemplified by Cumberland County, Tennessee: A Geographic Analysis." Unpubl. Master's thesis, Univ. of Tennessee, Knoxville, 1956. 282p.

A discussion of the settlement pattern, with some treatment of the location of roads.

Whitaker, J.R. "Tennessee—Earth Factors in Settlement and Land Use." *Tennessee Historical Quarterly*, V (Sept. 1946), 195–211.

Deals with selected aspects of settlement and land utilization affecting early settlers; fertile soil; climate; crops of cotton, corn and tobacco; livestock and dairy farming; travel routes; sectional contrasts.

IV. General Sources

This section consists of 135 titles ranging from scholarly surveys of Southern culture to personal reminiscences of life as it was. Articles on the importance and the methods of collecting folk materials, and their use in teaching, are scattered among almanacs and books covering manners, customs, possessions, songs, and stories. It is a heterogeneous section of entries which do not fit into any one subject division, but can be located by use of the Index.

Arnow, Harriette Simpson. *Flowering of the Cumberland*. New York: Macmillan, 1963. 441p.

A companion piece to *Seedtime on the Cumberland*, covering 1780–1803, concerned with the pioneer as a member of society: marriage and family life, language, education, agriculture, industry and trade.

―――― . *Seedtime on the Cumberland.* New York: Macmillan, 1960. 449p.

A good account of the everyday lives of the early settlers; how they built their homes; prepared their food; clothes; utensils; and tools. The author "tried to recreate a few of the more important aspects of pioneer life as it was lived on the Cumberland by ordinary men and women."

Barkley, Anna Mae. "Local History Stories for Third Grade Washington and Sullivan Counties, Tennessee." Unpubl. Master's thesis, East Tennessee State College, 1952. 83p.

Simple stories written on third grade vocabulary level, giving details about transportation, food, homes, and clothing of early settlers.

Berthelot, Dolly, ed. *Pioneer Spirit 76. Commemorative BicenTENNial Portrait Smoky Mountains Region Past and Present.* Knoxville: Dolly Berthelot, c1975. 69p.

Contains articles on regional dialects, mountain music, quilt revival, festivals, and other aspects of life in the Smoky Mountains Region.

Borah, Leo A. "Home Folk Around Historic Cumberland Gap." *National Geographic,* LXXXIV (Dec. 1943), 741–68.

The old customs seen in a modern time; descriptions accompanied by pictures of a country store; cutting sorghum cane; stirring off molasses; sacking meal at the mill; 'tater digging; "shoes in a circle" games; singing games; church service; and a footwashing ceremony.

Botkin, B.A., ed. *Lay My Burden Down; A Folk History of Slavery.* Chicago: Univ. of Chicago Press, 1945. 284p.

A selection of narratives from the Slave Narrative Collection of the Federal Writers' Project. Includes about a dozen stories from ex-slaves in Tennessee.

―――― , ed. *A Treasury of Mississippi River Folklore: Stories, Ballads, Traditions and Folkways of the Mid-Ameri-*can River Country. New York: Crown, 1955. 620p.

"Tennesseans will find much of specific local interest: DeSoto, the Natchez Trace, Murrell and the Harpes."

―――― , ed. *A Treasury of Southern Folklore: Stories, Ballads, Traditions, and Folkways of the People of the South.* New York: Crown, 1949. 776p.

An excellent collection including many items from Tennessee, and a good introduction. "Also basic to the book is the view of folklore as a part of folk culture."

Bowman, Elizabeth Skaggs. *Land of High Horizons.* Kingsport: Southern Publishers, 1938. 212p.

The chapter "Meet the Mountaineer" tells of the beliefs, cures, and speech of the natives of the Great Smoky Mountains.

Bowman, Virginia McDaniel. *Historic Williamson County, Old Homes and Sites.* Nashville: Blue & Gray Press, 1971. 194p.

A record of notable landmarks, with photographs, and accounts of incidents and events showing a changing way of life. Homes, schools, churches, inns, and covered bridges.

Braden, Beulah Brummett. *When Grandma Was a Girl.* Oak Ridge: Oak Ridger and Clinton-Courier News, 1976. 121p.

An interesting story of life in Anderson County at the turn of the century. Gives a detailed account of farm houses, yard and outbuildings, tools for riving wood, blacksmithing, carpentering, and descriptions of household equipment and chores, cooking and washing, food, games, toys, and the way of living, generally. Has many good drawings.

Breazeale, J.W.M. *Life As It Is; Or Matters and Things in General: Containing Amongst Other Things . . . Manners and Customs of the Inhabitants . . . .* Knoxville: Printed by James Williams at the Office of "The Post," 1842. 256p.

Manners and customs of the early settlers of Tennessee; tools, cooking utensils, methods of curing meat without salt; legislative, judicial, and ecclesiastical incidents; a history of the Harpes.

Burnett, Edmund Cody. "Big Creek's Response to the Coming of the Railroad: 'Old Buncombe' Promotes the Better Life in a Rural Community." *Agricultural History*, XXI (July 1947), 129–48.

A good article touching the influence of the railroad in bringing hitherto unavailable commercial articles but reverting to reminiscences of patent and home remedies, food, lye soap, clothes, farm implements, blacksmith shop, bedding, the gathering of berries, nuts, ginseng, and "yarbs."

Caldwell, Mary French. "Change Comes to the Appalachian Mountaineer." *Current History*, XXXI (Feb. 1930), 961–67.

Survey of conditions in the late 1920s; causes of illiteracy; isolated communities; customs and ballads; economic conditions.

Callahan, North. *Smoky Mountain Country*. New York: Duell, Sloan, 1952. 257p.

A native of Tennessee, the author recounts life as it used to be, and as he has found it on visits home. Discusses the mountain woman's routine day, food, superstitions, music, etc.

Campbell, John Charles. *The Southern Highlander and His Homeland*. New York: Russell Sage, 1921. 405p.

The author spent 25 years in the mountain country of the South, during a part of this time as principal of an academy in Tennessee. Gives an account of the mountaineers' homelife, religious life, living conditions, and health. Photographs of a grist mill, fence, schools, etc.

Caruso, John Anthony. *The Appalachian Frontier*. Indianapolis: Bobbs-Merrill, 1959. 408p.

The author concentrates his account of the settlement of the area within the period between 1750 and 1800. The chapter "Pattern of Life" tells of dress, food, household utensils, folk medicine, ways of dealing with wrong-doers, and religion.

Chambers, Will T. "Attempts to Adjust Political Life to Pioneer Environment in Tennessee." Unpubl. Master's thesis, Univ. of Chicago, 1924. 135p. (Copy in Univ. of Tennessee Library, Knoxville.)

Formation of governmental units as a result of the differing needs of individual settlements. Geography and environmental impact evidenced in the divisions of East, Middle, and West Tennessee today.

Chapman, Maristan. "The Mountain Man; An Unbiased View of Our Southern Highlanders." *Century Magazine*, CXVII (Feb. 1929), 505–11.

Description of the characteristics of the mountaineer formed by topography, early migration of different nationalities, and merging of languages and social conditions.

Clark, Joe. *Back Home*. Kingsport, Tenn.: Kingsport Press, 1965. Unpaged. (Privately printed for the Tennessee Squire Association.)

Excellent photographs, with accompanying verses, of people and scenes near Cumberland Gap, Tennessee, and life as it used to be.

――――. *Tennessee Hill Folk: Photographs and Captions by Joe Clark, with An Essay by Jesse Stuart*. Nashville: Vanderbilt Univ. Press, 1972. Unpaged.

Contains 81 photographs, including a baptizing, hoe-down, funeral, school, still, singing game, country store, several buildings, and interesting people. "A most important book that will preserve a segment of our Appalachia for centuries to come" —Stuart.

――――. *Up the Hollow From Lynchburg*. Photography by Joe Clark, introduction and descriptive text by Jesse Stuart. New York: McGraw-Hill, 1975. 128p.

Photographs include fences, one with a weather vane; bull-tongue plow; a one-horse drag-tooth harrow; a washtub and a bucket hanging on hewed log walls; a log barn, a mill, and a general store; strings of peppers in a window; and spearing tobacco. Captions "which are almost essays in themselves" are by Jesse Stuart.

Clark, Thomas D. *The Rampaging Frontier: Manners and Humors of Pioneer*

Days in the South and the Middle West.
Indianapolis: Bobbs-Merrill, 1939. 350p.

"Generally I have kept my story west of
the Allegheny Mountains, and within the
boundaries of Tennessee and south of the
Yankee line in Ohio, Indiana and Illinois.
My period covers generally from 1775–
1850." Includes transportation, accommodations, religion, law, military musters,
recreation, and much humor. Good bibliography with early travel accounts.

**Coffin, Tristram Potter, and Hennig Co-
hen,** eds. *Folklore From the Working
Folk of America.* Selected and edited
from the leading journals and archives of
folklore. Garden City, N.Y.: Anchor
Press/Doubleday, 1973. 464p.

State index locates a number of Tennessee items.

Cole, William E. "Some Contributions of
Folklore Studies to Social Planning."
Tennessee Folklore Society Bulletin, VIII
(March 1942), 2–4.

An understanding of folkways and mores
is essential to effective leadership and administration of community action agencies
and programs.

Corlew, Robert Ewing. "Some Aspects of
Slavery in Dickson County." *Tennessee
Historical Quarterly,* X (Sept. 1951),
224–48; X(Dec. 1951), 344–65.

The treatment of slaves, their use in
farming and in the development of iron
furnaces; the attitude of the churches.

Couch, W.T., ed. *Culture in the South.*
Chapel Hill: Univ. of North Carolina
Press, 1935. 711p.

"All the chapters taken together give a
picture of the more important aspects of
life in the present South and their historic
background." Pertinent chapters are listed
by author in this bibliography.

———. "The Negro in the South." In
Couch, W.T., *Culture in the South.*
Chapel Hill: Univ. of North Carolina
Press, 1935.

An account of the traditional way of life
of the Negro cropper in the Southern states.

Crowe, Dan. *The Horseshoe People.*

Johnson City, Tenn.: Don & Mignon,
1976. 196p.

Stories about life in the Horseshoe
Community in Carter County: the last will
and testament, listing all of a man's possessions; the fiddling cobbler; tales of a
schoolhouse and its special occasions;
churches and preachers and foot washings;
the doctor, the midwife, the mailman;
food; superstitions; death; the coming of
the railroad, and other events.

***Cumberland Almanac For the Year of
Our Lord*** . . . . Nashville: Various publishers. Various dates: Univ. of Tennessee Library, Knoxville, has 1882, American Book and Job Printing House, 32p.;
1887, Marshall & Bruce, 48p.; 1888,
Marshall & Bruce, 48p.; 1891,
Nashville-American, 34p. Published
1826–95.

Advice on farming, recipes of all kinds,
census of U.S. population, game and fish
laws, counting-out rhymes for the children,
etc.

Davidson, Donald. "Current Attitudes
Toward Folklore." *Tennessee Folklore
Society Bulletin,* VI (Dec. 1940), 44–51.

A classification of attitudes and activities
of the devotees of folklore, and an assess-
ment of the value to our culture of certain
collectors and writers.

DesChamps, Margaret Burr. "Early Days
in the Cumberland Country." *Tennessee
Historical Quarterly,* VI (Sept. 1947),
195–229.

Describes the houses, household possessions, and home life; the work of farmers,
traders, and merchants, ministers, doctors,
dentists; and transportation. Much information taken from wills and inventories.

———. "Pioneer Life in the Cumberland
Country." Unpubl. Master's thesis, Vanderbilt Univ., 1946. 81p.

Settling the land; the house, household
possessions, and home life (possessions
noted from wills and inventories); occupations; customs and amusements.

Dick, Everett. *The Dixie Frontier: A Social History of the Southern Frontier
From the First Transmontane Beginning*

to the Civil War. New York: Knopf, 1948. 374p.

> Description of frontier life in all of its aspects.

Dickens, Charles. "Old Settlers of Tennessee." *Household Words, A Weekly Journal*. Conducted by Charles Dickens. VIII (Oct. 22, 1853), 188–91.

> Discusses the way of living, houses, tools, school, and the importance of maize to the settlers. Much of the information taken from Ramsey's *Annals of Tennessee*.

Douglas, William O. "The People of Cades Cove." *National Geographic*, CXXII (July 1962), 60–95.

> A remnant of pioneer America. Excellent photographs.

Doyle, Bertram Wilbur. *The Etiquette of Race Relations in the South, A Study in Social Control*. Chicago: Univ. of Chicago Press, 1937. Rpt. Port Washington, N.Y.: Kennikat Press, 1968. 249p.

> The relationship of blacks with whites on plantations and farms before the Civil War. Tells of greetings and conversations, weddings, deaths and funerals, Christmas customs, and church activities.

Dykeman, Wilma. *The French Broad*. New York: Rinehart, 1955. 371p. Rpt. Knoxville: Univ. of Tennessee Press, 1965.

> Especially interesting are chapters 4 and 9. "Every Home Its Own Community," showing the pioneer way of life; and "The Great Drives," the story of the drovers of cattle, mules, ducks, turkeys, and hogs.

Edwards, Funson. *Profiles of Common Men; Dedicated to the Country Doctor and the Mountain Preacher Who Serve the Body and Soul Ailments of Their Constituants*. Knoxville: Privately Printed, 1969. 136p.

> Contains 38 sketches of rural people—doctors, teachers, philosophers, fiddlers, farmers—and their customs.

Edwards, Lawrence. *Speedwell Sketches*. Avon, Ill.: Hamlet Press, 1950. 103p. 2d ed., Boston: Bruce Humphries, 1951. 126p.

> Stories about a community in East Tennessee. "Deep-rooted in a pattern of culture which belongs to folklore."

———. *"Write That Down," She Said*. Knoxville: Holston Printing Co., 1977. 64p.

> Sketches reminiscent of people in Speedwell and those who passed along the road—coal miners; peddlers; carnival workers; turkey drovers.

Egypt, Ophelia Settle. *Unwritten History of Slavery: An Autobiographical Account of Negro Ex-Slaves*. Nashville: Social Science Institute, Fisk Univ., 1945. 322p. (Social Science Source Documents, No. 1.)

> "These documents . . . reveal some of the slaves in the declining days of the institution. They tell what the slaves saw and remembered; how they themselves, or others whom they knew lived. . . . They represent essentially the memories of childhood experiences." Interviews conducted in 1929–30. Subjects resided primarily in Tennessee and Kentucky.

Elrod, Geraldine Wilson. "Tennessee, 1796–1860, As Seen Through the Accounts of Travelers." Unpubl. Master's thesis, George Peabody College for Teachers, 1940. 78p.

> Presents comments on Tennessee by 22 travelers from other states and from European countries: sketches of homes, dress, food, towns, education, occupations, and religious and social life in Tennessee.

The Farmer's Almanac for the Year of Our Lord . . . . Knoxville: Printed and Published by James C. Moses, 1843.

> Gives advice, receipts, and stories as well as other usual almanac items.

Faulkner, Charles H., and Carol K. Buckles, eds. *Glimpses of Southern Appalachian Folk Culture: Papers in Memory of Norbert F. Riedl*. [Knoxville]: Tennessee Anthropological Association, 1978. 130p. (Miscellaneous Paper No. 3.)

> A collection of papers written by Dr. Riedl's students. (These papers also listed by subject in this bibliography.)

Fayte-Burnett, G.L. *Gap O'the Mountains, 1839–1939, Romantic Sketches Along the Trail of One Hundred Years.* Knoxville: n.p., 1939. 123p.

"Short sketches of the pioneers of the Great Smoky Mountains and the Appalachian region"—the Old Smithy, the General Store, the Mill, Country Doctor, Granny Woman, etc.

Federal Writers' Project, Works Project Administration, Tennessee. *Tennessee: A Guide to the State.* New York: Viking Press, 1939. 558p.

"Folklore: The Living Past," covers speech, superstitions and customs, with numerous examples. Also helpful are the chapters on agriculture, architecture, education, history, industry, Negroes in Tennessee, and transportation.

Fisher, Stephen L., J.W. Williamson, and Juanita Lewis. "A Guide to Appalachian Studies." *Appalachian Journal*, V (Autumn 1977), 1–192.

A survey of various aspects of Appalachian studies, with excellent articles and bibliographies. (Some individual articles are entered by subject in this bibliography.)

Ford, Thomas R., ed. *The Southern Appalachian Region: A Survey.* Lexington: Univ. of Kentucky Press, 1962. 308p.

A survey conducted by Southern Appalachian Studies to determine the changes that have taken place in the region with reference to health, education, religion, economic status, and other problem areas. Background information on traditional attitudes and culture is helpful, as is the section on folk arts in transition.

Fowler, James Alexander. "Memoirs." 6 vols. Mimeographed copy, Univ. of Tennessee Library, Knoxville.

Volumes 1 and 2 contain early memories of family life in East Tennessee: making of cloth; planting of corn, wheat, and cane; making of sorghum molasses; food; Easter customs; education; his training as a lawyer.

Frome, Michael. *Strangers in High Places: The Story of the Great Smoky Mountains.* Garden City, N.Y.: Doubleday, 1966. 394p. Rev. ed., Knoxville:

Univ. of Tennessee Press, 1980.

Accounts of early settlers, camp meetings, hunting, moonshining, and developments in education and medicine.

Glassie, Henry. *Pattern in the Material Folk Culture of the Eastern United States.* Philadelphia: Univ. of Pennsylvania Press, 1968. 316p.

Discusses the relation and the differences between popular and folk material. Contains sketches of a double-pen house, a two-level outbuilding type, and a cane or syrup mill in Tennessee. A basic book for the study of material folk culture, with an important bibliography.

Gray, John W. *The Life of Joseph Bishop, the Celebrated Old Pioneer in the First Settlements of Middle Tennessee, Embracing His Wonderful Adventures and Narrow Escapes with the Indians, His Animating and Remarkable Hunting Excursions.* Interspersed with Racy Anecdotes of Those Early Times. Spartanburg, S.C.: Reprint Co., 1974. 236p. (Reprint of the 1962 private edition published by J.R. Fleming. Originally published in Nashville by the author in 1858.)

"an impressive reflection of the raw reality of pioneer life in Tennessee"—Stanley F. Horn in the Introduction, 1974 edition.

Greene, Howard, and Alice E. Smith, eds. *The Journals of Welcome Arnold Greene.* 2 vols. Madison: State Historical Society of Wisconsin, 1956–57.

Vol. 2, *Journeys in the South, 1822–24* (Nashville, Tenn., April 8, 1824). In his narrative of a visit to Nashville in 1824 (v.2, pp. 242–53), Greene describes a woodman's house and furnishings, a country inn, a visit with Willie Blount, and an interest in the botany and geology of the surrounding country.

Guild, Josephus C. *Old Times in Tennessee, With Historical, Personal, and Political Scraps and Sketches.* Nashville: Tavel, Eastman and Howell, 1878. 503p.

Chapter XVI, "Some Odds and Ends of Early History and Customs," includes description of log cabins, dances, fashions, schooling, the barring out of the schoolmaster, the general muster, and reading the law.

Hale, Will T. *Backward Trail: Stories of the Indians and Tennessee Pioneers.* Nashville: Cumberland Press, 1899. 183p.

Conditions of living of early settlers, their pastimes and religion.

Hall, Frederick. *Letters From the East and From the West.* Washington, D.C.: F. Taylor and William M. Morrison, 1840. 168p.

Pages 150–60 tell of a visit to Nashville, describing, among other things, Sunday observance and a Fourth of July "Barbecue and Brandance."

Hall, Joseph S. *Smoky Mountain Folks and Their Lore.* Asheville: Gilbert Printing Co., 1960. 72p. (Published in cooperation with Great Smoky Mountains Natural History Association.)

A collection of stories told to the author by mountain people in the Great Smoky Mountains area in 1937.

Hall, Russell. "The Effect of Pittman Center on the Community Life." Unpubl. Master's thesis, Univ. of Tennessee, Knoxville, 1939. 134p.

The recreational, economic, and religious life of the people of Sevier County, and the effect of the work of Pittman Center on the community.

Hatcher, J. Wesley. "Appalachian America." In Couch, W.T., *Culture in the South.* Chapel Hill: Univ. of North Carolina Press, 1935.

Depicts a "close connection between genetic characteristics of the people and soil conditions" in the Southern Appalachians. Describes the homes and way of life of three classes of society: the people who live in the valleys, those who live farther upstream where the hills and mountains are higher, the mountaineers.

Hawkins, Donald. "A Note on Decatur County." *Tennessee Folklore Society Bulletin,* XIX (Sept. 1953), 64–65.

A brief account of life in the county, including recreation and superstitions. Fall,

1948. (From the Folklore Archive, Murray State College.)

Holt, Albert C. "The Economic and Social Beginnings of Tennessee." George Peabody College for Teachers. 1923. 107p.

A helpful account of the character of the settlers, and their military, economic, and social life. Topography, relations with Indians, population and early governments, travel, professions, industries, agriculture, and home and social life. Many maps.

———. "The Economic and Social Beginnings of Tennessee." *Tennessee Historical Magazine,* VII (Oct. 1921), 194–230; VII (Jan. 1922), 252–313; VIII (April 1924), 24–86.

Same as the diss. above.

Hunn, M. "Smoky's Hidden Annex." *Travel,* CXVII (April 1962), 38–40.

Cades Cove described for tourists. Good pictures of the John Oliver cabin, the Tipton-Oliver house, structures of the John P. Cable farm, the mill, and mulepower grinder.

Imlay, Gilbert. *A Topographical Description of the Western Territory of North America . . . .* 3rd ed. London: Printed for J. Debrett, 1797. 598p.

Contains a chapter on the state of "Tenassee," with a 1795 map. Gives physical description: roads and distances, climate and resources, with special reference to importance of salt.

Irwin, John Rice. "Pioneers Had It: A Need, a Knowhow, and Wood." *Tennessee Conservationist,* XL (April 1974), 16–19.

The many uses of wood: in home building, household items, storage, ashes for soap, tanning, lubricant, etc.

———. *The Story of Marcellus Moss Rice and His Big Valley Kinsmen.* Montevallo, Ala.: Times Printing Co., 1963. 161p.

Description of the way of life in Anderson County, including school, food, etc.

Johnson, Mary Elizabeth. "Stories and Legends of Donelson, Tennessee." Unpubl. Master's thesis, George Peabody College for Teachers, 1938. 188p.

A collection of miscellaneous brief remarks from interviews with people who lived in Donelson. Includes some place names, accounts of schools, homes, methods of travel, cattle and turkey droves, etc.

Jones, Lealon N., ed. *Eve's Stepchildren: A Collection of Folk Americana.* Caldwell, Idaho: Caxton Printers, 1942. 310p.

Two essays from Tennessee: "Dark Cabins" by Harry Harrison Kroll, and "John Barleycorn, Hillbilly" by Lawrence Edwards, "Rattlesnake Religion" by Keith Kerman has a reference to Tennessee.

Justus, May. "Growing Up in the Smokies." *Appalachian South,* II (Fall-Winter 1967), 16.

Brief account of the author's childhood, with mention of events in the log church and schoolhouse.

———. " A Smoky Mountain Mother." *Appalachian South,* II (Spring-Summer 1967), 43–44.

The author's memory of her mother, their family life, her charm as a story teller, her knowledge and use of herbs and homemade medicines.

Kephart, Horace. *Our Southern Highlanders: A Narrative of Adventure in the Southern Appalachians and a Study of Life Among the Mountaineers.* 1913; New York: Macmillan 1922. 469p. Rpt. Knoxville: Univ. of Tennessee Press, 1976. 517p.

"The real mountaineers are the multitude of little farmers living up the branches and on the steep hillsides, away from the main-traveled roads, who have been shaped by their own environment." Gives an account of many phases of life, including moonshining, religion, funerals, medical and dental treatment, home life, and speech.

The reprint edition of 1976 includes an introduction by George Ellison.

Lawlor, Virginia G., ed. "I, Mary Morriss Smith, Do Recollect . . . ." *Tennessee Historical Quarterly,* XXIX (Spring 1970), 79–87.

An interesting account from "five clear and legible manuscripts, handwritten in the late 1890's . . . recalling her arrival in Wilson County, Tennessee in the year 1812." Church services, camp meetings, school, food, and clothing.

Leonard, Roy C. "Rambling Around the Roof of Eastern America." *National Geographic,* LXX (Aug. 1936), 243–66.

Gives a brief account of pioneer speech and mountain homes. Clear pictures of a horsepowered sorghum press, basket weavers, a horse-drawn sled, a tub mill, swinging bridge, log cabin, and mountaineer's gun.

Lyle, Mary Willett. "Early Settlements of Memphis." 5p. (Read before the Memphis Historical Society, Jan. 1917; typescript in the Memphis Room, Memphis Public Library.)

Reminiscences of the author (who was born in 1833), telling of stage coaches; the Volunteer Fire Company, whose hose cart and pump was pulled through the streets by ropes, with 20 men on each side; school and church, and the scarcity of school books; and the building of roads.

McBride, Robert M., ed. *More Landmarks of Tennessee History.* Nashville: Tennessee Historical Society and Tennessee Historical Commission, 1969. 393p.

Contains 19 articles, by various authors, previously published in the *Tennessee Historical Quarterly.*

McNeil, W.K. "Appalachian Folklore Scholarship." *Appalachian Journal,* V (Autumn 1977), 55–64.

A brief survey.

Maloney, John. "Time Stood Still in the Smokies." *Saturday Evening Post,* CCXVIII (April 27, 1946), 16–17, 82–85.

A visit with the Walker Sisters in Little Greenbriar Cove, where they lived as if in the 19th century. Pictures of the four sisters spinning and carding, stretching and drying sheepskin; also shows their handmade coverlets and their log cabin home.

Manning, Ambrose. "Collecting Folklore: One Procedure." *Tennessee Folk-*

lore Society Bulletin, XXXV (Dec. 1969), 117–23.

An account of methods used by the author and Professor Thomas Burton in collecting folklore of southwestern Virginia, western North Carolina and eastern Tennessee.

Mansfield & Higbee's Memphis Family Almanac for the Use of Farmers, Planters, Mechanics, and All Others. 1873. Memphis: Mansfield & Higbee, Manufacturing Chemists . . . . 48p. 1845–. Title varies.

Has the usual almanac items, with hints to housekeepers, receipts, and many medicine ads.

Mason, Robert Lindsay. *The Lure of the Great Smokies.* Boston: Houghton Mifflin, 1927. 320p.

Describes the way of living of the mountain people, including "His Cabin is his Castle," "Oldtime Smoky Mountain Rifles and Riflemen" "Saddlebags, Firewater and Witches," and "A Raid in the Smokies."

Matthews, Elmora M. *Neighbor and Kin: Life in a Tennessee Ridge Community.* Nashville: Vanderbilt Univ. Press, 1966. 178p.

A sociological study of the effects of intermarriage on the way of living of a community of about sixty families. Farming, moonshining, superstitions, and joking relationships are also discussed.

Maxwell, Philip Herbert, and Edouard Evart Exline. *Valhalla in the Smokies.* Cleveland, Ohio: G.A. Exline, 1938. Unpaged. 25 plates.

An account of life in the Smokies as it has been lived from early days. Photographs of a cabin, pipe maker, weaver with loom, children, tanner, grist mill, basketmaker, and long rifle.

Melish, John. *A Geographic Description of the United States with the Contiguous British and Spanish Possessions . . . .* 182p. 1816; rpt. Nashville: Gazetteer Press, 1972.

Pages 115–18 give a topographic description of Tennessee, with a list of post offices and their distance from Washington.

Miles, Emma Bell. *The Spirit of the Mountains.* New York: J. Pott, 1905. Facsimile edition with a foreword by Roger D. Abrahams and introduction by David E. Whisnant. Knoxville: Univ. of Tennessee Press, 1975. 205p. (Tennesseana Editions.)

An account of mountain life, the log school, cabin home, religion, beliefs and customs, music, tales and rhymes. ". . . written by a bona fide 'insider,' a forgotten but welcome antidote to the many condescending books by 'outsiders' " —Introduction.

Miller, E.E. "Tennessee: Three-quarters of Bewilderment." *Nation,* CXV (Sept. 20, 1922), 273–76.

Brief but good description of background topography, population, and culture of East, Middle, and West Tennessee. Pessimistic description of 1920 condition and attitudes.

Mooney, Chase C. *Slavery in Tennessee.* Bloomington: Indiana Univ. Press, 1957. Rpt. Westport, Conn.: Negro Universities Press, 1971. 250p.

Chapters 4 and 7 give some aspects of the life of the slaves and of the planters, and the relationship between them.

Mooney, James. "Folk-lore of the Carolina Mountains." *Journal of American Folklore,* II (April-June 1889). 95–104.

"Most, if not all, of the beliefs and customs noted in this paper are known also in the adjacent region west of the Smoky Mountains." Houses and furniture, religion, dialect, holiday customs, superstitions, witchcraft, riddles and games, curing by touch, and folk medicine.

Oakley, Wiley. *Restin'.* Gatlinburg: Mountain Press, 1947. 62p.

A continuation of *Roamin' With the Roamin' Man of the Smoky Mountains.* Tells of hunting, milking, his father's gristmill, etc.

——— . *Roamin' With the Roamin' Man of the Smoky Mountains.* N.p. 1940. 64p.

Stories of the author's life in the Smoky Mountains, told in his own words. Includes customs and beliefs.

Odum, Howard W. *Southern Regions of the United States*. Chapel Hill: Univ. of North Carolina Press, 1936. 664p.

An important survey. "It must be clear that it is not possible either to understand or direct any society without a knowledge of its folk-regional culture and backgrounds."

———. *The Way of the South: Toward the Regional Balance of America*. New York: Macmillan, 1947. 350p.

A regional study, tracing development through many aspects of folk culture. Of especial interest are the following chapters: The People and the Way of the Folk; The Grandfathers to Grandchildren; In the Name of God, Amen; and Southern Symbols in Folk Song and Music.

Olmsted, Frederick Law. *Journey in the Back Country*. New York: Mason Brothers, 1860. 492p.

The chapter on The Highlanders gives the author's observations on agriculture and on domestic life in his journey through Tennessee.

Owsley, Frank Lawrence. *Plain Folk of the Old South*. Baton Rouge: Louisiana State Univ. Press, 1949. 235p. Rpt. Chicago: Quadrangle Books, 1965.

Focuses on landowning farmers and herdsmen, using county records and unpublished census reports among the sources of information. Tells of the selection of settlement sites and folk customs: house-raisings, work-swapping, recreation, wedding customs.

Pearsall, Marion. *Little Smoky Ridge: the Natural History of a Southern Appalachian Neighborhood*. University: Univ. of Alabama Press, 1959. 205p.

A study of an isolated Southern Appalachian neighborhood in East Tennessee. The effect of old cultural forms and values on family life, religion, and death.

———. "Some Aspects of Cultural Change in a Mountain Neighborhood of East Tennessee." Unpubl. Ph.D. diss. Univ. of California, 1950. 162p. (Microfilm copy in Univ. of Tennessee Library, Knoxville.)

Roles played by topography, climate and soil, timber and minerals in cultural change. Main arteries of travel by the settlers; the differentiation between valley and ridge culture; pioneer economy, education, and religion.

Peattie, Roderick, ed. *The Great Smokies and the Blue Ridge: The Story of the Southern Appalachians*. New York: Vanguard, 1943. 372p.

Peattie writes about the early settlers; Alberta Hannum about the mountain people, folk medicine, household tasks, preachers; John Jacob Niles on the folk ballad and carol; Ralph Erskin about craftsmen.

Pittman, Carolyn. "Memphis in the Mid-1840's." *West Tennessee Historical Society Papers*, XXIII (1969), 30–44.

Mentions a variety of building construction; commodities in the drug store; restaurant, hotel and livery stable rates, etc.

Poor Richard's Almanac, for the Year of Our Lord, 1848 ... Calculated for Tennessee, and the Road to Wealth, Honor and Distinction, and the Way to Put Money into Every Man's Pocket . . . . Nashville: George W. House. [1847] 34p.

Gives the usual information about eclipses, weather forecasts, when courts meet, general receipts, and comments.

Ramsdell, Charles W. "The Southern Heritage." In Couch, W.T. *Culture in the South*. Chapel Hill: Univ. of North Carolina Press, 1935.

A discussion of factors influencing change in the traditional cultural patterns in the Southern states.

Rawick, George P., gen. ed., *The American Slave: A Composite Autobiography*. Westport, Conn.: Greenwood, 1972. Vol. XVI.

"Tennessee Narratives" contains 26 interviews conducted by the Federal Writers' Project.

Rickard, J.A. "Folklore as an Aid to the Teacher of History." *Tennessee Folklore Society Bulletin*, V (Dec. 1939), 71–79.

Contains suggestions for coordination of the teaching of history and folklore.

Riedl, Norbert F. "Folklore and the Study of Material Aspects of Folk Culture." *Journal of American Folklore,* LXXIX (Oct.-Dec. 1966), 557–63.

A discussion of the difference in viewpoints of specialists in each field, and an appeal for more intensive research in material aspects of our folk culture.

———. "A Plan for the Organization of a Statewide Survey of the Folk Culture of Tennessee." *Tennessee Folklore Society Bulletin,* XXXII (Sept. 1966), 67–75.

An appeal and a proposal for research and for the collection of material concerning the folk culture of Tennessee.

Roark, Eldon. *Memphis Bragabouts: Characters I Have Met.* New York: Whittlesey House, 1945. 224p.

Stories of Memphis' colorful and eccentric characters who are bragged about.

Roberts, Bruce, and Nancy Roberts. *Where Time Stood Still; A Portrait of Appalachia.* London: Collier Macmillan, 1970. 114p.

Twentieth-century life in the mountains, still using many methods and customs of the past. Good photographs of chair-maker, broom-tier, sorghum mill, Decoration Day observance.

Rogers, E.G. "Some Odd Pickups from Here and There." *Tennessee Folklore Society Bulletin,* XVI (March 1950), 11–12.

Brief accounts of mail delivery, political musters, roadbuilding, guards as escorts for settlers, and burials.

Rogers, William Flinn. "Life in East Tennessee Near the End of the Eighteenth Century." *East Tennessee Historical Society Publications,* No. 1 (1929), 27–42.

Houses, dress, food, farming, crops and livestock, stores, and tanneries. Based on the diss. below.

———. "Life on the Kentucky-Tennessee Frontier Near the End of the Eighteenth Century." Unpubl. Master's thesis, Univ. of Tennessee, Knoxville, 1925. 99p.

Home life of the people, crops and livestock, commercial life, industrial life, education, and religious life.

Russell, Gladys Trentham. *Call Me Hillbilly; A Personal Account of Growing Up in the Smokies Near Gatlinburg.* Alcoa, Tenn.: Russell Publishing Co., 1974. 92p.

Sketches of the author's childhood and teenage years in her mountain home community tell of the sixteen buildings on the home place, school events, church meetings, weddings and funerals, games and other recreation, home remedies, farm planting, and chores.

Shannon, Augustine F. *Journal, 1848–50.* Nashville: Historical Records Survey, 1940. 54p. (From a typewritten copy produced by the Works Project Administration.)

The journal of a Methodist circuit rider. Brief, mostly travel, but has some mention of weddings, burials, shivarees, events of an election day, and the tragedy befalling the owners of a still.

Shaub, Earl L. "The New World of Today." *Tennessee Conservationist,* XXII (May 1956), 12–13.

Contrasts the old and new ways of living. Pictures of wielding old cradle in field, old bull-tongue plough drawn by an ox, and a woman carding and spinning yarn.

———. "Our Vanishing Mountaineers." *Tennessee Conservationist,* XXXIII (July 1967), 7–10.

Customs of yesterday described in contrast to changes appearing in mountain life. Pictures of individuals making a split-bottom chair, spinning, weaving, tanning leather, and plowing with an ox and bull-tongue plow.

———. "The Vanishing Mountaineers." *Tennessee Conservationist,* XIX (Dec. 1953), 6–8.

Brief account of "contemporary early Americans," with photographs of an old water wheel gristmill, a cabin, a basket-maker, an ox-drawn slide, and an old cradle still in use.

Smalley, Ruth, ed. *The Good Life Al-*

manac: *Being the Choicest Morsels of Wisdom for Readers Interested in Living, Rather Than Existing.* Written by Some Country Folk with Ties to Nature, Man, and God's Own World. Boone, N.C.: Appalachian Consortium Press, 1975. Unpaged.

Gathered in the Solway Community of East Tennessee, a compilation of "stories which would be interesting for the sake of the tales themselves or typical of the times to point up the era's dependence on water transportation, the excitement of the coming of the railroad, the self-contained nature of community recreation. . . . our regional recipes, our hints for living taken from both yesterday and tomorrow, and a few pithy comments on the human condition."

Smith, Betty N. "The Gap in Oral Tradition." In Williamson, J.W., ed., *An Appalachian Symposium: Essays in Honor of Cratis D. Williams.* Boone, N.C.: Appalachian State Univ. Press, 1977.

"A gap between parents and children in the transmission of songs, rhymes, and games . . . symptomatic of what happened to the quality of life."

Srygley, F.D. *Seventy Years in Dixie: Recollections, Sermons and Sayings of T.W. Caskey and Others.* Nashville: Gospel Advocate Publishing Co., 1891. 400p.

Hunters and their flint-and-steel guns, food, clothes, recreation, household furniture, dentistry, log-rolling, construction of cabins, soft-soap making, corn-shucking, quilt making, farm instruments, whiskey, funerals, church services, and preaching. Contains many interesting drawings.

Thomas, Jane H. *Old Days in Nashville, Tennessee.* Nashville: Publishing House, Methodist Episcopal Church, South, Barbee and Smith, Agents, 1897. 190p.

Recollections of life in Nashville in the early 1800s, written by a resident at the age of ninety-five. She tells of the people, their occupations, social events, food, clothes, and Christmas celebrations.

Thompson, Samuel H. *The Highlanders of the South.* New York: Eaton and Mains, 1910. 86p.

Brief treatment of the ethnic background of Tennessee mountaineers and their characteristics, manners, and way of living.

Thornborough, Laura. "Americans the Twentieth Century Forgot: A Visit to Our Contemporary Ancestors in the Great Smokies—Customs Surviving From the Elizabethan Age—The Results of Centuries of Isolation." *Travel*, L (April 1928), 25–29.

A visit to the homes of mountaineers before the National Park was established, observing their ways and hearing their recollections of how their parents lived. With photographs.

———. *The Great Smoky Mountains.* Rev. and enlarged ed. Knoxville: Univ. of Tennessee Press, 1956. 180p.

"Written from an actual, intimate knowledge of the Great Smoky Mountains and mountain people, covering many years," the book contains stories told by the Old Timers, giving their way of living, their customs, and their speech, as well as the history of the National Park, the mountain trails, and visits to various interesting places.

Tilly, Bette Baird. "Aspects of Social and Economic Life in West Tennessee Before the Civil War." Unpubl. diss. Memphis State Univ., 1974. 397p.

Discusses settlement patterns, food, clothing, life style, agriculture, transportation, religion, education, medicine, law and order, and entertainment.

Ulmann, Doris. *The Appalachian Photographs of Doris Ulmann.* Penland, N.C.: Jargon Society, 1971. 63p.

Sixty-two excellent photographs of the people, some showing them working at crafts such as weaving, basketmaking.

Vance, Rupert B. *Human Geography of the South: A Study in Regional Resources and Human Adequacy.* Chapel Hill: Univ. of North Carolina Press, 1932. 596p. Rpt. New York: Russell & Russell, 1968.

"The value to social science of these physical regions lives in the human uses to which they are devoted." Discusses the basic geographic regions of Tennessee.

Walker, Hugh. *Tennessee Tales.* Nashville: Aurora, 1970. 221p.

Brief descriptive and historical sketches of places in Middle Tennessee, originally published in the Sunday edition of the *Nashville Tennessean.* Contains some legends and tales, and some place names.

Walkup, Fairfax Proudfit. "My Southern Comfort." Pasadena, Calif.: n.p. 1970? (Reproduced from typescript copy; in Memphis Room, Memphis Public Library.)

Reminiscences of the author's childhood in Memphis: play, reading, food, Christmas celebration, home and family life, etc., in the late 19th and early 20th century.

Warner, James H. "Our Amazing Ancestors." *South Atlantic Quarterly*, XXXV (Jan. 1936), 62–73.

Gives "concrete examples of several phases of the pioneer life of our southern ancestors," including religion, treatment of slaves and criminals, cures for ailments. Taken from John Sevier's diary, court records, and 18th-century newspapers.

Webster, J.C. *Last of the Pioneers; or Old Times in East Tenn., Being the Life and Reminiscences of Pharaoh Jackson Chesney (Aged 120 Years).* Knoxville: S.B. Newman, Printer, 1902. 129p.

Customs and living conditions of the 19th century, as told to the author by an ex-slave living in Union County, Tennessee. Good description and detail on clothing, social gatherings for mutual assistance, transportation, harvesting and threshing, saw mills and corn mills, etc.

Wheeler, Lester R. "A Study of the Remote Mountain People of the Tennessee Valley." *Journal of the Tennessee Academy of Science*, X (Jan. 1935), 33–36.

A comparison of living conditions in the early 1900s with those of 1935. Describes the one-room log cabin, furniture, farm stock, and social life.

White, Newman Ivey, ed. *The Frank C. Brown Collection of North Carolina Folklore.* 7 vols. Durham, N.C.: Duke Univ. Press, 1952-1964.

An excellent collection. Reference is given to variants in other states, including

Tennessee. (Individual volumes are listed under their editors in this bibliography.)

Williams, Cratis D. "The Southern Mountaineer in Fact and Fiction." 3 vols. Ph.D. diss.: New York Univ., 1961.

Task set: "to seek out the evidence to establish historically the existence of a Southern Mountaineer and to identify him in terms of his differentiation from other Southern types, and then to study the presentation of this same mountaineer in fiction."

Williams, Joseph S. *Old Times in West Tennessee. Reminisces–Semi-Historic–of Pioneer Life and the Early Emigrant Settlers of the Big Hatchie Country.* By a Descendant of the First Settlers. Memphis: W.G. Cheeney, Printer and Publisher, 1873. 295p.

Reminiscences and anecdotes of early settlers in West Tennessee, jokes played on one another, and tall tales.

Williams, Samuel C. "Nashville As Seen By Travelers, 1801–1821." *Tennessee Historical Magazine*, Ser. 2, I (April 1931), 182–206.

Glimpses of youthful Nashville by 17 travelers, describing the people's generosity, business, etc.

Williamson, J.W., ed. *An Appalachian Symposium: Essays Written in Honor of Cratis D. Williams.* Boone, N.C.: Appalachian State Univ. Press, 1977. 223p.

Includes nineteen papers. (Two—"Old Christmas in Appalachia" by Chester Young, and "The Gap in Oral Tradition" by Betty N. Smith—are listed by subject in this bibliography.)

Wilson, Charles Morrow. "Elizabethan America." *Atlantic Monthly*, CXLIV (Aug. 1929), 238–44.

A general description of manners and customs in the Southern Highlands, including Tennessee. Mentions speech, diet, magic, weather signs, and moonshining.

Wirt, Alvin B. *The Upper Cumberland of Pioneer Times.* Washington, D.C.: The Author, 1954. 82p.

The development of roads and the listing of them by name; sketches of early hostelries; early industries; religious denominations and camp meetings; outlaws and lawlessness; early mail service.

Wood, Mayme Parrott. *Hitch Hiking Along the Holston River from 1792–1962: A Peep at East Tennessee from King's Meadows (Bristol) to White's Fort (Knoxville) Via McBee's Ferry (Strawberry Plains.)* Gatlinburg, Tenn.: The Author, 1964. 238p.

Telling of early settlers; early navigation of the Tennessee River; early merchants with some of their accounts; social life; schools; the first court; recipes for Sassafras Jelly, Blackberry Syrup for Cholera and Summer Complaint, Indian Bean Bread, and Chestnut Bread.

Woodward, F.G. "An Early Tennessee Almanac and Its Maker: Hill's Almanac, 1825–1862." *Tennessee Folklore Society Bulletin*, XVIII (March 1952), 9–14.

The influence on the Middle Tennessee household of "the most famous of early Tennessee almanacs," a description of its contents, and an interesting account of its history.

Yetman, Norman R., ed. *Voices From Slavery*. New York: Holt, Rinehart, 1970. 368p.

Interviews of ex-slaves from the Slaves Narrative Collection of the Federal Writers' Project. Index contains references to Tennessee.

V. History

The accompanying map will be helpful in giving a geographical location for the county or community names in many entries in this bibliography. For brief information on the three Grand Divisions see: Folmsbee, *History of Tennessee* (Section V); Hamer, *Tennessee, A History* (Section V); Holt, *Economic and Social Beginnings of Tennessee* (Section IV).

County histories have been selected somewhat at random. For a more complete list see: Smith, *Tennessee History, A Bibliography* (Section I).

General History

Abernethy, Thomas P. *From Frontier to Plantation in Tennessee; A Study in Frontier Democracy*. Chapel Hill: Univ. of North Carolina Press, 1932. 392p. Rpt. University: Univ. of Alabama Press, 1967. (*Southern Historical Publications*, No. 12.)

A chapter on the frontiersman describes the composition of society, houses, food, crops, products, roads; the chapter on the development of a frontier gives economic conditions, growth of educational institutions, transportation, trade; another covers frontier religion.

Carter, Hodding. "Tennessee." *Holiday*, VII (Nov. 1950), 34–51, 90–97.

An interesting history of the state, linking pioneer, frontier ways with present-tense, up-to-date developments.

Corlew, Robert E. *Tennessee, A Short History, Second Edition*. Knoxville: Univ. of Tennessee Press, 1981.

This completely rewritten edition of the 1969 work (see Folmsbee et al.) traces the history of the Volunteer State from its beginnings to the present.

Dykeman, Wilma. *Tennessee: A Bicentennial History*. New York: Norton, 1975. 206p.

"A story of people building on the past." Brings out the attitudes and ways of living developed from the heritage of Tennesseans.

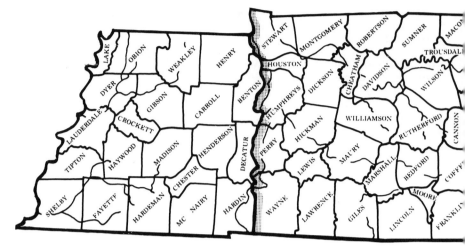

West Tennessee   Middle Tennessee

Folmsbee, Stanley J., et al. *History of Tennessee*. 4 vols. New York: Lewis Historical Publishing Co., 1960.

    Volume I, Chapter 12, Social and Economic Developments, describes the pioneer way of life, agriculture and industry, religious and educational institutions.

————. *Tennessee, A Short History*. Knoxville: Univ. of Tennessee Press, 1969.

    Based on the 4-volume edition of 1960. (See above S.V. Corlew, Robert E., for 2nd edition.)

Gilmore, James R. *John Sevier as a Commonwealth-Builder*. New York: Appleton, 1887. 321p.

    Chapter XI, Pioneer Life in 1796, tells of farm life, social gatherings, Sunday meetings, a backwoods physician, postal service, and Cowan's store.

Hale, Will T., and Merrit L. Dixon. *A History of Tennessee and Tennesseans*. 8 vols. Chicago: Lewis Publishing Co., 1913.

    Volume I contains chapters on the progress of the settlements, the Melungeons, religion, early schools and textbooks, superstitions, attire, amusements, and vices and shortcomings.

Hamer, Philip M. *Tennessee, A History, 1673–1932*. 4 vols. New York: American Historical Society, 1933.

    Volume I has chapters on the frontier state and early transportation on land and water, the early railroad movement, and coal mining.

Historical Records Survey. "Tennessee." Nashville: U.S. Works Project Administration, 1936–1942.

    Numerous typewritten volumes of records copied by WPA workers include church records, county court records, estate books, and wills. Gives useful information on property, way of living, etc.

History of Tennessee from the Earliest Time to the Present, Together with a Biographical Sketch of --- County . . . Besides a Valuable Fund of Notes, Original Observations, Reminiscences, Etc., Etc. 6 vols. Nashville: Goodspeed Publishing Co., 1887. 1482p. Rpt. Columbia, Tenn.: Woodward and Stinson Printing Co., 1971–79. Original paging.

    An account from frontier days to the Civil War, with a history of certain counties in each of the six volumes. Gives the location of grist mills, stores, courts, etc.

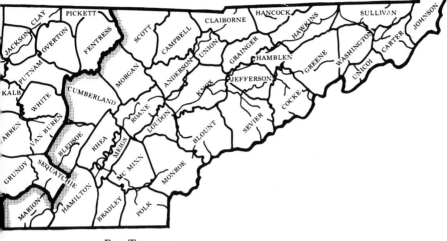

East Tennessee

Imlay, Gilbert. *A Topographical Description of the Western Territory of North America* . . . . 3rd ed. London: Printed for J. Debrett, 1797. 598p.

Contains a chapter on the state of "Tenassee," with a 1795 map. Gives physical description, roads and distances, climate and resources, with special reference to the importance of salt.

Moore, John Trotwood, and Austin P. Foster. *Tennessee, the Volunteer State, 1769–1923.* 4 vols. Nashville: S.J. Clarke Publishing Co., 1923.

Volume I offers a brief account of early life; clothing; religion; the Melungeons; and Tennessee desperados: the Harpes, Tom Mason, John A. Murrell, Daniel Crenshaw.

Phelan, James. *History of Tennessee: The Making of a State.* Boston: Houghton Mifflin, 1889. 478p.

Includes cabins, furniture, food, manners and customs, legislative and judicial beginnings, religion and the circuit rider, and a chapter on John A. Murrell and the reign of disorder. Good bibliography.

Ramsey, J.G.M. *The Annals of Tennessee to the End of the Eighteenth Century* . . . . 1853; rpt. Knoxville: East Tennessee Historical Society, 1967. 821p.

Frontier dwellings, food, Christmas celebrations, camp meetings, and education.

Roosevelt, Theodore. *The Winning of the West: An Account of the Exploration and Settlement of Our Country from the Alleghanies to the Pacific.* 6 vols. New York: G.P. Putnam and Sons, 1889.

The development of a way of life and of self-government is traced from the time of the backwoodsmen and the Holston and Cumberland settlements to the establishment of the state government in Tennessee.

Rothrock, Mary U. *Discovering Tennessee.* Chapel Hill: Univ. of North Carolina Press, 1962. 597p.

An elementary text, "an account of a people and their growth, in relation to their environment," giving good, clear detail. Travel and transport: boats, wagons, stagecoach; family household tasks; household industries; farming; mining; schools; law; religion; weddings.

Warden, D.B. *A Statistical, Political and Historical Account of the United States of North America, From the Period of*

Their First Colonization to the Present Day. 3 vols. Edinburgh: Printed for Archibald Constable and Co., 1819.

"To put his readers in possession of a full and authentic collection of the most interesting facts regarding the population, industry, wealth, power and resources of the United States." Volume II, pp. 345–63, tells of the manners and character, health, government, and military organization of Tennesseans.

White, Robert H. *Tennessee, Its Growth and Progress.* Nashville: The Author, 1947. 709p.

An elementary textbook but very good in details, sometimes with illustrations, concerning houses of the pioneers, furniture, food, clothing, occupations, religion, education, recreation, and government.

East Tennessee History

Armstrong, Zella. *History of Hamilton County and Chattanooga, Tennessee.* 2 vols. Chattanooga: Lookout Publishing Co., 1931 (v.I), 553p.; 1940 (v.II), 343p.

Volume I is a biography with photographs. Volume II covers early settlement, courts and courthouses, churches and schools.

Battaglia, Joseph C. "The Social and Economic History of Maryville Since 1890." Unpubl. Master's thesis, Univ. of Tennessee, Knoxville, 1936. 78p.

Brief description of early settlement and way of living: clothes, meals, and occupations.

Brewer, Alberta, and Carson Brewer. *Valley So Wild: A Folk History.* Knoxville: East Tennessee Historical Society, 1975. 382p.

History of the Little Tennessee watershed. "Seeks to place a finger over the pulse of the valley and let the people tell their story. The flavor of their language, their everyday customs, their love of the wild beauty of the region, and their identity with the river."

Burns, Inez E. *History of Blount County, Tennessee: From War Trail to Landing Strip, 1795–1955.* Maryville, Tenn.:

Sponsored by Mary Blount Chapter Daughters of American Revolution and Tennessee Historical Commission, 1957. 375p.

Useful chapters on early inns and watering places, churches of Blount County, education, industries, and occupations.

Dunn, Durwood Clay. "Cades Cove During the Nineteenth Century." Unpubl. Ph.D. diss. Univ. of Tennessee, Knoxville, 1976. 252p.

A scholarly study, "analyzing the nature and degree of change within the community, and the extent to which cultural continuity existed throughout the nineteenth century." Includes the life of early settlers, hunting and trapping, herb and ginseng collecting, farming, the development of industries—among them the Cades Cove Bloomery Forge—churches, and place-names.

———. "The Folk Culture of Cades Cove, Tennessee." *Tennessee Folklore Society Bulletin,* XLIII (June 1977), 67–87.

A revised and expanded chapter from the above dissertation.

Fink, Miriam. "Some Phases of the Social and Economic History of Jonesboro, Tennessee, Prior to the Civil War." Unpubl. Master's thesis, Univ. of Tennessee, Knoxville, 1934. 103p.

Accounts of early justice, with punishments for misdeeds; the growth of religious and educational institutions; means of travel and the building of roads; the first stores, their wares and prices.

Fink, Paul M. *Jonesborough: The First Century of Tennessee's First Town.* Washington, D.C.: U.S. Dept. of Housing and Urban Development, 1972. (Publication No. 394.)

A helpful account of the "daily lives and activities of the people who made the town in the early days" tells of the judgment and penalties of major and lesser crimes; stage lines carrying mail and passengers; public buildings; trade and commerce (local manufacturing); travel and accommodations; churches and schools.

Foscue, Edwin J. *Gatlinburg: Gateway*

to the Great Smokies. Dallas: Southern Methodist Univ. Press, 1946. 19p.

A history of the region and its physical setting, exploration and settlement, logging and lumbering industry, Pi Beta Phi Settlement School, and the Great Smoky Mountains National Park. An enlargement of the material in *Economic Geography*, below.

———. "Gatlinburg: A Mountain Community." *Economic Geography*, XXI (July 1945), 192–205.

A history of the community, origin of the name, first settlers, and influence of the Pi Beta Phi Settlement School.

Govan, Gilbert E., and James W. Livingood. *The Chattanooga Country, 1540–1976: From Tomahawks to TVA*. New York: Dutton, 1952; 3rd ed. Knoxville: Univ. of Tennessee Press, 1977. 536p.

The third edition is revised and updated by James W. Livingood. A good history.

Greve, Jeanette S. *The Story of Gatlinburg*. Strasburg, Va.: Shenandoah Publishing House, 1931. 136p. Rpt. Gatlinburg, Tenn.: Brazos Printing Co., 1964.

Story of the settlement of White Oak Flats, now Gatlinburg. Description of cabins, clothes, manner of living, Old Harp singing, "Music Makin's," and other community gatherings.

———. "The Traditions of Gatlinburg." *East Tennessee Historical Society Publications*. No. 3 (Jan. 1931), 62–77.

Description of the early settlers of White Oak Flats, now Gatlinburg: their homes, clothing, and way of living, with emphasis on the work of the women.

Krechniak, Helen Bullard, and Joseph Marshall Krechniak. *Cumberland County's First Hundred Years*. Crossville, Tenn.: Centennial Committee, 1956. 377p.

Early settlements and how the settlers lived: flax spinning and weaving, log rolling parties, quilting bees, molasses making, and soap making.

Lillard, Roy G. *The History of Bradley County*. Cleveland, Tenn.: Bradley

County Chapter, East Tennessee Historical Society, 1976. 481p.

Early history, telling of the settlement, towns and communities, transportation, churches, education, and social life.

Merritt, Frank. *Early History of Carter County, 1760–1861*. Knoxville: East Tennessee Historical Society, 1950. 213p.

"This study has been limited to four aspects of the early county history, namely, government and politics, religious development, educational development, and slavery and secession."

O'Dell, Ruth Webb. *Over the Misty Blue Hills: The Story of Cocke County, Tennessee*. N.p., c1950. 369p.

A history of Cocke County, with a backlog of tradition, legend, and lore.

Raulston, J. Leonard, and James W. Livingood. *Sequatchie: A Story of the Southern Cumberlands*. Knoxville: Univ. of Tennessee Press, 1973. 273p.

Early settlers, their "courthouses and boundary lines," their way of life, social events (including "infares"), medical practices, circuit riders, and the last days of John Murrell, outlaw.

Rule, William, ed. *Standard History of Knoxville, Tennessee . . . .* Chicago: Lewis Publishing Co., 1900. 590p.

Early industries and stores, postal service, fire-fighting methods, and laws of Sabbath observance.

Sanderson, Esther Sharp. *County Scott and Its Mountain Folk*. Huntsville, Tenn.: The Author, 1958. 254p.

Early pioneer living, food, clothing, industries, churches, schools, and hunting. A chapter on medicine and folk remedies and one on superstitions.

Seeber, R. Clifford. "A History of Anderson County, Tennessee." Unpubl. Master's thesis, Univ. of Tennessee, Knoxville, 1928. 116p.

The exploration and settlement, early development, social problems under the care of the county court (paupers and insane, homeless children), schools, churches, building of roads, and other internal improvements.

Shields, A. Randolph. "Cades Cove in the Great Smoky Mountains National Park." *Tennessee Historical Quarterly*, XXIV (Summer 1965), 103–20. (Rpt. in McBride, Robert M., *More Landmarks of Tennessee History*.)

   Brief history of the settlers and their ways, and the projects of the National Park to preserve the mountain culture.

———. *The Cades Cove Story*. Gatlinburg: Great Smoky Mountains Natural History Association, 1977. 116p.

   An interesting discussion of life in Cades Cove—harvest events and their social occasions, weddings, Christmas Eve, death and burial customs, cemetery Decoration Day programs, churches and revivals, school activities such as spelling bees, country stores, postal service. Good photographs and descriptions of homes and farm buildings.

Taylor, Oliver. *Historic Sullivan: A History of Sullivan County, Tennessee with Brief Biographies of the Makers of History*. Bristol: King Printing Co., 1909. 330p.

   Frontier women; industries including iron works; churches; agriculture; schools; hunters; travelways: roads, stage coach, river traffic, steamboats; and postal service.

Wooten, John Morgan. *A History of Bradley County*. Cleveland: Bradley County Post 81, American Legion, with the cooperation of the Tennessee Historical Commission. 1949. 323p.

   A brief history of institutions. Gives rules of the camp meetings: seating, sounding of the horn, location of camp grounds; location of mills and mill sites.

Middle Tennessee History

Blanton, John O. "My Native Heath: An Historical Sketch of Coffee County, Tennessee and Other Things." *Coffee County Historical Society Quarterly*, II (Summer-Fall 1971), 1–33.

   Gives placenames; industries: grist mills, saw mills, cotton gin, carding factory,

hemprope factory, saltpeter cave; churches; the use of cotton, hemp, and flax for clothing; social events: log-rolling, quilting bees, corn huskings, singings, and musters.

Brandon, Helen Gould. "A History of Stewart County Tennessee." Unpubl. Master's thesis, Univ. of Tennessee, Knoxville, 1944. 101p.

   Political and organizational growth; iron works; agriculture; lumbering and miscellaneous industries; schools; churches; and transportation.

Brown, Sterling Spurlock. *History of Woodbury and Cannon County, Tennessee*. Manchester, Tenn.: Press of Doak Printing Co., 1936. 235p.

   Scattered through the history are anecdotes and descriptions of local customs.

Century Review, 1805–1905, Maury County, Tennessee: A Condensation of the Most Important Events of the Past One Hundred Years, and Descriptive Sketches of the Cities and Villages, Columbia and Mt. Pleasant in Detail. Columbia, Tenn.: Auspices of the Board of Mayor and Aldermen of Columbia, 1905. 216p. Rpt. with supplement and corrections, Maury County Historical Society, 1970. 336p.

   Early courts, business and industry developments, churches and schools, and some placename origins.

Clayton, W. Woodford. *History of Davidson County, Tennessee*. Philadelphia: J.W. Lewis, 1880. 499p.

   Brief account of pioneer life and customs, location of buildings, and biographical sketches of early families.

Corlew, Robert Ewing. *A History of Dickson County, Tennessee*. Nashville: Tennessee Historical Commission and Dickson County Historical Society, 1956. 243p.

   An account of early settlement, building of cabins, establishment of county courts, schools, churches and their ruling of the conduct of members, treatment of slaves.

Durham, Walter T. *The Great Leap*

Westward: A History of Sumner County, Tennessee from Its Beginnings to 1805. Nashville: Parthenon Press, 1969. 225p.

Building of the first homes, religion and the church, schools, social activities, and commerce.

———. *Old Sumner: A History of Sumner County, Tennessee from 1805 to 1861.* Nashville: Parthenon Press, 1972. 530p.

Early industries included a fulling mill "where cloth will be dressed"; quarrying and cutting millstones; distilleries; cabinet makers; merchants; inns and hotels for stage coach passengers; horseracing; schools and churches. The story of Elisha Cheek and what befell travelers at Cheek's tavern.

Fleming, William Stuart. *A Historical Sketch of Maury County, Read at the Centennial Celebration in Columbia, Tennessee, July 4th, 1876.* Columbia, Tenn.: Excelsior Printing Office, C.W. Kent, Manager, 1876. 65p.

An interesting account of the settlement and organization of Maury County, giving geographical details; place names; names of early settlers and their occupations; location of mills, country stores, and churches; religious events; amusements; and social gatherings.

Garrett, Jill Knight. *History of Humphreys County, Tennessee,* N.p.: The Author, 1963. 376p.

Early transportation—flat boats, keelboats, ferries, and stage line; the establishment of towns; place names; and early economic development.

Goodpasture, Albert V. *Overton County: Address of Albert V. Goodpasture Delivered at Livingston, Tennessee, July 4, 1876.* Nashville: The Author, 1877. 27p. Facsimile edition Nashville: B. C. Goodpasture, 1954.

A brief account of the settlements, schools, manner of living, and household utensils. "Two great occasions which brought the people together were the camp meeting and the general muster."

Hale, Will T. *Early History of Warren*

County. McMinnville, Tenn.: Standard Printing Co., 1930. 59p.

Interesting for brief reminiscences of elderly residents on mills, stores, flintlock rifles, farming, and clothing.

———. *History of DeKalb County, Tennessee.* Nashville: P. Hunter, 1915. 254p. Facsimile edition McMinnville, Tenn.: Ben Lomond Press, 1969.

Describes pastimes such as dances, horse races, musters, fox hunts, and social visits; farming and merchandising; food and clothing; school customs; religion; slaves and free Negroes; and stagecoach and tavern days, with many anecdotes.

Henderson, C.C. *The Story of Murfreesboro.* Murfreesboro, Tenn.: News-Banner Publishing Co., 1929. 145p.

A collection of accounts of the life of early settlers, development of government, punishment of criminals and other offenders, etc.

Jones, N.W. *A History of Mount Pleasant, Especially, and the Western Part of Maury County, Generally, As He Remembers It.* Nashville: McQuiddy Printing Co., 1903. 78p. Rpt. Columbia, Tenn.: Maury County Historical Society, 1965.

An informal history, giving personal names; locations of stores, mills; and so forth. Describes methods of farming, medical practices, and various events.

Kinard, Margaret. "Frontier Development of Williamson County." *Tennessee Historical Quarterly,* VIII (March, June 1949), 3–33, 127–53.

Homes, furniture, housekeeping articles, farming and stock raising. Duties of a frontier county court: records of stock marks, stray animals; appointment of local officials; administration of justice for the poor, insane and orphans; militia musters. Much information is taken from county records.

———. "Frontier Development of Williamson County, Tennessee." Unpubl. Master's thesis, Vanderbilt Univ., 1948. 112p.

County Court minutes, wills, and inventories give a picture of the development of an agricultural economy, land holdings, farm implements, and household possessions, and of the influence of the county court on community life.

Knight, George Allen. *My Album of Memories*. Knoxville: Southeastern Composition Services, 1971. 134p.

Reminiscences of the author's home, customs, and good manners in Overton County.

McCallum, James. *A Brief Sketch of the Settlement and Early History of Giles County, Tennessee*. 1876. Pulaski, Tenn.: Pulaski Citizen, 1928. 134p.

Describes the early settlers: their character, domestic habits, and economy; camp meetings; mills; the production of cotton; the manufacture of powder.

McClain, Iris Hopkins. *A History of Houston County*. N.p.: The Author, 1966. 241p.

A history with brief accounts of mills, iron works, schools, etc.

————. *A History of Stewart County, Tennessee*. N.p.: The Author, 1965. 152p.

Early happenings taken from court records; the iron industry, with names and location of furnaces; taverns and 1811 tavern rates; road building; ferries, flat boats, keelboats, and steamboats.

MacKellar, William H. *Chuwalee— Chronicles of Franklin County*. Winchester, Tenn.: Chronicle Publishing Co., 1973. 135p.

Pioneer cabins; furniture; food; Jesse Bean's gun shop; muster day; cotton growing, processing and use; transportation.

Merritt, Dixon, ed. *The History of Wilson County: Its Land and Its Life*. Compiled and written by History Associates of Wilson County. Lebanon, Tenn.: County Court of Wilson County, 1961. 453p.

Settlement patterns, place names, early roads, and early industry. "The Life of the People (Settlement to Civil War)," pp. 436–53, is especially useful for customs. Detailed description of ash-hopper and soap

making. Pictures of exterior of pioneer cabin, hearth with articles used by pioneers.

Parker, Elizabeth C. "History of Giles County, Tennessee." Unpubl. Master's thesis, Middle Tennessee State College, 1953. 101p.

Early settlers and routes by which they came; their way of life, crops; variety of goods in a general store; early government and first ordinances passed in the town of Pulaski, showing offenses and punishment; the establishment of schools, churches and camp meetings; place names.

Prater, Otto. "Economic History of White County, Tennessee." Unpubl. Master's thesis, George Peabody College for Teachers, 1932. 126p.

Describes the life of the settlers; their homes and furnishings; farm implements; food and clothing; their use of agricultural, forest, and industrial resources.

Putnam, A.W. *History of Middle Tennessee: or, Life and Times of General James Robertson*. Nashville: The Author, 1859. Facsimile edition, with introduction by Stanley F. Horn, Knoxville: Univ. of Tennessee Press, 1971. 682p. (Tennesseana Editions.)

Seals, Monroe. *History of White County, Tennessee*. 1935; rpt. Spartanburg, S.C.: Reprint Co. Publishers, 1974. 152p.

Contains good information on the way of living of early settlers: food, clothing, time keeping, education, religion, buildings, utensils, and industries.

Sims, Carlton C., ed. *A History of Rutherford County*. N.p., 1947. 236p.

Chapters by nine contributors, for the sesquicentennial celebration of the state. Tells of the importance and duties of the county court, including the register of stock marks. Cock fights are among the listed recreations. Gives a brief history of the medical profession, education, and religion, with biographical sketches.

Spence, W., Jerome D. Spence, and David L. Spence. *A History of Hickman County, Tennessee*. Nashville: Gospel Advocate Publishing Co., 1900. 509p.

A history of each of the first through the fifteenth districts, giving the names of residents, occupations, place names. Incidents termed "a characteristic of 'the good old days' " include a description of shooting matches and flintlock rifles.

Turner, William Bruce. *History of Maury County, Tennessee.* Nashville: Parthenon Press, 1955. 404p.

History of the towns and early settlers. Gives place names, and information about the turnpikes.

Titus, W.P. *Picturesque Clarksville, Past and Present: A History of the City of the Hills.* N.p.: The Author, 1887. 522p.

A carriage factory, merchants, banking, newspapers, doctors, preachers, ladies' fairs, horseracing, and "free fights."

Winters, Ralph L. *Historical Sketches of Adams, Robertson County, Tennessee and Port Royal, Montgomery County, From 1799 to 1968.* Clarksville: The Author, 1968. 280p.

Largely personal and family sketches, but tells of tools and their use, old methods and equipment of housework, a Negro church, the location of mills and factories. Pictures of buildings, tools, bridges, etc.

Womack, Walter. *McMinnville at a Milestone 1810–1960.* McMinnville, Tenn.: Standard Publishing Co. and Womack Printing Co., 1960. 327p.

The original plat of 1810 given, with history of the landowners and type of construction used. Organizations listed with their history; agriculture and industry discussed.

West Tennessee History

Alexander, Mai. *Dyer County: Garden Spot of the World.* Dyersburg, Tenn.: Wallace Printing Co., 1974. 166p.

Principally family histories, followed by accounts of social activities and miscellaneous bits from diaries—a peddler's visit, old school days, etc.

Carmichael, Claudia Jeter. "A History of Weakley County, Tennessee, Through

1861." Unpubl. Master's thesis, Univ. of Tennessee, Knoxville, 1970. 75p.

Tells of the settlement and establishment of the county; a brief account of buildings, clothing and recreation; business, professions; agriculture; religion; education; transportation, especially railroads.

Carroll County Historical Society. *Carroll County.* N.p., 1972. 192p.

Sesquicentennial booklet. Tells of a county fair, a carding mill, some place names, and some recipes.

Culp, Frederick M., and Mrs. Robert E. Ross. *Gibson County, Past and Present: The First General History of One of West Tennessee's Pivotal Counties.* Trenton: Gibson County Historical Society, 1961. 583p.

Organization of the county, incorporated towns, and communities; schools; churches; industries; place names; special events and customs, such as the First Monday celebration held in August (mule and horse sale); and anecdotes.

Davis, James D. *History of Memphis: The History of the City of Memphis, Being a Compilation of the Most Important Documents and Historical Events Connected with the Purchase of Its Territory, Laying Off of the City and Early Settlement.* Memphis: Hite, Crumpton & Kelly, 1873. 320p.

Includes "The Old Times Papers" which appeared in *The Appeal,* "a series of stories of early days." Many reminiscences and anecdotes of characters and events, given in an entertaining manner.

Deming, Raymond M. "Hardeman County: Its Origin and Economic Development." Unpubl. Ph.D. diss. George Peabody College for Teachers, 1958. 276p.

Migration routes and ways of travel; types of houses; preparation of the land for farming (cotton being the principal crop); clothing; industrial pursuits; the legal status, food, and clothing of slaves.

Gardner, John A. "Early Times in Weakley County." *West Tennessee Historical Society Papers,* XVII (1963). 68–84.

An address delivered at Dresden, Tennessee, July 4, 1876, by one of the early residents of Weakley County. Gives "a synopsis of the scenes and incidents in the county for the past fifty years."

Humphreys, Cecil C. "The History of the Reelfoot Lake Region." Unpubl. Master's thesis, Univ. of Tennessee, Knoxville, 1939. 95p.

Tells of the early settlers of the Reelfoot region in Tennessee. Includes the Indian legend concerning the earthquake and has a chapter on the Night Riders.

Keating, J.M. *History of the City of Memphis and Shelby County, Tennessee.* 2 vols.: I by J.M. Keating; II by O.F. Vedder. Syracuse, N.Y.: D. Mason & Co., Publishers, 1888.

Life in and about Memphis in 1827: social events; camp meetings; militia musters; beginnings of commerce; John Murrell and his clan. Includes a map of Memphis as originally laid out by William Lawrence in 1819.

Lowe, Walter Edgar. "History of Reelfoot Lake." Unpubl. Master's thesis, George Peabody College for Teachers, 1930. 196p.

Gives the Indian legend, the accounts of residents of the area who experienced the earthquakes, of travelers on flatboats and other boats, and reports of the Night Riders.

Majors, C.L. *McNairy-Hardin Counties: Gen. Marcus J. Wright's Reminiscences of the Early Settlements and Early Settlers of McNairy County, Tennessee,* originally published in 1882 by the author, and P.M. Harbert's *Early History of Hardin County, Tennessee,* taken from the *West Tennessee Historical Society Papers,* No.1, (1947). Rpt. C.L. Majors. Memphis: Tri-State Printing & Binding Co., 1968. 96p.

Sketches of individuals and families in McNairy County, telling of occupations, etc., and a brief early history of Hardin County.

Marshall, E.H., ed. *History of Obion County: Towns and Communities,*

Churches, Schools, Farming, Factories, Social and Political. Union City, Tenn.: Daily Messenger, 1941. 272p.

Accounts from various communities concerning businesses, schools, churches, crimes, etc.

Peters, Kate Johnston, ed. *Lauderdale County From Earliest Times.* Written by Descendants of its Pioneer Citizens. Ripley, Tenn.: Sugar Hill Lauderdale County Library, 1957. 377p.

Sketches of individuals and families, giving occupations, etc.

Powers, Auburn. *History of Henderson County; Comprising an Account of the Facts Connected with the Early Settlement of the County . . . .* N.p., 1930. 169p.

Chapter II, The Pioneers, tells of cooking roasting ears, hoecake, ash cake; household utensils; clothing; workings and parties; manner of living; churches and schools. Chapter VIII, Miscellaneous Facts, recounts legendary individuals, tells of Mills Darden and "Uncle Henry" Armstrong.

Smith, Jonathan Kennon Thompson. *Historic Benton—A People's History of Benton County, Tennessee.* Memphis: Richard H. Harris, 1975. 231p.

Chapter VI, Folkways, is a brief account of houses, churches, agriculture, tobacco, cotton ginning, medical services, roads, and farriers.

Stewart, J.B., Sr. *"As It Was": Plantation Life in West Tennessee Beginning 1832.* N.p.: The Author, 1974. 240p.

Story of the author's background, childhood and youth, "a way of life gone from southern cotton plantations."

Van Dyke, Roger Raymond. "A History of Henry County, Tennessee, Through 1865." Unpubl. Master's thesis, Univ. of Tennessee, Knoxville, 1966. 144p.

A history of early settlement; legislative, social, and economic development; education; and transportation. Cotton and tobacco are given as the principal agricultural and economic resources.

Williams, Emma Inman. *Historic Madison; The Story of Jackson and Madison*

County, From the Prehistoric Mound-builders to 1917. Jackson: Madison County Historical Society, 1946. 553p.

Frontier politics; early transportation including river trade and roads; mail service; medicine; the planter and farmer; social events; John A. Murrell, the outlaw.

Williams, Samuel Cole. *Beginnings of West Tennessee in the Land of the Chic-kasaws, 1541–1841.* Johnson City, Tenn.: Watauga Press, 1930. 331p.

Brief accounts of the country; its soil, forests, and animals; grants that were made in the Western District; migration and settlement; place names of counties; river transportation; militia musters; John A. Murrell, the outlaw; religion; education; agriculture; customs and way of life.

VI. Buildings

General

In this General section are titles containing information concerning materials and methods of pioneer construction; folk architectural recording; historic sites; the building of riverboats, ferries, and tunnels; and some titles covering more than one phase of the subject Buildings.

Burnett, Edmund Cody. "Shingle Making on the Lesser Waters of the Big Creek of the French Broad River." *Agricultural History*, XX (Oct. 1946), 225–35.

Sawed shingle making in the Big Creek Valley.

Creighton, Wilbur Foster. *Building of Nashville.* Rev. and enlarged by Wilbur F. Creighton, Jr., and Leland R. Johnson. Nashville: n.p., 1969. 205p.

"To record the history of a few of the prominent structures and utilities": includes accounts of pioneer construction; building materials and tools; toll roads; transportation of timber resources by river; building river boats, tunnels, bridges, ferries, etc.

Fielder, George F. "Folk Architecture in Tennessee." *Tennessee Anthropologist,* I (Spring 1976), 48–57.

The author summarizes the procedure of architectural recording necessary to provide a statistically adequate data base and calls for a new organized effort in folk architectural research in Tennessee.

Historic Sites Survey. Prepared by the First Tennessee-Virginia Development District Under Contract with the Tennessee State Planning Office, 1977. 99p.

Contains good photographs of houses, inns, farm buildings, and iron furnace in northeast Tennessee.

Historic Sites Survey for Anderson, Campbell, Claiborne, Grainger, Knox, Scott, and Union Counties. Knoxville: East Tennessee Development District, 1974. 120p.

Brief description of buildings, often giving materials and methods of construction.

Historical Album of East Tennessee. N.p., 1898. Unpaged.

Twenty-four photographs of old buildings, monuments, etc., including log houses, smokehouse, mill, school, and log fence.

Kniffen, Fred. "On Corner-Timbering." *Pioneer America,* I (Jan. 1969), 1–8.

"The student of pioneer America should always observe the type of corner-timbering employed in every log structure." With drawings by Henry Glassie.

McBride, Robert M. "Historic Sites in Tennessee, Preservation and Restoration." *Antiques*, C (Sept. 1971), 394–401.

Pictures of Old Deery Inn, Netherland Inn, Ramsey House, Blount Mansion interior, Davy Crockett cabin, and Magevney House.

"Making Split and Shaved Shingles." *American Agriculturalist*, XXXVIII (June 1879), 223.

A good description of the step-by-step process from splitting to packing, with illustrations.

Morse, Mike. "The Chimney, An Important Part of Traditional Life," 1973–179. Unpubl. MS. 6p. with 24 photographs. Western Kentucky Univ. Folklore, Folklife, and Oral History Archives.

Discusses stone and brick, single hip, double hip, and stepped chimneys in southeastern Kentucky and northeastern Tennessee. Clear photographs of old chimneys.

The National Register of Historic Places. Prepared in the Office of Archeology and Historic Preservation. Washington, D.C.: Government Printing Office, 1976. 961p.

Arranged by state and county, contains a brief history and description of all properties added to the National Register through December 31, 1974. Section on Tennessee, pp. 711–24.

Nelson, Lee H. "Nail Chronology As An Aid to Dating Old Buildings." *History News*, XXIII (Nov. 1968), 203–214.

Covers the 18th and 19th centuries. No mention of Tennessee, but useful.

Patrick, James. *Architecture in Tennessee, 1768–1897*. Contemporary photography by Michael A. Tomlan. Knoxville: Univ. of Tennessee Press, 1981. 280p.

A critical history of Tennessee architecture, illustrated with 260 photographs, and including a location and ownership catalog. It is an important source of information about dwellings, schools, churches, courthouses, and inns.

"Pioneer Relics." *Tennessee Conservationist*, XXI (March 1955), 12–13.

Pictures of a log cabin, covered bridge, grist mill, corn crib, blockhouse, swinging bridge, foot log, and sorghum making.

"Pioneer Relics." *Tennessee Conservationist*, XXXI (Aug. 1965), 8–9.

Pictures of a covered bridge, a waterwheel grist mill, Andrew Johnson's tailor shop, blockhouse at Benton, a swinging bridge, a pioneer barn, first courthouse at Lewisburg, Sam Houston's schoolhouse, and Davy Crockett's tavern in Tennessee (all exteriors).

Riedl, Norbert F., Donald B. Ball, and Anthony P. Cavender. *A Survey of Traditional Architecture and Related Material Folk Culture Patterns in the Normandy Reservoir, Coffee County, Tennessee*. Knoxville: Tennessee Valley Authority, 1976. 261p. (Report of Investigations No. 17, Dept. of Anthropology, Univ. of Tennessee.)

A detailed study of log and frame buildings; dwellings, barns, and other farm structures; grist mills, cemeteries, nonmodern fencing, and miscellaneous tools and other objects. With photographs, floor plans, and drawings.

Spoden, Muriel C., comp. *Historic Sites of Sullivan County* by the Sullivan County Historical Commission and Associates. Kingsport: Kingsport Press, 1976. 233p.

"A record showing the houses and buildings which have survived . . . There are some comments on architecture, some references to genealogy, and some threads of history." Brief accounts with photographs.

United States, National Park Service. *Historic American Buildings Survey*. Washington, D.C.: Government Printing Office, 1941. 470p. Rpt. 1971.

A list of early houses in existence in 1941, for which a permanent graphic record was deposited in the Library of Congress. The list gives location, material, type, period, architect if known, and the number of drawings and photographs on file.

Dwellings

Evans, E. Raymond. "The Strip House in Tennessee Folk-Architecture." *Tennessee Folklore Society Bulletin*, XLII (Dec. 1976), 163–66.

A type of housing developed by rural Blacks in East Tennessee during the Great Depression.

Fielder, George F., Jr. "Log Structures in the Tellico Reservoir, Eastern Tennessee." 1972. 11p., drawings. Riedl Collection, Univ. of Tennessee Library, Knoxville.

Buildings "that will be affected by construction and use of the Tennessee Valley Authority (TVA) Tellico Dam and reservoir."

Glassie, Henry. "The Appalachian Log Cabin." *Mountain Life and Work*, XXXIX (Winter 1963), 5–14.

"The log cabin is a fit symbol of Southern architecture, as in it were brought together the best of German and British architectural traditions." The history and structure of the log cabin, with sketches of adaptations.

————. "Southern Mountain Houses: A Study in American Folk Culture." Unpubl. Master's thesis, State Univ. of New York College at Oneonta, 1965. 244p. (Copy in Univ. of Tennessee Library, Knoxville.)

A carefully researched study covering construction, elements of form, and house types in a part of the Appalachian region including eastern Tennessee.

————. "The Types of the Southern Mountain Cabin." In Brunvand, Jan Harold. *The Study of American Folklore*. New York: Norton, 1968. pp. 338–70.

Includes types of cabins in the Great Smokies and their foothills, giving details of structure and sketches of interior and exterior items. Has excellent bibliographic notes.

Grossman, Charles S. *The Chandler Jenkins Cabin Building and Pig Pen: Historic Structures Report, Great Smoky Mountains National Park*. Washington, D.C.: U.S. National Park Service, Office of Archeology and Historic Preservation. 1965.

————. "Great Smoky Pioneers." U.S. National Park Service, Region One. *Regional Review*, VII (July-Aug. 1941), 2–6.

Describes the routes of the first settlers in the area which is now the Great Smoky Mountains National Park, noting "how topography and environment influenced the activities and architecture," the building of shelters and homes, and the possessions of the people. Photographs of two homes, a corncrib and gear shed.

Hicks, Nannie Lee. *Historic Treasure Spots of Knox County, Tennessee*. Knoxville: Simon Harris Chapter, DAR. 1964. 82p.

Pictures and history of houses still standing; log houses and early frame houses.

Hudson, J. Paul. "Appalachian Folk Ways." *Antiques*, LVII (May 1950), 368–69.

A brief article with photographs of a cabin of sawn logs, detail of a door with wooden hinge and peg catch, riflemaker, woman spinning yarn, pine chest with horseshoe hinges, a blacksmith, interior of the Walker Sisters' cabin in the Great Smoky Mountains.

Hulan, Richard H. "Middle Tennessee and the Dogtrot House." *Pioneer America*, VII (July 1975), 37–46.

Four early Middle Tennessee houses, with pictures and a floor plan.

Kilgore, Sherry J. "A Brief Survey of Frontier Architectural Characteristics in Robertson and Sumner Counties." *Tennessee Folklore Society Bulletin*, XLIV (Sept. 1978), 116–26.

"Three houses—one log, one brick and one stone—still stand as frontier examples of the colonial influence in construction and style." Photographs and sketches of floor plans.

Kniffen, Fred, and Henry Glassie. "Building in Wood in the Eastern United States: A Time-Place Perspective." *Geographical Review*, LVI (Jan. 1966), 40–66.

An examination of a basic aspect of settlements, the method of constructing buildings. Concerned principally with horizontal notched-log construction, with details of corner-notching. Pictures of houses.

————. "Folk Housing: Key to Diffusion." *Annals of the Association of American Geographers*, LV (Dec. 1965), 545–77.

The "Dogtrot" log house and the four-crib barn cited as especially relevant to Tennessee.

Kroll, Harry Harrison. "Dark Cabins." In Jones, Lealon N., *Eve's Stepchildren*. Caldwell, Idaho: Caxton Printers, 1942. pp. 75–82.

"You can know folks by the shacks they live in"—a description of sharecroppers' cabins.

Madden, Robert R., and T. Russell Jones. *Alfred Reagan House and Tub Mill: Historic Structures Report, Great Smoky Mountains National Park, Historic Data Section*. Washington, D.C.: U.S. National Park Service, Office of Archeology and Historic Preservation, 1969. 33p.

Historical and architectural information with illustrations, plans, and plates.

————. *Walker Sisters Home: Historic Structures Report, Part II and Furnishing Study, Great Smoky Mountains National Park Historical Data Section*. Washington, D.C.: U.S. National Park Service, Office of Archeology and Historic Preservation, 1969. 58p. 53 photographs, 9 plans.

The story of the Walker family, their land and house, and their way of living; a list of pioneer culture items; photographs of the family, home, and garden, barn, spring house, pig pen, blacksmith shop; detailed condition of construction.

Olinger, Danny E. "Folk Architecture on the North Fork of the Holston River—Log Structure." 1968. 46p. Riedl Collection, Univ. of Tennessee Library, Knoxville.

Includes photographs and sketches.

O'Malley, James R. "Functional Aspects of Folk Housing: A Case for the 'I' House, Union County, Tennessee." *Tennessee Folklore Society Bulletin*, XXXVIII (March 1972), 1–4.

Considers the validity of a house form as an indication of economic attainment, concluding that "the validity of I houses as indicators can provide the layman and professional alike with a useful element of field observation." A picture of an I house in Union County is on the cover of this issue.

————. "The 'I' House: An Indicator of Agricultural Opulence in Upper East Tennessee." Unpubl. Master's thesis, Univ. of Tennessee, Knoxville, 1972. 102p.

In this thesis the basic form of houses and outbuildings is studied and used as an expression of agricultural attainment. Three farms are given as examples. "It is felt that a form, whether a housetype or other manifestations of man's cultural traits, can be used as a quick, visible, and in many cases very reliable, indicator of the importance most men place on achieving economic status."

————. "The I House in Union County, Tennessee." 1971. 11p. Riedl Collection, Univ. of Tennessee Library, Knoxville.

Gives location, construction materials, and settlement patterns.

Scofield, Edna. "The Evolution and Development of Tennessee Houses." *Journal of the Tennessee Academy of Science*, XI (Oct. 1936), 229–40.

Diagrams and photographs of rural houses, showing "double-pen" houses and their variations.

Tate, Susan Douglas. "Thomas Hope of Tennessee, c. 1757–1820, Home Carpenter and Joiner." Unpubl. Master's thesis, Univ. of Tennessee, Knoxville, c. 1972. 163p.

"Virtually the only Knoxville craftsman of the period whose name has endured, Hope was in general demand. The works and the influence of Thomas Hope contributed to the evolution of Knoxville from frontier survival to successful settlement." Describes architectural details and furniture attributed to Hope.

Weslager, C.A. *The Log Cabin in America From Pioneer Days to the Present*. New Brunswick, N.J., Rutgers Univ. Press, 1969. 382p.

Treats "the part played by the log cabin in early American family life." Discusses the structural aspects, and tools and furniture, as well as the tasks of father and sons, and mother and daughter in providing food and clothing and caring for all the needs of the family. Photographs of several Tennessee buildings are included.

Wilson, Eugene H. "The Single Pen Log House in the South." *Pioneer America*, II (Jan. 1970), 21–28.

A report on some existing single pen log houses in the Southeast. Tables give date of construction, type of corner, and dimensions.

Farm and Utility Buildings

Arthur, Eric, and Dudley Witney. *The Barn: A Vanishing Landmark in North America.* Greenwich, Conn.: New York Graphic Society, 1972. 256p.

A well illustrated book, containing two Blount County barns in Tennessee, with photographs and diagrams.

Brakebill, David. "Folk Architecture: The Cantilevered Barns of Eastern Tennessee." Unpubl. Bachelor of Architecture thesis, Univ. of Tennessee, Knoxville, 1973. 52p. Copy in Riedl Collection, Univ. of Tennessee Library, Knoxville.

Types and construction of barns.

"Brown's Mill, Near Murfreesboro." *Tennessee Folklore Society Bulletin*, XXXIII (March 1967).

Cover photograph.

Crabb, Alfred Leland. "The Disappearing Smokehouse." *Tennessee Historical Quarterly*, XXV (Summer 1966), 155–68.

A description of remaining smokehouses in Kentucky and Tennessee, with a brief account of curing methods and two recipes.

"Double Crib Barn, Wayne County, Tennessee." *Tennessee Folklore Society Bulletin*, XXX (Dec. 1964).

Cover photograph.

"Double Crib Log Barn, Polk County,

Tennessee." *Tennessee Folklore Society Bulletin*, XXXI (March 1965).

Cover photograph.

Evans, E. Raymond. "The Palen Fence: An Example of Appalachian Folk Culture." *Tennessee Anthropologist*, III (Spring 1978), 93–99.

Observations concerning the construction and the use of the palen fence, with a sketch and two photographs.

Glassie, Henry. "The Old Barns of Appalachia." *Mountain Life and Work*, XLI (Summer 1965), 21–30.

Describes the construction and use of log barns. Gives clear sketches of various structures including corncrib, double-crib, four-crib, and transverse-crib barns in Monroe, Greene, Blount, Sevier, and Polk counties in Tennessee.

———. "The Pennsylvania Barn in the South." *Pennsylvania Folklife*, XV (Winter 1965-66), 8–19.

Description of the construction and floor plans. Pictures of individual barns with their locations. Gives a map showing areas of distribution of barns in Tennessee.

———. "The Smaller Outbuildings of the Southern Mountains." *Mountain Life and Work*, XL (Spring 1964), 21–25.

Three basic forms built of log or stone: smoke or meat houses, tool sheds, spring houses, milk houses, pump houses, well houses, wash houses, root cellars, and apple houses.

"Grist Mill in the Great Smoky Mountains National Park." *Tennessee Folklore Society Bulletin*, XXXIV (Dec. 1968).

Cover photograph.

Hart, John Frazer, and Eugene Cotton Mather. "The American Fence." *Landscape*, VI (Spring 1957), 4–9.

The importance of fences and fence types. "The fence is a significant index of settlement stage and character."

———. "The Character of Tobacco Barns and Their Role in the Tobacco Economy of the United States." *Annals of the Association of American Geographers*, LI (March 1961), 274–93.

Includes tobacco barns in western Kentucky and Tennessee.

Jones, Russell. *Ephraim Bales Woodshed and Meathouse.* Architectural data by Russell Jones; historical data by Robert Madden. Washington, D.C.: U.S. National Park Service, Office of Archeology and Historic Preservation, 1970. 15p. 10 plates.

————. *Leige Oliver Barn and Corn Crib, Historic Structures Report.* Washington, D.C.: U.S. National Park Service, Office of History and Historic Architecture, Eastern Service Center, 1970. 7p., 16 plates, 4 sketches and plans.

Architectural data, with photographs and plans.

Kearfott, Clarence Baker. *Highland Mills.* New York: Vantage Press, 1970. 192p.

"A story in word and picture of the history and legends of the old grist mills in the Appalachian Highlands and adjoining territory." Includes photographs of 25 mills in Tennessee.

Killebrew, J.B. *Report of the Bureau of Agriculture, Statistics and Mines for 1876 . . . .* Nashville: Tavel, Eastman and Howell, 1877. 435p.

Details concerning tobacco raising, building of tobacco barns, etc.

Leiper, Bart. "Time Stands Still in Cades Cove." *Tennessee Conservationist*, XXIII (Dec. 1957), 8–9.

Pictures of an old corn crib, water wheel gristmill, and church.

Mather, Eugene Cotton, and John Frazer Hart. "Fences and Farms." *Geographical Review*, XLIV (April 1954), 201–23.

The authors carried out a "fence traverse" along two routes between Athens, Georgia, and Cleveland, Ohio. Includes Tennessee fences and farms, with maps and illustrations. Shows the development of the American fence from pioneer times.

Montell, Lynwood. "Barns of the Upper

South: An Instructional Manual for Folklore and Folklife Classes," 1972–542. Unpubl. MSS. 69p. Western Kentucky Univ. Folklore, Folklife, and Oral History Archives.

A catalog of barn types, plan of building, mode of construction, and area where each type is found. Numerous drawings.

Sloane, Eric. *An Age of Barns.* New York: Funk and Wagnalls, 1967. 94p.

A sketchbook giving attractive and clear details, including a tobacco barn, a corncrib, and a salt-box barn in Tennessee.

————. *American Barns and Covered Bridges.* New York: Wilfred Funk, 1954. 112p.

Interesting material on tools, barns, bridges, with numerous sketches. The only identification of Tennessee is a sketch of a covered bridge at Elizabethton.

Tennessee Bureau of Agriculture, Statistics and Mines. *Report for 1876, Tobacco—Little Sequatchee Coal Field—Ocoee and Hiwassee Mineral District—Region of Cincinnati Southern R.R.—Tennessee as a Stock-Producing State—Southern States Coal and Iron Association.* By J.B. Killebrew. Nashville: Tavel, Eastman & Howell, 1877. 435p.

Among other things, the discussion of construction of tobacco barns is of interest.

Public Buildings

"Ancient Meeting House Has Quaint History." *Tennessee Conservationist*, XXIV (Dec. 1958), 6–7, 19.

Strother's Meeting House, a log structure which housed the first Middle Tennessee Methodist Conference in 1802, now a Methodist museum on Scarritt College campus, Nashville. Pictures of a log meeting house; corner logs notched to fit; Bible and Bishop's chair; mourner's bench.

Fink, Paul M. "Jonesboro's Chester Inn." *East Tennessee Historical Society Publications*, No. 27, (1955), 19–38.

A description of the inn built about 1798 in Tennessee, and an account of prominent guests and events. Also indicates modes of travel.

Harper, Herbert L. "The Antebellum Courthouses of Tennessee." *Tennessee Historical Quarterly*, XXX (Spring 1971), 3–25.

Description of the seven courthouses which survived the Civil War; original buildings and their use.

Lathrop, Elise. *Early American Inns and Taverns*. New York: Tudor, 1926. 365p.

A brief history and listing of Tennessee inns.

Mathews, Maxine. "Old Inns of East Tennessee." *East Tennessee Historical Society Publications*, No. 2 (1930), 22–33.

Describes about 12 early inns, relating their importance, giving some of the rates, etc.

Price, Edward T. "The Central Court-House Square in the American County Seat." *Geographical Review*, LVIII (1968), 29–60.

The place and function of the courthouse square in early communities, with mention of the Shelbyville and Nashville squares.

Radford, P.M. "Block Houses." *American Historical Magazine*, I (July 1896), 247–52.

Describes the construction of Ridley's Block House, near Buchanan's Fort, in Tennessee.

Shell, William S., ed. *Historic Jonesboro*. Produced by 19 students of design studio in the School of Architecture, Univ. of Tennessee. N.p., n.d. 16p.

Photographs of 54 buildings with a brief history and description of architectural features.

Williams, Samuel Cole, and S.W. Tindell. *The Baptists of Tennessee*. Kingsport: Southern Publications, 1930. 67p.

Contains "Tennessee's First Pastor," by Williams and "Tennessee's First Church," by Tindell, articles on Tidence Lane, and the Buffalo Church.

Young, S.M. "The Old Rock House." *Tennessee Historical Magazine*, Series 2, III (Oct. 1932), 59–64.

Description of a house near Dixon Springs, Tennessee, built by John Shelton, and for years occupied as a tavern.

Covered Bridges

Beach, Ursula Smith. "Tennessee's Covered Bridges—Past and Present." *Tennessee Historical Quarterly*, XXVIII (Spring 1969), 3–23. (Also in McBride, Robert M., *More Landmarks of Tennessee History*.)

Construction and use of covered bridges, with an account of each known remaining bridge in the state; several photographs.

"State's Covered Bridges Retain Romantic Charm." *Tennessee Conservationist*, XXXII (Nov. 1966), 10–11.

Comments on the old use of covered bridges and pictures of three such bridges remaining in Tennessee.

"Tennessee's Covered Bridges." *Tennessee Conservationist*, XXIII (Dec. 1957), 13–14.

Pictures of Port Royal bridge over Red River; bridge over Sulphur Fork near Cedar Hill; historic covered bridge at Elizabethton.

VII. Agriculture

Allred, Charles E., et al. *How the Swiss Farmers Operate on the Cumberland Plateau*. Knoxville: Dept. of Agricultural Economics and Rural Sociology, Univ. of Tennessee Agricultural Experiment Station, 1937. 30p. (Monograph No. 33.)

A study of conditions in 1935 "of a group of sixteen farms operated by Swiss farmers near Gruetli, Grundy County, Tennessee."

Arnow, Harriette Simpson. "The Pioneer Farmer and His Crops in the Cumberland Region." *Tennessee Historical Quarterly*, XIX (Dec. 1960), 291–327.

Farming as a way of pioneer life; planting, cultivating, harvesting of corn, flax, tobacco, and hemp crops; description of hoes, iron plow points.

Bokum, Hermann. *The Tennessee Hand-book and Immigrant's Guide: Giving a Description of the State of Tennessee; Its Agricultural and Mineralogical Character; Its Waterpower, Timber, Soil, and Climate; Its Various Railroad Lines, Completed, In Progress, and Projected; Its Adaptation for Stock-raising, Grape Culture, Etc., Etc. With Special Reference to the Subject of Immigration.* Philadelphia: Lippincott, 1868. 164p.

Good background material.

Boom, Aaron M. "Early Fairs in Shelby County." *West Tennessee Historical Society Papers*, X (1956), 38–52.

First Shelby County fair, 1856. Awards for the best cooked ham; baked goods; preserves; handwork, including handkerchiefs and woolen hose; agricultural products; animals; implements; oratory; and a trial of skill in buggy driving.

Bridgewater, Betty Anderson. "The First Manchester Street Fair." *Coffee County Historical Society Quarterly*, II (Winter 1971), 19–25.

Lists events, and entries of vegetable products and handwork, 1898.

Brookman, Rosemary. "Folk Veterinary Medicine in Southern Appalachia." In Faulkner, Charles H., and Carol K. Buckles, eds., *Glimpses of Southern Appalachian Folk Culture: Papers in Memory of Norbert F. Riedl.* [Knoxville]: Tennessee Anthropological Association, 1978. (Miscellaneous Paper No. 3.)

Diseases and treatment of cattle, horses, hogs, and chickens.

Burnett, Edmund Cody. "Hog Raising and Hog Driving in the Region of the French Broad River." *Agricultural History*, XX (April 1946), 86–103.

As observed through the years by the author.

Clark, Blanche Henry. *The Tennessee Yeomen, 1840–1860.* Nashville: Vanderbilt Univ. Press, 1942. 200p.

Gives some information on early farming and farm implements, as well as on the status of slave holding and non-slaveholding farmers.

"Curing Dark Fired Tobacco." *Tennessee Folklore Society Bulletin*, XXXVI (March 1970).

Cover photograph.

Durand, Loyal, Jr., and Elsie Taylor Bird. "The Burley Tobacco Region of the Mountain South." *Economic Geography*, XXVI (Oct. 1950), 274–306.

Includes "the historical background of East Tennessee Burley Production."

East Tennessee, Historical and Biographical. Chattanooga: A.D. Smith & Co., 1893. 545p.

Agricultural crops grown for home use, and implements used; variety of timbers and their use; livestock; country store; women's work.

Gray, Lewis Cecil. *History of Agricultural in the Southern United States to 1860.* 2 vols. Washington, D.C.: Carnegie Institution of Washington, 1933; rpt. Clifton, N.J. Kelley, 1969.

"extending to a wider horizon that includes also an attempt to understand the way of life of a great section of our country, which was almost entirely agricultural."

Guthrie, Charles S. "Corn: The Mainstay of the Cumberland Valley." *Kentucky Folklore Record*, XII (July-Sept. 1966), 87–91.

Methods of planting and cultivation, with accompanying terminology, folk style.

Hatcher, Mildred. "An Old Fashioned Hog Killing." *Mississippi Folklore Register*, V (Summer 1971), 51–59.

An account of the event, with the assistance given by neighbors.

Jackson, Frances Helen. "The German Swiss Settlement at Gruetli, Tennessee." Unpubl. Master's thesis, Vanderbilt Univ., 1933. 70p.

Describes the community life of settlers, agricultural pursuits, devotion to school, church, music, and woodcarving.

Killebrew, J.B. *Information for Immigrants Concerning Middle Tennessee and the Counties in That Division . . . .* Nashville: Marshall & Bruce Co., 1898. 148p.

"Homeseekers may rely with confidence upon all the statements made concerning the soils, timber, crops, minerals, markets, etc."

————. *Tennessee: Its Agricultural and Mineral Wealth*, with an Appendix Showing the Extent, Value and Accessibility of its Ores, with Analysis of the Same. Nashville: Tavel, Eastman & Howell, 1876. 196p.

Contains information on coal, iron, copper, marble, and farm products, with an agricultural and geological map of Tennessee.

Knox, John. "A Hundred Years for Breakfast." *Tennessee Conservationist*, XL (Oct. 1974), 16–18.

An account of an old place on the Cannon County-Rutherford County line in Tennessee where buckwheat was planted, harvested with a cradle, threshed, flailed, sacked, and taken to the mill.

Kollmorgen, Walter M. *The German-Swiss in Franklin County, Tennessee: A Study of the Significance of Cultural Considerations in Farming Enterprises.* Washington, D.C.: U.S. Dept. of Agriculture, Bureau of Agricultural Economics, 1940. 113p.

"The agricultural practices of the German- Swiss and of the control groups in Franklin County sustain the belief that cultural backgrounds are extremely significant in farming enterprises."

————. "Observations on Cultural Islands in Terms of Tennessee Agriculture." *East Tennessee Historical Society Publications*, No. 16 (1944), 65–78.

"Agriculture is definitely tied in with culture and has a basis in tradition and folklore." A consideration of the German-Swiss and Pennsylvania German cultural-agricultural islands in Tennessee and their contribution to Tennessee agriculture.

————. "A Reconnaissance of Some Cultural-Agricultural Islands in the South." *Economic Geography*, XVII (Oct. 1941), 409–30.

The effect of immigrants of different nationalities on farming methods; Germans in Wartburg; Poles in Deer Lodge; Germans and Swiss in Gruetli; Germans in Lawrenceburg.

————. "Agricultural-Cultural Islands in the South—Part II." *Economic Geography*, XIX (April 1943), 109–17.

(See description above.)

Neskaug, Selmer Reinhart. "Agricultural and Social Aspects of Swiss Settlement in Grundy County, Tennessee." Unpubl. Master's thesis, Univ. of Tennessee, Knoxville, 1936. 184p.

Characteristics of Swiss agriculture in Grundy County: lay-out of farms, soil resources, fruit and vegetable crops, and livestock. Includes a brief history of the social and religious aspects of the settlement.

O'Dell, Ruth W. "Old Mills." *Tennessee Folklore Society Bulletin*, XI (Sept. 1945), 1–4.

Description of corn, wheat, and cane milling.

Rogers, E.G. "Switching for Water." *Tennessee Folklore Society Bulletin*, XXI (Dec. 1955), 108–11.

How to switch for water. Examples of use and practice from Middle and East Tennessee counties.

Rothrock, Mary U., ed. *The French Broad-Holston Country; A History of Knox County, Tennessee.* By the Knox County History Committee, East Tennessee Historical Society. Knoxville: East Tennessee Historical Society, 1946. 573p.

Part I discusses Farming from the Beginning to 1860, and Transportation Prior to the Civil War.

Shaub, Earl L. "The New World of Today." *Tennessee Conservationist*, XXII (May 1956), 12–13.

Contrast of the old and new ways of living. Pictures of wielding old cradle in field, old bull-tongue plough drawn by an ox, and woman carding and spinning yarn.

Smith, J. Gray. *A Brief Historical, Statistical and Descriptive Review of East Tennessee, United States of America: Developing Its Immense Agricultural, Mining and Manufacturing Advantages, With Remarks to Emigrants . . .* London: Published by J. Leath, 1842. 71p. Rpt. Spartanburg, S.C.: Reprint Co., 1974.

"Designed and published as a promotion of the East Tennessee Land Company, was intended to aid in the sale of farm lands in the area." Describes crops, marketable products, agricultural methods, stock raising, silkworm raising, forest and fruit trees, game, and industries.

Stephens, Wendell. "Hog-Killing Time in Middle Tennessee." *Tennessee Folklore Society Bulletin*, XXXVI (Dec. 1970), 83–91.

Interviews with a dozen or so old-timers on their recollection of hog-killing customs.

Tennessee State Agricultural Bureau. *Second Biennial Report to the Legislature of the State, Comprising the Transactions of 1856 and 1857.* By E.G. Eastman. Nashville: G.C. Torbett and Co., 1858. 588p.

Premium lists of the district and county

fairs are interesting, and the proceedings of county societies tell of farming methods.

"Tennessee Wheat Harvest with Cradle." *Tennessee Folklore Society Bulletin*, XXIX (June 1963).

Cover photograph.

Vogt, Evon Z., and Peggy Golde. "Some Aspects of the Folklore of Water Witching in the United States." *Journal of American Folklore*, LXXI (1958), 519–31.

A history and distribution of the pattern, with theoretical implications as to whether the practice really works.

Wayland, Mrs. Charles F., Sr. "An Old Book of Stock Marks and Brands of Knox County, Tennessee." *East Tennessee Historical Society Publications*, No. 22 (1950), 148–57.

A record book of stock marks of cattle and other stock; the brands of horses; authorizations for building public grist mills.

Williams, Samuel C. "Journal of Events (1825–1873) of David Anderson Deaderick." *East Tennessee Historical Society Publications*, No 8, (1936), 121–37.

Comments on the conditions of agriculture and industry in Tennessee: cotton, corn, cotton spinning, silk culture, ploughs, etc.

See also:
Section IV, General Sources: Cumberland Almanac; Farmer's Almanac; Mansfield & Higbee's Memphis Family Almanac.

Section XIII, Speech: Fitzpatrick, Language of the Tobacco Market; Harder, Haymaking Terms; Harder, Vocabulary of Hog-killing; Harder, Vocabulary of Wagon Parts; Woodbridge, Tobacco Words.

VIII. Crafts, Business and Industries

General Crafts

Bullard, Helen. *Crafts and Craftsmen of the Tennessee Mountains*. Falls Church, Va.: Summit Press, 1976. 213p.

Tells of East Tennessee craftsmen, modern and traditional, with background information on how things were done in relation to pioneer living. Includes Charles Decker and his Keystone Pottery, Frank Tabor and Tabor chairs, and Alex Stewart, cooper.

Chambliss, Bill. "Mountain Crafts; Legacy from the Lonesome Past." *Tennessee Conservationist*, XXVI (Sept. 1960), 12–13, 17.

Useful for pictures of craftsmen making chairs, brooms, baskets, dolls, and spinning and carding.

"Crafts of the Southern Highlands." *Craft Horizons*, XXVI (June 1966), 35–67.

"Crafts born out of an agrarian seventeenth-century attitude, but real expressions of flesh and blood humans made in 1966." Good photographs of craftsmen and their products.

Dupuy, Edward L., and Emma Weaver. *Artisans of the Appalachians*. Asheville: Miller Printing Co., 1967. 121p.

Photographs of about 60 craftsmen at work, with interviews concerning their trade.

Durrance, Jill, and William Shamblin, eds. *Appalachian Ways: A Guide to the Historic Mountain Heart of the East.* Washington, D.C.: Appalachian Regional Commission, 1976. 220p.

"This book introduces some of the places and, most importantly, some of the people who make Appalachia so uniquely American." Sketches by various authors on personalities, their crafts and activities, with photographs. Includes lists of craft fairs, music and theater, and festivals.

Eaton, Allen H. *Handicrafts of the Southern Highlands, with an Account of the Rural Handicraft Movement in the United States and Suggestions for the Wider Use of Handicrafts in Adult Education and in Recreation.* New York: Russell Sage Foundation, 1937; rpt. New York: Dover, 1973. 370p.

Describes the mountain handicrafts of pioneer days, and their revival in the present. Includes the "work of the mountaineer in the building and furnishing of his home, the making of equipment by which he works and lives, and the articles which he fashions." Spinning and weaving; coverlets and counterpanes; quilting and patchwork; native dyes and herbs; furniture; baskets; dolls, toys; mountain music and instruments; and pottery. Excellent photographs.

Erskine, Ralph. "Adventures among the Mountain Craftsmen." In Peattie, Roderick, *The Great Smokies and the Blue Ridge*. New York: Vanguard, 1943.

Chairmakers, weavers, potters, whittlers, gem-cutters—most of them in North Carolina, with mention of some in Tennessee.

Hodges, Sidney Cecil. "Handicrafts in Sevier County, Tennessee." Unpubl. Master's thesis, Univ. of Tennessee, Knoxville, 1951. 74p.

The pioneer background, and the revival of crafts: spinning and weaving, native dyes and herbs, furniture and woodwork, basket making, whittling and carving, and pottery.

Horwitz, Elinor Lander. *Mountain People, Mountain Crafts*. Philadelphia: Lippincott, 1974. 143p.

A brief history of crafts in the Appalachian region and their revival by contemporary craftsmen. Good photographs of crafts and craftsmen by Joshua and Anthony Horwitz.

Krechniak, Helen (Bullard). "Handicrafts: Ceramics, Dolls, Baskets, Brooms Are Made by Tennessee Rural Folk." *Tennessee Conservationist*, XIX (July 1953), 12–13, 21.

A brief account of the revival of handicrafts in Tennessee, with pictures of craftsmen at work.

——. "Tennessee Mountain Crafts." *Appalachian South*, I (Summer, Fall, and Winter 1965), 24–26.

Revival of crafts.

Made in Tennessee: An Exhibition of Early Arts and Crafts. Sponsored by National Life and Accident Insurance Co. and WSM. Sept. 15–Oct. 31, 1971. Nashville: Tennessee Fine Arts Center. 67p.

Photographs, with descriptive captions, of furniture, silver, firearms, brass, ceramics, textiles, musical instruments, etc., made by Tennessee craftsmen from the late 18th century through 1870.

Southern Highland Handicraft Guild. *Crafts in the Southern Highlands, with Seventy-three Photographic Illustrations*. Asheville: The Guild, 1958. 46p.

Describes homes, furniture and utensils, dyeing and weaving of materials in the early days, with the revival of crafts, sometimes using modified materials.

Stevens, Bernice A. *Our Mountain Craftsmen*. Gatlinburg, Tenn.: Buckhorn Press, 1969. 41p.

Sketches of contemporary craftsmen, and their work, in the Smoky Mountain area.

———. "The Revival of Handicrafts." In Ford, Thomas R., ed., *The Southern Appalachian Region*. Lexington: Univ. of Kentucky Press, 1962.

Deals with craft revival "built upon a foundation of old crafts that had never completely died out in the area."

Basketmaking

Teleki, Gloria Roth. *The Baskets of Rural America*. New York: Dutton, 1975. 202p.

Ethnic, communal and regional origins include a brief discussion of the Southern Appalachian Highlands. The book is well illustrated with photographs and sketches.

See also Eaton, Hodges, Horwitz, and Krechniak, above.

Dyeing

Davidson, Mary Frances. "Dye It Yourself From Field and Forest." *Mountain Life and Work*, VI (April 1930), 31–32.

Directions for dyeing wool with vegetable dyes.

———. *The Dye-Pot*. Middlesboro, Ky.: The Author, 1950. 27p.

Recipes for vegetable dyeing.

Furry, Margaret S., and Bess M. Viemont. *Home Dyeing with Natural Dyes*. Washington, D.C.: Government Printing Office, 1935. 36p. (U.S. Dept. of Agriculture, Miscellaneous Publication 230.)

"This publication reports the result of tests on about sixty-five natural dye materials when used for dyeing cotton and wool cloth." The result of widespread interest in

handicraft work, it contains directions and recipes for dyes.

Krechniak, Helen Bullard. "Dyeing Can Be Fun: Vegetable Dyeing Revival in the Southern Appalachians." *Mountain Life and Work*, XXXVII (Winter 1961), 25–28.

Brief history of the art and its revival.

———. "Vegetable Dyeing Revival in the Southern Appalachians." *Tennessee Folklore Society Bulletin*, XXVII (September 1961), 48–51.

Includes several very old recipes.

Stone, Helen Wilmer. "Vegetable Dyes." *Mountain Life and Work*, VI (April 1930), 31–32.

How to use vegetable dyes; the necessity of a mordant; how to get dye from a plant; some useful plants.

Thornburgh, Kathleen. "Colors from Nature." *Tennessee Conservationist*, XL (July 1974), 14–15.

Instructions for vegetable dyeing, with a short list of dye plants and the colors they yield.

Furniture Making

Beasley, Ellen. "Tennessee Cabinetmakers and Chairmakers Through 1840." *Antiques*, C (Oct. 1971), 612–21.

A checklist of Tennessee craftsmen, with a "view of how cabinetmaking and chairmaking crafts functioned in early Tennessee."

———. "Tennessee Furniture and Its Makers." *Antiques*, C (Sept. 1971), 425–31.

Comments on simplicity of form and decoration, and woods used; includes 13 pictures.

Ellesin, Dorothy E. "Robert Black, Middle Tennessee Cabinetmaker." *Antiques*, CIX (May 1976) 950.

Photographs of a cherry chest of drawers made about 1820(?), found in the vicinity of Dixon Springs, Smith County.

Jones, Michael Owen. "The Study of

Traditional Furniture: Review and Preview." *Keystone Folklore Quarterly*, XII (Winter 1967), 233–45.

"to comment briefly on the kind of studies of traditional American furniture now available and to suggest the type of crucial investigation that still needs to be carried out if we are ever to approach a fuller understanding of the processual and contextual aspects of folk craft production." Discusses the fieldwork involved, actual techniques, tools, materials, etc.

Krechniak, Helen Bullard. "Handicrafts: High Standards of Arts and Crafts Expressed in Exclusive Furniture." *Tennessee Conservationist*, XIX (June 1953), 14–15.

Chairmaking and other types of furniture as a revival of handicrafts. Includes pictures of craftsmen working on chairs.

———. "Tabor Family Noted as Stout Chair Makers Over 150 Years." *Tennessee Conservationist*, XXII (July 1956), 14–15. Rpt. in *Mountain Life and Work*, XXXII (1956), 27–29.

"The Tabor family, which in 1806 settled near Black Drowning Creek north of Crossville, is rounding out 150 years of woodcrafting, principally chairmaking." Comments on the kinds of wood used and some of the processes.

Rabun, Josette Hensley. "Lewis Buckner, c.1856–1924, Country Cabinetmaker and House Carpenter." Unpubl. Master's thesis, Univ. of Tennessee, Knoxville, c1979. 164p.

"To present an Afro-American artisan . . . who lived and worked as a cabinetmaker and house carpenter in Sevier County, Tennessee." Good photographs of details.

Rains, B. Mickey. "The Crafting of Hickory Bottomed Chairs." 1972–77. Unpublished MS. 35p., 25 photographs. Western Kentucky Univ., Folklore, Folklife, and Oral History Archives.

Includes interviews with craftsmen in Macon County, Tennessee.

Reed, Ann. "Southern Appalachian Culture in the Tennessee Valley: A Study of Traditional Furniture." 1970. 54p. Student paper, Riedl Collection, Univ. of Tennessee Library, Knoxville.

Construction of chairs, beds, cradles, tables, chests, cupboards, and kitchen safes, in the Little Tennessee Valley. With drawings.

Pottery

Burbage, Beverly S. "The Remarkable Pottery of Charles Decker and His Sons." *Tennessee Conservationist*, XXXVII (Nov. 1974), 6–8.

Tells of a pottery operated in East Tennessee from 1872 until shortly after the turn of the century. Has photographs of the Deckers and their wares.

Guilland, Harold F. *Early American Folk Pottery*. Philadelphia: Chilton Book Co., 1971. 322p.

Describes pioneer life and the folk potter's craft, his materials, equipment, methods, and his strictly utilitarian wares. Gives a brief mention of the Keystone Pottery, Washington County, Tennessee, with a photograph of the Decker family and their work.

Miller, David Kent. "The Pottery Patriarch." *Tennessee Conservationist*, XXXVII (Nov. 1974), 9–11.

Gives the biography and family history of Charles Frederick Decker, Sr., with photographs of family members, buildings and pottery.

See also entries under General Crafts; and Clay Products, under Business and Industry.

Quilting

Bowling, Brenda M. "Quilts and Quiltmaking in Southern Appalachia." 1972. 12p. Student paper, Riedl Collection, The Univ. of Tennessee Library, Knoxville.

Gives 44 patterns. Quilting bees, and beliefs and customs. Five Tennessee informants.

Bracken, Lorene. "The Quilt and the Quilter in Southern Appalachia." 1974.

19p. Student paper, Riedl Collection, Univ. of Tennessee Library, Knoxville.

"A brief overview of the folk art of quilting in its form and function is given." Six Tennessee informants give quilt patterns, and the social aspects of quilting bees.

Finley, Ruth E. *Old Patchwork Quilts and the Women Who Made Them*. Philadelphia: Lippincott, 1929. 202p.

History of designs; details of patches and how to cut them; quilting patterns; origin of quilt names; a few dye recipes; photographs of quilts.

McClaskey, Bettie. "East Tennessee Quilts: Are They Distinctive?" 1965. 13p. Student paper, Riedl Collection, Univ. of Tennessee Library, Knoxville.

Six Tennessee informants tell of quilting bees and superstitions.

Richardson, Elizabeth F. "The Art of Patchwork." *Tennessee Folklore Society Bulletin*, XVI (Sept. 1950), 54–61.

Importance of quilts and quilting parties. Includes quilt pattern names.

Weatherford, Sally E. "Profile of a Murfreesboro Quiltmaker and Her Craft." *Tennessee Folklore Society Bulletin*, XLIV (Sept. 1978), 108–14.

Pictures and instructions for 12 patterns.

Webster, Marie D. *Quilts, Their Story and How to Make Them* . New York: Doubleday, 1926, 178p.

This general history touches Tennessee and the Appalachian chain. Good pictures of quilts and a list of quilt names.

Weaving

Atwater, Mary Meigs. *The Shuttle-Craft Book of American Hand-Weaving*. New York: Macmillan, 1928. 275p.

Explanation of the old ways of preparing flax and wool for spinning and dyeing; dressing the loom; weaving; patterns and instruction.

Bullard, Helen. "Romantic Story of Weaving." *Tennessee Conservationist*, XXVII (Dec. 1961), 16, 21.

The story of looms and weaving, a craft revived in the mountains of Tennessee. Picture of a loom.

Huff, Vicki. "The Craft of the Southern Appalachian Coverlet." 1973. 18p. Student paper, Riedl Collection, Univ. of Tennessee Library, Knoxville.

"Using the tools and coverlets found in John Rice Irwin's Museum of Appalachia in Norris, Tennessee as examples, this paper will describe the way in which a coverlet is made, beginning with the growing of the flax to the actual weaving of the coverlet." Includes pictures and sketches of tools, equipment, and coverlets.

Hulan, Richard H. "Tennessee Textiles." *Antiques*, C (Sept. 1971), 386–89.

Pictures of a loom, pattern drafts, and the finished product.

Krechniak, Helen (Bullard). "Handicrafts: Kiverlid Inspires Revival of Weaving in Tennessee Mountains." *Tennessee Conservationist*, XIX (May 1953), 10–11.

The fostering of home industries by the Pi Beta Phi Settlement School and others.

Obenchain, Eliza C. *A Book of Hand-Woven Coverlets*. Boston: Little, Brown, 1927. 279p.

Sixty-four good plates, some in color, with names of patterns and designs; recipes for dyeing. References to Tennessee.

Reeves, Florence. "A Mountain Coverlet." *Mountain Life and Work*, XI (Oct. 1935), 16–19.

Told in dialect. Deals largely with preparing the dyes and wool.

Woodworking

Callahan, Terri, and Jill Dye. "Jim Spier—Wood Carver." *Tennessee Folklore Society Bulletin*, XLIV (March 1978), 1–6.

An interview with a craftsman, most of whose carvings are of animals. Tells of the kinds of wood he uses.

Echols, Stan, et al. "Alex Stewart: Cooper and Churnmaker." *Foxfire*, VII (Summer 1973), 144–63.

A resident of Sneedville, Tennessee, who makes churns, buckets, and large tubs, working with handmade tools in the traditional way. Includes diagrams and photographs on making a churn.

"A Wife, a Knife, and a Strong Right Arm." *Tennessee Conservationist*, XXIV (July 1958), 14–15.

The knife as the frontiersman used it. Whittling not an art but a way of life.

Business and Industries: General

"Antiques in Tennessee." A special regional issue of *Antiques*. Rpt. from issues of Aug., Sept. ,Oct., and Dec., 1971.

Includes textiles, furniture, cabinetmakers, and silversmiths.

Coxe, Tench, comp. *Statement of the Arts and Manufactures of the United States of America for the Year 1810: Digested and Prepared by Tench Coxe, Esquire, of Philadelphia.* Philadelphia: Printed by A. Cornman, Junr., 1814. 169p.

Tables of numerous products and agricultural stock, by states and counties.

Morris, Eastin. *Tennessee Gazetteer or Topographical Dictionary, Containing a Description of the Several Counties, Towns, Villages, Post Offices, Rivers, Creeks, Mountains, Valleys, &c. in the State of Tennessee . . . .* by W. Hasell Hunt & Co. Nashville: Banner & Whig Office, 1834. 178p.

Gives the number of professions and businesses, such as hatters, saddlers, coachmakers. Some place names.

Clay Products

Cummings, James Barnett. "The Clay Products Industries of the City of Nashville." Unpubl. Master's thesis, George Peabody College for Teachers, 1928. 83p.

Includes a brief account of claymixing process and making bricks by hand.

Guilland, Harold F. *Early American Folk Pottery.* Philadelphia: Chilton, 1971. 322p.

Gives a brief account of the Keystone (or Decker) Pottery in Washington County, Tennessee, with a photograph of the Decker family and their wares. Reference is made to an article by Dorothy Hamill in the *Johnson City* (Tennessee) *Chronicle*, Dec. 3, 1967, on the pottery.

Harney, Andy Leon. "Appalachian Stoneware for America's Dinner Table, the Iron Mountain Story." *Appalachia*, VI (Oct.-Nov. 1972), 48–56.

An industry begun in the early 1960s to make pottery by hand and machine, in the village of Laurel Bloomery in the northeastern corner of Tennessee.

Smith, Samuel D., and Stephen T. Rogers. *A Survey of Historic Pottery Making in Tennessee.* Nashville: Tennessee Department of Conservation, Division of Archeology, 1979. 159p. (Research Series, No. 3).

A survey recording the location and distribution of 163 pre-1940 pottery-making operations in Tennessee. "For each site an attempt has been made to summarize the information obtained on the type of operation, period of production, persons associated, wares produced, and marks or other distinguishing attributes of the pottery." A helpful bibliography is included.

Webb, Thomas G. "The Pottery Industry of Dekalb, White, and Putnam Counties." *Tennessee Historical Quarterly*, XXX (Spring 1971), 110–12.

The process probably used from 1822 to 1938, from mixing of the clay to stacking of the ware in the kiln and firing it.

Whitlach, George I. "Mileposts in Tennessee's Clay Indsutry." *Journal of the Tennessee Academy of Science*, XI (July 1936), 153–63.

The use of clay by early pioneers. No methods of brickmaking or pottery are given, but names, dates, locations, and notations are indicated of plants still standing in 1936 for brick chimneys, brick houses, and potteries.

Coal Mining

Hutson, Andrew C.,Jr. "The Coal Miners' Insurrections, 1891–1892." Unpubl.

Master's thesis, Univ. of Tennessee, Knoxville, 1933. 167p.

>   Accounts of the four insurrections at Coal Creek, Tennessee, and their underlying causes. *See* Work Songs (Section XX) for ballads based on these and other mining incidents.

―――. "Coal Miners' Insurrections of 1891 in Anderson County, Tennessee." *East Tennessee Historical Society Publication*, No. 7 (1935), 103–21.

―――. "The Overthrow of the Convict Lease System in Tennessee." *East Tennessee Historical Society Publication*, No. 8 (1936), 83–103.

>   Both of the above items are taken from Hutson's thesis.

Turpin, Jane A., and William D. Bradley. "Scratching the Coal Creek Valley for Coal and Lore." 1972. 75p. Student paper, Riedl Collection, Univ. of Tennessee Library, Knoxville.

>   Tells of the life style of the early miner, reminiscences, mining terms, tools, etc.

Cotton Industry

Williams, Emma Inman. "Jackson and Madison County: An Inland Cotton Center of the Growing West." *Tennessee Historical Quarterly*, III (March 1944), 24–45.

>   Development of business and industry, with emphasis on cotton; efforts to develop transportation; use of Negroes as a labor supply; laws to protect property.

Williams, Samuel C. "The South's First Cotton Factory." *Tennessee Historical Quarterly*, V (March-Dec. 1946), 212–21.

>   The effort of John Hague to establish a factory near Nashville in 1790 for cotton cloth and thread. No details of the process are given. The plant lasted only a few years. Several later manufacturers are mentioned.

Fishing

Cobb, James E. "Historic Fish Traps on the Lower Holston River." *Tennessee*

Anthropologist, III (Spring 1978), 31–58.

>   "Three well-preserved fish trap sites located on the lower Holston River are defined and described. An historical sketch of each trap is presented to document its period of operation . . . early 1800 to ca. 1940." With diagrams and photographs.

Kear, Steve R., David C. Stout, and Robert H. Ross. "Fishing Folk Culture in East Tennessee." In Faulkner, Charles H., and Carol K. Buckles, eds., *Glimpses of Southern Appalachian Folk Culture: Papers in Memory of Norbert F. Riedl.* [Knoxville]: Tennessee Anthropological Association, 1978. (Miscellaneous Paper No. 3.)

>   Nets, trotlines, fish traps, fish baskets, and pole fishing.

Horseshoeing

Smith, Douglas. "Traditional Horseshoeing in East Tennessee—The Present as Influenced by the Past." 1973. 68p. Student paper, Riedl Collection, Univ. of Tennessee Library, Knoxville.

>   "This paper hopes to give a basic knowledge in this art and to compare past and present whenever the opportunity develops." Illustrated with good drawings and photographs.

Iron Industry

Brandon, Helen Gould. "A History of Stewart County, Tennessee." Unpubl. Master's thesis, Univ. of Tennessee, Knoxville, 1944. 101p.

>   Of particular interest is the account of the iron industry and the description of hillside iron furnaces.

Chamberlain, Morrow. *A Brief History of the Pig Iron Industry of East Tennessee.* Chattanooga: The Author, 1942. 28p.

>   A brief description of charcoal furnaces supplying pioneer needs, with a history and directory of later iron companies.

Clark, Joseph Harold. "History of the Knoxville Iron Company." Unpubl. Master's thesis, Univ. of Tennessee, Knoxville, 1949. 153p.

A brief account of the development of the iron industry in Tennessee, explaining the two methods of production used in the early years.

Fink, Paul M. "The Bumpass Cove Mines and Embreville." *East Tennessee Historical Society Publications*, No. 16 (1944), 48–64.

Process of iron production by forge or "bloomery" and by furnace, in Washington County, Tennessee.

Foster, A.P. "History of Tennessee Industry—Iron." *Tennessee Industry*, I (Jan. 1931), 7–9; (March 1931), 11–13; (May 1931), 11–13; (June 1931), 9–10.

The location, history, and processes of iron companies, including the Tennessee Coal, Iron and Railroad Company, the Roane Iron Company, and the Knoxville Iron Company.

French, B.F. *History of the Rise and Progress of the Iron Trade of the United States from 1621 to 1857:* With Numerous Statistical Tables, Relating to the Manufacture, Importation, Exportation, and Prices of Iron For More Than a Century. New York: Wiley & Halsted, 1858. 179p.

Tennessee is included in the tables from 1810 to 1856.

"Furnaces and Forges." *Tennessee Historical Magazine*, IX (Oct. 1925), 190–92.

Environmental, social, and economic surroundings of pioneer industrial enterprises, such as the Cumberland Furnace, built in 1793, with brief references to other plants.

Hersh, Alan. "The Development of the Iron Industry in East Tennessee." Unpubl. Master's thesis, Univ. of Tennessee, Knoxville, 1958. 61p.

Chapter IV, The Iron Industry, Early Period: 1790–1860, locates deposits and furnaces and describes processes.

Hunt, Raymond F., Jr. "The Pactolus Ironworks." *Tennessee Historical Quarterly*, XXV (Summer 1966), 176–96.

History of the operations of iron manufacture from charcoal to blacksmith shop, from 1789 to 1830, Sullivan County, Tennessee.

Luther, Frank. "Laurel Furnace, A Walk Back in Time." *Tennessee Conservationist*, XXXIX (Aug. 1973), 15–17.

Early mining operation and iron works in Middle Tennessee.

Nave, Robert Tipton. "A History of the Iron Industry in Carter County to 1860." Unpubl. Master's thesis, East Tennessee State College, 1953. 114p.

Early history and methods used.

Phelps, Dawson A., and John T. Willett. "Iron Works on the Natchez Trace." *Tennessee Historical Quarterly*, XII (Dec. 1953), 309–22.

Processing of timber into charcoal; primitive mining operations; furnace processes.

Van Benthuysen, Robert N., Jr. "The Sequent Occupance of Tellico Plains, Tennessee." Unpubl. Master's thesis, Univ. of Tennessee, Knoxville, 1951. 129p.

Of principal interest are iron mining industries, goldmining, and timber.

Williams, Samuel C. "Early Iron Works in the Tennessee Country." *Tennessee Historical Quarterly*, VI (March 1947), 39–46.

Location of early iron works.

Merchants

Clark, Thomas D. "The Country Store in Post-Civil War Tennessee." *East Tennessee Historical Society Publications*, No. 17 (1945), 3–21.

Describes stores as supply centers for their communities, as centralizing influences, and as reflecting community life.

———. *Pills, Petticoats and Plows; The Southern Country Store*. Indianapolis: Bobbs-Merrill, 1944. 359p. Rpt. Norman: Univ. of Oklahoma Press, 1964. 306p.

"The country store in a way was more symbolic of the southern way of rural life than were other institutions." Tells of stock, business methods, and the social and political influence of store gatherings. 1865–1915.

Crowder, James. "The Old Country Store." *Tennessee Folklore Society Bulletin*, XIV (June 1948), 34–36.
The social function of the store.

Provine, W.A. "Lardner Clark, Nashville's First Merchant and Foremost Citizen." *Tennessee Historical Magazine*. III (March 1917), 28–50; (June 1917), 115–33.
Merchant and ordinary keeper. Tells of home, education, town activities, the Salt Works, and an estate listing of books and household utensils. "Horses and cows, axes and cow-bells constituted the ready circulating medium."

Spears, James E. "Where Have All the Peddlers Gone?" *Kentucky Folklore Record*, XXI (July-Sept. 1975), 77–81.
An account of the peddlers' circuit, wares, and relations with families, taken by interviews with people "who knew the breed firsthand."

Wassom, Earl E. "The Rolling Store." 1973–83. Unpubl. MS. 69p. Western Kentucky Univ. Folklore, Folklife, and Oral History Archives.
A transcription of taped interviews with the operator of a traveling store in Bedford County, Tenn. Tells of crops, bartering, folk beliefs, contributions to special occasions such as Christmas and the Fourth of July, as well as the equipment and produce.

Wright, Richardson. *Hawkers and Walkers in Early America; Strolling Peddlers, Preachers, Lawyers, Doctors, Players, and Others, from the Beginning to the Civil War*. Philadelphia: Lippincott, 1927. 317p.
An interesting account of peddlers and their wares, as well as itinerant practitioners of various kinds.

Moonshine Making

Atkinson, George Wesley. *After the Moonshiners, By One of the Raiders; A Book of Thrilling Yet Truthful Narratives*. Wheeling, W.Va.: Frew and Campbell, Steam Book and Job Printers, 1881. 239p.
Explanation of equipment and methods of distilling moonshine whiskey; stories of efforts to apprehend mountaineers engaged in the business.

Carr, Jess. *The Second Oldest Profession; An Informal History of Moonshining in America*. Englewood Cliffs, N.J.: Prentice-Hall, 1972. 250p.
History, methods, and customs of moonshiners.

Dabney, Joseph Earl. *Mountain Spirits: A Chronicle of Corn Whiskey From King James' Ulster Plantation to America's Appalachians and the Moonshine Life*. New York: Scribner's, 1974.
"In this book I have tried to recreate his (the moonshiner's) individualistic, exciting, but disappearing world." History and stories, many from East Tennessee; includes photographs and a corn whiskey glossary.

Durand, Loyal, Jr. " 'Mountain Moonshining' in East Tennessee." *Geographical Review*, XLVI (April 1956), 168–81.
Depicts conditions in the 1940s and 1950s, with some references to "a tradition of local whiskey-making in certain mountain and hill-country locations." Pictures of stills.

Edwards, Lawrence. "John Barleycorn, Hillbilly." In Jones, Lealon N., ed., *Eve's Stepchildren*. Caldwell, Idaho: Caxton, 1942.
Distilling as a part of the life of the mountaineers.

Kellner, Esther. *Moonshine; Its History and Folklore*. Indianapolis: Bobbs-Merrill, 1971. 235p.
The locale is chiefly Kentucky, but Tennessee is mentioned a few times, and methods and folk aspects would be applicable.

O'Dell, Ruth W. "Moonshine in the Tennessee Mountains." *Tennessee Folklore Society Bulletin*, XII (Sept. 1946), 1–5.

Brief history, with description of the process of whiskey making.

Pendleton, Charles S. "Illicit Whiskey-Making." *Tennessee Folklore Society Bulletin*, XII (March 1946), 1–16.

Moonshining from the meaning of the phrase to the finished product. Vocabulary, locations of stills, and process of making whiskey.

Williams, Cratis D. "Moonshining in the Mountains." *North Carolina Folklore*, XV (May 1967), 11–17. (Page 16 is a duplicate of page 15.)

A description of the whiskey-making process.

Rifle Making

Dillin, John G.W. *The Kentucky Rifle: A Study of the Origin and Development of a Purely American Type of Firearm, Together with Accurate Historical Data Concerning Early Colonial Gunsmiths, and Profusely Illustrated with Photographic Reproductions of Their Finest Work*. New York: Ludlum and Beebe, 1946. 136p.

Names 11 Tennessee riflemakers before 1840.

Fink, Paul M. "The Beans of Tennessee, Master Gunsmiths." *Muzzle Blasts* (Oct. 1946), 3–4.

An account of William Bean, first permanent settler of Tennessee, and his descendants, gunsmiths for a century and a half. Pictures of rifles.

Kendall, Arthur Isaac. "Rifle Making in the Great Smokies." U.S. National Park Service, Region I, *Regional Review*, VI (Jan.-Feb. 1941), 21–31.

Methods of making "the rifled gun, the American rifle, or as it frequently is called, the Kentucky rifle" used by the mountain settlers.

———. "Rifle Making in the Great Smoky Mountains." *National Park Service Popular Study Series: History, No. 13*. Washington, D.C.: Government Printing Office, n.d. 34p.

Step-by-step explanation of the making of rifles, with illustrations.

Saltpeter Mining

Tarkington, Terry W. "Saltpeter Mining in the Tennessee Valley." *Tennessee Valley Historical Review*, II (Summer 1973), 17–25.

Describes caves, equipment, and process of extracting saltpeter.

Silversmithing

Caldwell, Benjamin H. "Tennessee Silversmiths." *Antiques*, C (Sept. 1971), 382–85.

The use of coins as raw material. Photographs of four articles.

———. "Tennessee Silversmiths Prior to 1860: A Checklist." *Antiques*, C (Dec. 1971), 906–13.

An alphabetical list by name, giving addresses, dates, and products.

IX. Food, Clothing, Furniture, Household Utensils, Tools

Food

Brown, David. "Buying Habits of the Middle Tennessee Area Between 1900 and 1920." *Tennessee Folklore Society Bulletin*, XLII (March 1976), 21–33.

Interviews with individuals who remember bygone ways of providing, preserving, and storing food, meat, milk, fruit, and vegetables; hog and beef killing; hunting and cooking rabbits; buying materials for clothing; and prevailing prices.

Burrell, Vivian, Mary Thomas, et al. "Apple Butter Made in a Brass Kettle." *Foxfire*, VII (Winter 1973), 268–272.

An interview with Mr. and Mrs. Pat Brooks of Rogersville, Tennessee, with photographs on the process of making apple butter.

Byrd, James W. "Poke Sallet from Tennessee to Texas." *Tennessee Folklore Society Bulletin*, XXXII (June 1966), 48–54.

A defense of poke for food and other uses, and instructions for preparing it.

Carr, Lillian R. "Mammy's Ho'made Soap and Hominy." *Tennessee Conservationist*, XL (June 1974), 20.

A brief account of the process of making hominy.

Chiles, Mary Ruth, and Mrs. William P. Trotter, eds., *Mountain Makin's in the Smokies: A Cookbook*. Gatlinburg, Tenn.: Great Smoky Mountains Natural History Association, 1957. 54p.

Old-timey recipes using cornmeal, molasses, and honey, all staple commodities of early settlers in the Great Smokies.

Clark, Emily H. "The Foods of Southern Appalachia." 1970. 23p. Student paper, Riedl Collection, Univ. of Tennessee Library, Knoxville.

Traditional foods in the Little Tennessee Valley.

Hilliard, Sam Bowers. *Hog Meat and Hoecake: Food Supply in the Old South, 1840–1860*. Carbondale: Southern Illinois Univ. Press, 1972. 296p.

Describes the distinctive character of Southern food habits and the persistence of food preferences; agriculture and food production; food preparation; slave diet; routes used in the droving trade, etc.

Hills, J.L., Charles E. Wait, and H.C. White. "Dietary Studies in Rural Regions in Vermont, Tennessee, and Georgia." *U.S.D.A. Office of Experiment Stations Bulletin 221*. Washington, D.C.: Government Printing Office, 1909. 142p.

The Tennessee portion consists of dietary studies of 63 families living in the mountain region of eastern Tennessee, conducted by Dr. Wait. He notes the peculiarities of diet; foods most commonly eaten; and the amounts, costs, and nutrients.

Kolasa, Kathryn Marianna. "Food and the Southeastern United States." 1972. 28p. Student paper, Riedl Collection, Univ. of Tennessee Library, Knoxville.

"A review of literature . . . particular note was made of foods mentioned, techniques of food preservation and preparation, hunting and other methods of food procurement and any miscellaneous references to foods." A good annotated bibliography.

———. "Foodways of Selected Mothers and Their Adult-Daughters in Upper East Tennessee." Unpubl. diss., Univ. of Tennessee, Knoxville, 1974. 238p.

A study conducted in Hancock County and some nearby areas concerning the transmission of foodways, with some mention of "old-timey" foods. Lists of food preferences and food terminology are given. A brief discussion of accounts of Melungeon food behavior is included, but "Melungeons were not separated out of the random or purposive sampling procedures."

Lane, Virgil. "Tennessee Vittles." *Farm Quarterly*, XI (Autumn 1956), 42–43.

Family meals in Tennessee in the early years of the 20th century: breakfast, dinner, and supper; what was served, and how it was prepared.

Maclachlan, Emily Stevens. "The Diet Pattern of the South, A Study in Regional Sociology." Unpubl. Master's thesis, Univ. of North Carolina, 1932. 140p.

"The Southern diet pattern has its roots in frontier life." Gives an interesting account of "habits of food getting, cooking, and eating . . . folkways handed down through the generations."

Morton, Joan E. "Teas in Southern Appalachia: An Annotated Bibliography." 1976. 12p. Student paper, Riedl Collection, Univ. of Tennessee Library, Knoxville.

"Made from many things . . . but mainly they were made from herbs and for the most part these teas were the main source of medicine in Appalachia." Has 46 entries.

Poplin, Dick. "Like Hominy? Let Lane Make It." *Tennessee Conservationist*, XXX (Aug. 1964), 14.

Instructions for making hominy, with illustrations.

Schaeffer, Elizabeth. *Dandelion, Poke Weed, and Goosefoot, How the Early Settlers Used Plants for Food, Medicine, and In the Home*. Reading, Mass.: Addison-Wesley, 1972. 94p. (Young Scott Books.)

"Describes the various plants used by the early settlers as food and medicine and includes recipes, as well as instructions for starting a garden."

Shackelford, Neryle. "Wild Sallit Greens." *Mountain Life and Work*, XXXVII (Spring 1961), 57–58.

A brief account of greens and beverages used in olden times.

Shelton, Ferne. *Southern Appalachian Mountain Cookbook*. High Point, N.C.: Hutcraft, 1964. 32p.

Recipes and comments on traditional foods.

Spears, James E. "Favorite Southern Negro Folk Recipes." *Kentucky Folklore Record*, XVI (Jan.-March 1970), 1–5.

Has 18 recipes "peculiar to Negro folk": chitterlings, coon, possum, sow belly, collards, corn bread, crackling bread, and others.

Taylor, Joe Gray. "The Food of the New South, 1875–1940." *Georgia Review*, XX (Spring 1966), 9–28.

A good article by a native of West Tennessee. "From the pioneer period through the Great Depression the eating habits of the Southern United States changed relatively little . . . I realized recently that my generation was the last one which grew to maturity on a regional diet."

Wait, Charles E. "Dietary Studies of Families Living in the Mountain Region of Eastern Tennessee." U.S. Dept. of Agriculture, *Office of Experiment Stations Bulletin 221*. 1909. Pp.21–116.

The introductory description of the region and people studied gives information on houses and meager furnishings. Dietary case studies show cost of foods and peculiarities of diet.

"A Week in the Great Smoky Mountains." *The Southern Literary Messenger*, XXXI (Aug. 1860), 117–31.

Tells of a trip in 1859 along the Little Pigeon River; describes the hospitality of the natives and lists their food.

Wheeler, Lester R. "Changes in the Dietary Habits of Remote Mountain People Since 1900." *Journal of the Tennessee Academy of Science*, X (July 1935), 167–74.

A comparison of the earlier study by C.E. Wait. Buttermilk, cornbread, and biscuits used in both; pork the most used meat, etc.

Clothing

Gilbert, Gerry Beth. "An Examination of the Influence of Social and Economic

Development of East Tennessee Dress From 1790–1850." Unpubl. Master's thesis, Univ. of Tennessee, Knoxville, 1971. 68p.

A good account of women's and men's dress, giving details of costumes, fabrics, and colors. Also reviews the way of living as to furniture, foods, social gatherings, etc.

Moffat, Adelene. "The Mountaineers of Middle Tennessee." *Journal of American Folk-Lore,* IV (Oct.-Dec. 1891), 314–20.

Homes, dress, and personal characteristics of the people of the Cumberland Ridge.

"Pioneer Social Life in Overton County." *Tennessee Folklore Society Bulletin,* XIV (March 1948), 6–7.

Told by J.R. Copeland to A.V. Goodpasture and used in a centenary address in Livingston, Tenn., in May 1876. Especially interesting for the description of clothing.

Furniture and Household Utensils

See:
Section VIII, Crafts
Beasley, "Tennessee Cabinet-makers"; Echols, "Alex Stewart, Cooper and Churnmaker"; Reed, "Southern Appalachian Culture"; Southern Highland Handicraft Guild, *Crafts of the Southern Highlands.*

Section IV, General Sources
Braden, *When Grandma Was a Girl;* Caruso, *The Appalachian Frontier;* Des-Champs, "Early Days in the Cumberland Country"; ——— , "Pioneer Life in the Cumberland Country"; Srygley, *Seventy Years in Dixie.*

Section V, History
Historical Records Survey, "Tennessee"; Kinard, "Frontier Development of Williamson County"; Phelan, *History of Tennessee;* Seals, *History of White County;* White, *Tennessee.*

Tools

See:
Section VI, Buildings
Creighton, *Building of Nashville;* Riedl, *Survey of Traditional Architecture.*

Section IV, General Sources
Braden, *When Grandma Was a Girl;* Breazeale, *Life As It Is;* Burnett, "Big Creek's Response"; Crowe, *Horseshoe People.*

Section V, History
Historical Records Survey, "Tennessee"; Kinard, "Frontier Development"; Prater, "Economic History of White County."

X. Transportation

Alldredge, J. Haden, et al. *A History of Navigation on the Tennessee River System: An Interpretation of the Economic Influence of this River on the Tennessee Valley.* Washington, D.C.: Government Printing Office, 1937. 192p. (75th Congress, 1st Sess. House Doc. 254.)

A report "prepared from a strictly historical point of view" traces the influence of the river on the early settlement of the region. Sketches of the keelboat, dugout canoe, raft, and flatboat show the types of craft in early use.

Baldwin, Leland D. *The Keelboat Age On Western Waters.* Pittsburgh: Univ. of Pittsburgh Press, 1941. 268p.

Chapters on boats and boat building, the art of navigation, the boatmen, and river pirates give important information on Mississippi transportation.

Barbee, John D. "Navigation and River Improvement in Middle Tennessee, 1807–1834." Unpubl. Master's thesis, Vanderbilt Univ., 1934. 90p.

Discusses the early settlers' use of and

dependence upon navigable streams, and the efforts made to improve means of travel, including financing by lotteries.

Beard, William E. "A Saga of the Western Waters." *Tennessee Historical Quarterly*, II (Dec. 1943), 316–30.

Travel on the Mississippi River by various means, from the Indian canoe to the steamboat.

Botkin, Benjamin Albert, and Alvin F. Harlow, eds., *A Treasury of Railroad Folklore: The Stories, Tall Tales, Traditions, Ballads and Songs of the American Railroad Man.* New York: Crown, 1953. 530p.

Includes the stories of Casey Jones' railroad career and the wreck of the "Cannonball."

Brooks, Addie Lou. "Early Plans for Railroads in West Tennessee, 1830–1845." *Tennessee Historical Magazine*, Series 2, III (Oct. 1932), 20–39.

Describes other means of transportation such as river travel, wagon transportation, turnpikes.

Campbell, Thomas Jefferson. *The Upper Tennessee: Comprehending Desultory Records of River Operations in the Tennessee Valley . . . .* Chattanooga: The Author, 1932. 144p.

The story of early transportation on the upper Tennessee, from rafts and flatboats to steamboats.

Clark, T.D. "The Building of the Memphis and Charleston Railroad." *East Tennessee Historical Society Publication*, No. 8 (1936), 9–25.

"The first coaches to be used on the new road were horse-drawn English stagecoaches equipped with flange wheels." Tells of festivities when the first locomotive was brought to Memphis by boat, and the giant celebration when the road was completed.

Condon, James E. "Tennessee's Vanishing Ferries." *Tennessee Conservationist*, XXXV (Feb., March 1969), 4–9, 4–10.

Historical sketches of ferries, continuing to those in operation in 1969.

Davidson, Donald. *The Tennessee. The Old River: Frontier to Secession.* Facsimile edition of Volume I, with an introduction by Thomas Daniel Young. Knoxville: Univ. of Tennessee Press, 1978. 342p. (Tennesseana Editions.)

Flatboat and Keelboat Days; Boatmen and Outlaws on the Natchez Trace; Early Steamboat Days; and How It Was in the Old Days giving the way of life with its humor and song.

Ferrell, Mallory Hope. *Tweetsie Country: The East Tennessee & North Carolina Railroad.* Boulder, Colo.: Pruett Publishing Co., 1976. 219p.

The story, with photographs, of the narrow gauge railroad from Johnson City, Tennessee, to Boone, North Carolina, 1866–1950.

Gauding, Harry Hendricks. "A History of Water Transportation in East Tennessee Prior to the Civil War." Unpubl. Master's thesis, Univ. of Tennessee, Knoxville, 1933. 106p.

"Largely the story of a mountain-locked people seeking access to the sea," from canoe to the steamboat. Pictures the life of the rivermen.

Hoagland, H.E. "Early Transportation on the Mississippi." *The Journal of Political Economy*, XIX (Feb. 1911), 111–23.

Tells of the means of transportation from the Indian canoe and raft to the coming of the steamboat, and the method of construction and propelling.

Holland, James Wendell. "A History of Railroad Enterprise in East Tennessee, 1836–1850." Unpubl. Master's thesis, Univ. of Tennessee, Knoxville, 1930. 448p.

In addition to an extensive history, a list of East Tennessee railroad promoters is given—"men who were, in any manner or to any degree, involved in railroad enterprise in ante-bellum East Tennessee."

Hubbard, Freeman H. *Railroad Avenue: Great Stories and Legends of American Railroading.* New York: McGraw-Hill, 1945. 374p.

With several references to Tennessee.

MacGill, Caroline E. *History of Transportation in the United States Before 1860.* Prepared under the Direction of Balthasar Henry Meyer. 1917; rpt. New York: Peter Smith, 1948. 678p. Rpt. with permission of the Carnegie Institution of Washington.

Early trails, roads, natural waterways, and railroads in the South.

Moore, Tyrel Gilce, Jr. "The Role of Ferry Crossings in the Development of the Transportation Network in East Tennessee, 1790–1974." Unpubl. Master's thesis, Univ. of Tennessee, Knoxville, 1975. 96p.

"Ferries functioned as vital transportation linkages, reference points for travel, and sometimes contributed to the development of local trade centers."

Neville, Bert. *Directory of Tennessee River Steamboats (1821–1928) With Illustrations.* Selma, Ala.: n.p., 1963. 272p.

A directory of steamboats, table of landings giving distances, and over two hundred pictures of boats, including keelboats and flatboats.

Quick, Herbert, and Edward Quick. *Mississippi Steamboatin'.* New York: Holt, 1926. 342p.

Tells of the types of boats used before the steamboat. Accounts of bandits on the river include Micajah and Wiley Harpe, and John A. Murrell.

Ringwalt, J.L. *Development of Transportation Systems in the United States, with Illustrations of Hundreds of Typical Objects.* Philadelphia: The Author, 1888. 398p.

Roads, turnpikes, canals, railways, vessels, vehicles, cars, locomotives, with notable incidents in railway history, construction, and operation. Mention of some Tennessee railroads. Interesting illustrations.

Sulzer, Elmer G. *Ghost Railroads of Tennessee.* Indianapolis: Vane A. Jones, 1975. 328p.

The history of railroads, with anecdotes and illustrations.

See also (Section IV) Burnett, "Big Creek's Response to the Coming of the Railroad"; (Section V), Carmichael, *History of Weakley County*; (Section IV), Crowe, *The Horseshoe People*.

XI. Travel

Baily, Francis. *Journal of a Tour in Unsettled Parts of North America in 1796 & 1797.* Ed. Jack D.L. Holmes. Carbondale: Southern Illinois Univ., 1969. 336p.

The fascinating journal of a 21-year-old Englishman; the last chapter covers the Tennessee River-Duck River-Nashville-Knoxville part of his journey. Tells of the difficulties of transporting baggage across a river on a barge, of the trails followed, the places for lodging, and the response of the settlers.

Boniol, John Dawson, Jr. "The Walton Road." *Tennessee Historical Quarterly,* XXX (Winter 1971), 402–12.

Building more than 100 miles of the road (1799–1802) from Southwest Point to Nashville; describing the inns along it; carrying the mail twice a month; and toll rates.

Buckingham, James Silk. *The Slave States of America.* 2 vols. London: Fisher, Son & Co., 1842.

Volume 2, pp. 225–71, includes an account of a trip by stagecoach from Warm Springs, North Carolina, to Greeneville, Raystown, Jonesborough, and Blountsville, Tennessee. Comments on inns, covered wagons, people, the press, and political attitudes and gatherings.

Cotterill, R.S. "The Natchez Trace." *Tennessee Historical Magazine*, VII (April 1921), 27–35.

Conditions of road travel on the homeward journey from New Orleans by boatmen who transported merchandise down the Mississippi River. Until the coming of the steamboat there was little up-river travel.

Counce, Paul Atkins. "Social and Economic History of Kingsport Before 1908." Unpubl. Master's thesis, Univ. of Tennessee, Knoxville, 1939. 96p.

The settlement of the frontier village of Boat Yard, later Kingsport. Describes the effects of travel along the stage road and river.

Daniels, Jonathan. *The Devil's Backbone; The Story of the Natchez Trace.* New York: McGraw-Hill, 1962. 278p.

A narrative of the travelers and conditions of travel on the Natchez Trace, from Natchez, Mississippi, to Nashville, Tennessee.

Devol, George H. *Forty Years a Gambler on the Mississippi.* Cincinnati: Devol & Haines, 1887. 300p.

The numerous exploits of a gambler on Mississippi River boats.

Dunbar, Seymour. *A History of Travel in America* . . . . 4 vols. Indianapolis: Bobbs-Merrill, 1915.

"A history of the devices originated by the people, primarily for their personal use, in moving from place to place." Pictures the pioneer as a traveler, the qualities of the people, their appearance and manner of living, their log cabins and furnishings, and their industries. Contains a map of westward travel routes.

Featherstonhaugh, George William. *Excursion Through the Slave States* . . . . 2 vols. London: John Murray, 1844.

An Englishman's account of his journey, 1834–35, from Washington, D.C., to Mexico, going by stagecoach through Tennessee from Blountsville to Nashville. Comments on the people and the accommodations for travelers, as well as the geology of the region.

Herndon, Marion. "Tennessee Is on the Move: From Oxcart to Airplane." *Tennessee Conservationist*, XXVIII (Sept. 1962), 16–20.

A narrative of various modes of travel during the history of Tennessee, with illustrations.

Kelly, James K. "Early Migrations in Tennessee 1769–1800." Unpubl. Master's thesis, Indiana Univ., 1947. 98p.

Discusses the routes which were the principal lines of travel for immigrants.

Natchez Trace Parkway Survey. Washington, D.C.: Government Printing Office, 1941. 167p. (76th Congress, 3rd Sess. Senate Doc. 148.)

History of the Natchez Trace, including transportation facilities and accommodations for travelers. Good bibliography.

Phelps, Dawson A. "Stands and Travel Accommodations on the Natchez Trace." *Journal of Mississippi History*, XI (Jan. 1949), 1–54.

Locates, and in some cases, describes the accommodations for travelers.

————— . "Travel on the Natchez Trace: A Study of Its Economic Aspects." *Journal of Mississippi History*, XV (Jan.-Oct. 1953), 155–64.

"Economic aspects of a road which began as a series of Indian trails and for a period of more than two decades was a post road and frontier highway."

Rogers, E.G. "Some Experiences at Staging." *Tennessee Folklore Society Bulletin*, XII (May 1946), 6–13.

Stories of stagecoach days, inns, roads, and mail carriers.

White, Kate. "John Chisholm, Solder of Fortune." *East Tennessee Historical Society Publications*, No. 1 (1929), 60–66.

Tells of the establishment of a post route from Knoxville to Abingdon.

See also: Section IV, General Sources Arnow, *Flowering of the Cumberland*;

Clark, *The Rampaging Frontier*; Wirt, *The Upper Cumberland of Pioneer Times.*

Section V, History
Burns, *History of Blount County*; Dem-ing, *Hardeman County*; Durham, *Old Sumner*; Fink, *Some Phases of the Social and Economic History of Jonesboro*; Fink, *Jonesborough*; Taylor, *Historic Sullivan.*

XII. Education

Anderson, Paul Fain. "The History of Educational Development in Sullivan County, Tennessee." Unpubl. Master's thesis, Univ. of Tennessee, Knoxville, 1936. 91p.

Accounts of early schools, their buildings, customs, and teachers.

Arnow, Harriette Simpson. "Education and the Professions in the Cumberland Region." *Tennessee Historical Quarterly*, XX (June 1961), 120–58.

The schooling of pioneer children; textbooks and other books used; the rise of professional men—teachers, lawyers, physicians—most practicing at least two professions.

Blair, Reuben Moore. "The Development of Education in Polk County, Tennessee." Unpubl. Master's thesis, Univ. of Tennessee, Knoxville, 1941. 94p.

A history of common school lands; specifications of a log schoolhouse; an account of the selection and qualification of teachers; the conduct of schools, and subjects taught. Two photographs of the exterior of log schoolhouses.

Edwards, Lawrence. *School at Speedwell.* N.p., n.d. 25p.

Author's account of his first days at a rural school.

Hatcher, Mildred. "Folklore of Our Early Schools." *Southern Folklore Quarterly*, XXI (June 1957), 110–18.

A description of early American schools, their rules and punishments, games and special events.

Lewis, Claudia. *Children of the Cumber-land.* New York: Columbia Univ. Press, 1946. 217p.

An account of family life in a section of the Cumberland Plateau, with a special emphasis on the mountain children from pre-school age to adolescence.

"Mrs. Opal Myers—A Lady with a Mission." *Foxfire*, X (Spring 1976), 77–94.

Experiences in teaching one-room schools in the Del Rio, Tennessee, area. Also gives an account of burial customs, and a brief treatment of food and a way of living.

Murray, Lena Davis, and Alvin H. Harlow. [Published under the pseudonym of Ella Enslow.] *Schoolhouse in the Foothills.* New York: Simon and Schuster, 1935. 239p.

The story of teaching experiences in a mountain community in East Tennessee during the Depression of the 1930s.

Wilson, Gordon. "Traditional Aspects of the One-Roomed School." Part I, The Schoolhouse; Part II, Books; Part III, Playtime; Part IV, The Teacher. *Kentucky Folklore Record*, XIII (Jan.-March 1967), 14–19; (April-June 1967), 43–49; (July-Sept. 1967), 62–67; (Oct.-Dec. 1967), 90–95.

Description of the building, and activities and subjects studies. Set in Kentucky but could be descriptive of Tennessee also.

Woodson, Carter G. *The Education of the Negro Prior to 1861, A History of the Education of the Colored People of the United States from the Beginning of Slavery to the Civil War.* 2d ed. Washington, D.C.: Association for the Study of Negro Life and History, 1919. 454p.

The chapter Learning in Spite of Opposition tells of the interest of persons in Maryville and Knoxville in the enlightenment of the black people. Various references to Tennessee occur throughout the book.

See also: Section IV for other accounts of the development of education, of school buildings, school customs, and books. Most of the histories in Section V give some treatment of these subjects.

XIII. Law and Crime

Accounts of early justice and the punishment of offenders; the training of lawyers; the importance of the county court and its influence on community life; and many stories of the outlaws may also be found in Sections IV and V.

Law

Caldwell, Joshua W. *Sketches of the Bench and Bar of Tennessee*. Knoxville: Ogden Brothers and Co., Printers, 1898. 402p.

An explanation of the early court system; the riding of circuits by lawyers; description of an early jail in Knoxville; old statutes regulating lawyers; a feeling of opposition to lawyers; a love of oratory.

Calhoun, Daniel H. *Professional Lives in America: Structure and Aspiration, 1750–1850*. Cambridge, Mass.: Harvard Univ. Press, 1965. 231p.

Chapter III, Branding Iron and Retrospect: Lawyers in the Cumberland River Country, describes riding the judicial circuit and the changing bar in Tennessee.

Caruthers, R.L., and A.O.P. Nicholson. *A Compilation of the Statutes of Tennessee, of a General and Permanent Nature, From the Commencement of the Government to the Present Time . . . .* Nashville: Printed at the Steam Press of James Smith, 1836. 808p.

A good index—helps in locating items of interest.

Duncan, Hannibal G. "The Southern Highlanders." *Journal of Applied Psychology*, X (July-Aug. 1926), 556–61.

Attitude toward law and outside authority.

Dynes, Russell Rowe. "Almshouse Care in Tennessee." Unpubl. Master's thesis, Univ. of Tennessee, Knoxville, 1950. 132p.

Contains early legislative provisions for care of the poor by county courts.

Fink, Miriam L. "Judicial Activities in Early East Tennessee." *East Tennessee Historical Society Publications*, No. 7 (1935), 38–49.

Tells of the building of the court house and the "interests and activities of the tribunals," and describes crimes and the methods of punishment in Washington County.

Hallum, John. *The Diary of an Old Lawyer: Or Scenes Behind the Curtain*. Nashville: Southwestern Publishing House, 1895. 458p.

Anecdotes of the author's experiences.

Haywood, John, comp. *The Duty and Authority of Justices of the Peace, in the State of Tennessee*. Nashville: Printed and Sold by Thomas G. Bradford, 1810. 372p.

Contains regulations, laws, and penalties.

Henry, H.M. "The Slave Laws of Tennessee." *Tennessee Historical Magazine*, II (Sept. 1916), 175–203.

"An examination of statute law and judicial interpretation." Gives the legal status of slaves and the regulations governing their lives.

Imes, William Lloyd. "The Legal Status of Free Negroes and Slaves in Tennessee." *Journal of Negro History*, IV (July 1919), 254–72.

Laws and regulations which concerned their way of living.

Mitchell, James Coffield. *The Tennessee Justice's Manual and Civil Officer's Guide.* Nashville: J.C. Mitchell and C.C. Norvell, 1834. 534p.

Intended to be "the People's Law Book . . . made to bring knowledge of the law to the door and comprehension of every man."

Pitts, John A. *Personal and Professional Reminiscences of an Old Lawyer.* Kingsport, Tenn.: Southern Publishers, 1930. 381p.

Reminiscences, originally published by the *Citizens Appeal* of Nashville, give some account of rural life about the middle of the 19th century: building the cabin home, making sugar and maple syrup, early school days, and characteristics of "Saddlebag" practice.

Thompson, E. Bruce. "Reforms in the Penal System of Tennessee 1820–1950." *Tennessee Historical Quarterly*, I (Dec. 1942), 219–308.

Early methods of punishment for various offenses, and efforts for more humanitarian and effective legislation.

Crime

Coates, Robert M. *The Outlaw Years: The History of the Land Pirates of the Natchez Trace.* New York: Macaulay Co., 1930. 308p.

The Harpes, Hare, Samuel Mason, and Murrell, with an introductory description of the way of life of the pioneers, their cabins, clothing, and food.

Elliott, Mabel A. "Crime and the Frontier Mores." *American Sociological Review*, IX (April 1944), 185–92.

Maintains that "the mainsprings of antisocial conduct are as much rooted in the past as they are a function of the present and that in America, crime bears a particular relationship to the folkways and mores of the frontier."

Hall, James. *Letters From the West; Containing Sketches of Scenery, Manners and Customs; and Anecdotes Connected With the First Settlements of the Western Sections of the United States (1828).* Facsimile edition with an introduction by John T. Flanagan. Gainesville, Fla.: Scholars Facsimiles and Reprints, 1967. 385p.

Has a chapter on the Harpes.

Harrison, C. William. *Outlaw of the Natchez Trace.* New York: Ballentine, 1960. 128p.

The life of John A. Murrell.

Howard, H.R., comp. *The History of Virgil A. Stewart and His Adventure in Capturing and Exposing the Great "Western Land Pirate" and His Gang . . . .* New York: Harper & Brothers, 1836. 273p.

Association with and capture of John A. Murrell.

Marshall, Park. "John A. Murrell and Daniel Crenshaw. Some Facts with Regard to These Criminals . . . ." *Tennessee Historical Magazine*, VI (April 1920), 3–9.

Questions some of the accusations that have accumulated concerning these outlaws.

Morgan, Marshall. *Tennessee Town.* Franklin, Tenn.: James D. Dustin, 1936. 116p.

Includes an account of John A. Murrell, highwayman.

National Police Gazette Editors. *The Life and Adventures of John A. Murrell: The Great Western Land Pirate,* with twenty-one spirited illustrative engravings. New York:H. Long & Brother, 1847. 126p.

> Murrell was born in Middle Tennessee in 1804.

Nye, Russell B. *A Baker's Dozen: Thirteen Unusual Americans*. East Lansing: Michigan State Univ. Press, 1956. 300p.

> John A. Murrell, outlaw, pp. 116–37.

Rothbert, Otto A. *The Outlaws of Cave-In-Rock: Historical Accounts of the Famous Highwaymen and River Pirates Who Operated in Pioneer Days Upon the Ohio and Mississippi Rivers and Over the Old Natchez Trace*. Cleveland: Arthur H. Clark Co., 1924. 364p.

> Full accounts of the Harpes and Samuel Mason.

Vanderwood, Paul J. *Night Riders of Reelfoot Lake*. Memphis: Memphis State Univ. Press, 1969. 159p.

> Discussion of the crimes, the trials, and legal maneuvers.

Walton, Augustus Q. *A History of the Detection, Conviction, Life and Designs of John A. Murel* [sic] *The Great Western Land Pirate; Together With His System of Villany, and Plan of Exciting a Negro Rebellion Also, a Catalogue of the names of Four-Hundred and Fifty-Five of His Mystic Clan Fellows and Followers, and a Statement of Their Efforts For the Destruction of Virgil A. Stewart, the Young Man Who Detected Him . To Which Has Been Added a Biographical Sketch of V. A. Stewart*. Cincinnati: n.p., n.d. 84p.

XIV. Religion

Alexander, Frank D. "Religion in a Rural Community of the South." *American Sociological Review*, VI (April 1941), 241–51.

> Ruralville, a fictitious name for an open-country community in Southwest Tennessee, is analyzed as to religious beliefs and practices.

Alexander, Theron, Jr. "The Covenanters Come to East Tennessee." Unpubl. Master's thesis, Univ. of Tennessee, Knoxville, 1939. 84p.

> History of the Scotch-Irish migration; early work of Presbyterian preachers in the area; the Great Revival; the establishment of "log colleges."

Anderson, T.C. *Life of Reverend George Donnell, First Pastor of the Church in Lebanon; With a Sketch of the Scotch-Irish Race*. Nashville: Published for the Author, 1858. 334p.

> Camp meetings stressed.

Asbury, Francis. *The Journal and Letters of Francis Asbury*. Elmer E. Clark, editor-in-chief. 3 vols. London:Epworth Press, and Nashville: Abingdon Press, 1958.

> Volume I, The Journal, 1771–1793; Volume II: The Journal, 1794–1816; Volume III, Letters.
> Shows conditions from the viewpoint of the itinerant preacher and bishop, with numerous references to Tennessee.

Beard, Richard. *Brief Biographical Sketches of Some of the Early Ministers of the Cumberland Presbyterian Church*. Second series. Nashville: Cumberland Presbyterian Board of Publication, 1874. 408p.

> The way of life and the manner of preaching of Tennessee ministers in the Cumberland Presbyterian Church.

Bowyer, John Wilson, and Claude Harrison Thurman, eds. *The Annals of Elder Horn: Early Life in the Southwest*. New

York: Richard R. Smith, 1930. 225p.

The autobiography of a minister and school teacher whose early career was spent in Sumner County in the late 1800s. Religion, law and order, and education in a pioneer community.

Bruce, Dickson D., Jr. *And They All Sang Hallelujah: Plain-Folk Camp-Meeting Religion, 1800–1845.* Knoxville: Univ. of Tennessee Press, 1973. 155p. (Winner of the first James Mooney Award.)

A helpful account of life and religion on the Southern frontier, of the camp meetings, and of the singing of the spiritual choruses which "concisely summarized what religion meant to the frontier saints."

Burnett, James J. *Sketches of Tennessee's Pioneer Baptist Preachers.* Nashville: Marshall & Bruce Co., 1919. 567p.

Biographical sketches show the way of life and the circumstances under which the ministers' work was done.

Byrne, Donald E., Jr. *No Foot of Land: Folklore of American Methodist Itinerants.* Metuchen, N.J.: Scarecrow Press and American Theological Library Association, 1975. 354p. (ATLA Monograph Series, No. 6.)

"Folklore culled . . . from the autobiographies, biographies, and reminiscences of the nineteenth century Methodist itinerant ministers, has constituted the core data used in this volume." A good background study.

Carr, John. *Early Times in Middle Tennessee.* Nashville: E. Stevenson & F.A. Owen, 1857. 248p. Rpt. Nashville: Parthenon Press, 1958. 112p.

An interesting contemporary account of religious gatherings, preachers, and customs.

Cartwright, Peter. *Autobiography of Peter Cartwright, the Backwoods Preacher.* Ed. W.P. Strickland. New York: Carlton & Porter, 1857. 525p.

Includes accounts of his various experiences as a member of Tennessee Methodist Conferences, among them revivals and camp meetings.

Cassell, C.W., et al., eds. *History of the Lutheran Church in Virginia and East Tennessee.* Strasburg, Va.: Shenandoah Publishing House, 1930. 401p.

History of individual congregations, buildings, etc., and names of members and pastors.

Christ Church, Nashville 1829–1929. Nashville: Marshall & Bruce Co., 1929. 297p.

A chapter by Silas B. McKinley called "Religious Conditions in Tennessee in 1829" tells about circuit-riders, camp meetings, church services, and the attitude of the people toward religion. "Nashville in Those Days" by Elizabeth P. Elliott briefly describes the town, its buildings, roads, military muster grounds, schools, etc.

"Christianburg Baptist Church Minutes 1828–1917. Monroe County, Tennessee." Typed copy made by Works Progress Administration, 1938. 113, 53, 27, 18, 24p.

Very brief minutes include frequent reference to individual offenses against the church, and their treatment.

Ciaramitaro, Bridget. "Anabaptists in Tennessee." 1972. 16p. Student paper, Riedl Collection, Univ. of Tennessee Library, Knoxville.

The Old Order Amish in Tennessee; Menonites in Lawrence County, in Knoxville, Concord, and Muddy Pond. Interviews concerning their beliefs, clothing, and way of life.

Cleveland, Catharine C. *The Great Revival in the West, 1797—1805.* Chicago: Univ. of Chicago Press, 1916. 215p.

Description of frontier religious conditions and customs; the rise of revivals and camp meetings; revival leaders; phenomena of the revival, and its effect on communities.

Cockrum, James Earl. "A Study of the Development of Organized Religion in Jefferson County, Tennessee (1785–1950)." Unpubl. Master's thesis, Univ. of Tennessee, Knoxville, 1951. 138p.

Presbyterians, Baptists, Methodists, and Quakers. An account of the organization of individual churches, the principles of training and selection of ministers, and something of their influence.

Coulter, E. Merton. *William G. Brownlow: The Fighting Parson of the Southern Highlands.* Chapel Hill: Univ. of North Carolina Press, 1937. 432p.

"Crusading in the Southern Highlands" as experienced by a fiery Tennessee circuit rider who became a journalist and politician.

Daniel, W. Harrison. "Frontier Baptist Activities, 1780–1803." Unpubl. Master's thesis, Vanderbilt Univ., 1947. 118p.

Describes the buildings and furnishings, and the practices, ordinances, and discipline of the frontier church.

Davenport, Franklin Morgan. *Primitive Traits in Religious Revivals; A Study in Mental and Social Evolution.* New York: Macmillan, 1905. 323p.

Contains a chapter on the religion of the American Negro and one on the Scotch-Irish revival in Kentucky in 1800.

Dickinson, Eleanor. *Revival!* . . . text by Barbara Benziger. New York: Harper & Row, 1974. 180p.

"For a number of summers she [the artist] traveled in rural and urban areas of Tennessee, Kentucky and West Virginia, drawing from life as the people worshiped in tents and churches." Also photographs and tape recordings made as she "covers the varied culture and customs of revival country, from footwashings and baptisms in mountain creeks to snake handlings and healing the sick."

Edwards, Lawrence. "History of the Baptists of Tennessee with Particular Attention to the Primitive Baptists of East Tennessee." Unpubl. Master's thesis, Univ. of Tennessee, Knoxville, 1941. 110p.

The effect of migration of religious groups in the early settlement; religious awakening on the frontier in the 1800s, and the Great Revival.

———, ed. *Minutes of Davis Creek Church, 1797–1907.* N.p.: The Author, 1968. 244p.

Minutes of the Baptist Church of Christ at Davis Creek, Powell Valley community later to be called Speedwell. Many instances of exclusion of individuals because of "worldly" behavior.

Flanigen, George J., ed. *Catholicity in Tennessee; A Sketch of Catholic Activities in the State, 1541–1937.* Nashville: Ambrose Printing Co., 1937. 176p.

History of early Catholic activities, and the development of churches and other institutions. Includes biographical sketches.

Fuller, T.O. *The Story of the Church Life Among Negroes in Memphis: For Students and Workers, 1900–1938.* Memphis: n.p. 1938. 52p.

A history of various denominations, including some doctrines, customs, and incidents.

Gallaher, James. *The Western Sketchbook.* Boston: Crocker and Brewster, 1850. 408p.

Contains a chapter on the Great Western Revival.

Green, William M. *Life and Papers of A. L. P. Green, D. D.* Ed. T. O. Summers. Nashville: Southern Methodist Publishing House, 1877. 592p.

Camp meetings and the life of a Methodist Circuit Rider.

Hooker, Elizabeth R. *Religion in the Highlands; Native Churches and Missionary Enterprises in the Southern Appalachian Area.* . . . New York: Home Missions Council, 1933. 319p.

A survey which "reproduces to a considerable extent the churches and religious attitudes of their ancestors of colonial days." Considers racial stocks, distribution of settlers, total religious inheritance, and pioneer ethics.

Howse, Ruth Whitener. "The Old Fashioned Campmeeting Church." *Tennessee Folklore Society Bulletin,* XVII (Dec. 1951), 83–84.

Historical legend in verse about the Tabernacle Methodist Church, Brownsville, Tenn.

Johnson, Charles A. "The Frontier Camp Meeting: Contemporary and Historical Appraisals, 1805–1840." *Mississippi Valley Historical Review*, XXXVII (June 1950), 91–110.

"The pioneer revival, although a crude and imperfect institution, was an expression of the times."

———. *The Frontier Camp Meeting: Religion's Harvest Time*. Dallas: Southern Methodist Univ. Press, 1955. 325p.

"This study is an attempt to capture the essence of the camp meeting; to place it in proper perspective . . . as a natural product of a frontier environment, and as one of the most important social institutions in the trans-Allegheny West in the first half of the nineteenth century." Includes sketches of the arrangement of the camps, the events of a day, the hymns, and the sociability of the groups.

Johnson, Clifton H., ed. *God Struck Me Dead: Religious Conversion Experiences and Autobiographies of Ex-slaves*. Foreword by Paul Radin. Fisk Univ. Social Sciences Institute. Philadelphia: Pilgrim Press, 1969. 172p.

Has interviews from Tennessee.

Jones, Alice Marie. "The Negro Folk Sermon: A Study in the Sociology of Folk Culture." Ph.D. diss., Fisk Univ., 1942. 86p.

"This study aims finally to define a point of view and eventually to formulate a frame of reference for understanding the Negro folk sermon as a part of Negro folk culture."

Jones, Loyal. "Studying Mountain Religion." *Appalachian Journal*, V (Autumn 1977), 125–30.

Resources for Appalachian studies.

Kane, Steven M. "Holy Ghost People: The Snakehandlers of Southern Appalachia." *Appalachian Journal*, I (Spring 1974), 255–62.

Based on field work in Kentucky, Tennessee, West Virginia, South Carolina, and Virginia.

Kincheloe, Joe Lyons. "The Camp Meet-

ing and the Political Rally." Unpubl. Master's thesis, Univ. of Tennessee, Knoxville, 1975. 141p.

A comparison of the principles, manners, techniques, and influences of evangelical camp meetings and political gatherings.

La Barre, Weston. *They Shall Take Up Serpents; Psychology of the Southern Snake-Handling Cult*. Minneapolis: Univ. of Minnesota Press, 1962; rpt. New York: Schocken Books, 1969. 208p.

Apparently originated in Tennessee in the early 1900s. Meetings are described and are considered as "a psychological phenomenon in the American South of our day."

Ledford, Allen James. "Methodism in Tennessee, 1783–1866." Unpubl. Master's thesis, Univ. of Tennessee, Knoxville, 1941. 125p.

History of the expansion of Methodism in Tennessee, including the story of the circuit riders, and of the temperance efforts.

McBride, Robert M. "A Camp Meeting at Goshen Church." *Tennessee Historical Quarterly*, XXII (June 1963), 137–42.

An annual meeting in Franklin County, with preaching and dinner on the grounds.

McDonnold, B.W. *History of the Cumberland Presbyterian Church*. Nashville: Board of Publication of the Cumberland Presbyterian Church, 1899. 687p.

The way of living in the early 19th century in Kentucky and Tennessee, the Great Revival, and the "planting" of the churches throughout the area.

McTeer, Will A. *History of the New Providence Presbyterian Church, Maryville, Tennessee, 1786–1921*. Maryville: New Providence Church, 1921. 111p.

A brief description of church buildings, burial grounds, camp meetings and Sabbath schools.

M'Ferrin, John B. *History of Methodism in Tennessee*. 3 vols. Nashville: A.H. Redford, 1872–79.

Tells of the Great Revival of 1800, the origin and manner of conducting camp meetings, their grounds and shelter, and "the Jerks," and gives accounts of annual conferences and other events, 1783–1840.

Miller, Harriet Parks. *Pioneer Colored Christians.* Clarksville, Tenn.: W.P. Titus, Printer and Binder, 1911. 103p.

Interviews with members of a Black family, telling of religious experiences and other activities, including a corn shucking.

Peacock, Mary Thomas. *The Circuit Rider and Those Who Followed; Sketches of Methodist Churches Organized Before 1860 in the Chattanooga Area With Special Reference to Centenary.*Chattanooga: Hudson Printing and Lithographing Co., 1957. 465p.

A description of the life of the circuit rider, and a brief account of camp meetings.

Pioneer Presbyterianism in Tennessee: Addresses Delivered in Connection With the Observance of "Presbyterian Day" at the Tennessee Centennial and International Exposition, Nashville, October 28, 1897. Richmond, Va.: Presbyterian Committee of Publication, 1898. 83p.

Address by C.W. Heiskell gives an imaginary picture of the church building, the service, and the Sunday behavior of the family.

Posey, Walter Brownlow. *The Baptist Church in the Lower Mississippi Valley, 1776–1845.* Lexington: Univ. of Kentucky Press, 1957. 166p.

Tells of the work of itinerant preachers, camp meetings, and the development of churches.

———, ed. "Bishop Asbury Visits Tennessee, 1788–1815: Extracts from His Journal." *Tennessee Historical Quarterly,* XV (Sept. 1956), 253–68.

The hardships of travel of a circuit rider.

———. *The Development of Methodism in the Old Southwest 1783–1824.* Tuscaloosa, Ala.: Weatherford Printing Co., 1933. 151p.

Includes experiences of the circuit rider and detailed description of various phases of camp meetings—the necessity for pre-

serving order, the need for giving medical advice, and the demonstration of the power of music.

———. *Frontier Mission: A History of Religion West of the Southern Appalachians to 1861.* Lexington: Univ. of Kentucky Press, 1966. 436p.

The work of frontier preachers, the early camp meeting era, and the relation of various denominations to the growth of the state.

———. *The Presbyterian Church in the Old Southwest, 1778–1838.* Richmond, Va.: John Knox Press, 1952. 192p.

"Religion, virtue and knowledge had been the three cardinal possessions of the Scotch-Irish" and are pictured in the organization of churches, the qualifications of the ministers, fostering of education, and regulation of moral life on the frontier. The physical structure of church buildings and their furnishings are also described.

Preece, Harold, and Celia Kraft. *Dew On Jordan.* New York: Dutton, 1946. 221p.

An account of meetings of "the little sects," principally in East Tennessee: snake-handlers, faith healers, footwashings, dinner on the grounds, and many others.

Price, Richard Nye. *Holston Methodism: From Its Origin to the Present Time.* 5 vols. Nashville: Publication House of the M.E. Church, South, Smith & Lamar, Agents, 1904–14.

Volume I, Itinerant Preachers and the Great Revival, tells of the early work of itinerant preachers, their personalities, where and how they preached, church discipline, the Great Revival, etc.

Puckett, Newbell N. "Religious Folk-Beliefs of Whites and Negroes." *Journal of Negro History,* XVI (Jan. 1931), 9–35.

"Such religious folk-beliefs and customs arrange themselves naturally into the creed, what folk believe in a religious way, and the cult, or what the folk practice in a religious way."

Rogers, E.G. "Pioneering Accounts of Frontier Religion." *Tennessee Folklore Society Bulletin,* XVII (June 1951), 32–40.

Accounts of early preachers and their work.

Ross, James. *Life and Times of Elder Reuben Ross*. Philadelphia: Grant, Faires & Rodgers, n.d. 426p.

An account of Elder Ross's work as a Baptist minister in Robertson, Montgomery, and Stewart counties in the early 1800s, with sketches of other ministers and churches. The Great Revival is included. Also described are customs and manner of living, food, clothing, making sugar, reaping wheat, procuring salt, recreation, and schools.

Schwarz, Berthold E. "Ordeal By Serpents, Fire and Strychnine, A Study of Some Provocative, Psychosomatic Phenomena." *Psychiatric Quarterly*, XXXIV (July 1960), 405–29.

An account of visits by a psychiatrist to groups of "the Free Pentacostal Holiness Church, a religious sect in the mountainous, rural regions of eastern Kentucky, Tennessee and parts of Virginia."

Shurter, Robert L. "The Camp Meeting in the Early Life and Literature of the Mid-West." *East Tennessee Historical Society Publications*, No. 5 (1933), 142–49.

"It is the purpose of this paper to give something of the history of the camp meeting, to present some of the best contemporary accounts of it, and to analyze the attitude of early literary men toward it."

Simmons, Hugh L. "Religion in the Old Southwestern Environment." Unpubl. Master's thesis, Vanderbilt Univ., 1933.

The development of frontier religion and its relation to living conditions, 1770 to 1800. Places of worship, accommodations for traveling preachers, and revivals.

Spaulding, Arthur W. *The Men of the Mountains; The Story of the Southern Mountaineer and His Kin of the Piedmont; With an Account of Some of the Agencies of Progress Among Them*. Nashville: Southern Publishing Assoc., 1915. 320p.

Tells of the life of the mountain people, circuit riders, and camp meetings and the work of one denomination in the development of schools and health care.

Sullins, David. *Recollections of an Old Man, Seventy Years in Dixie, 1827–1897*. Bristol: King Printing Co., Leroi Press, 1910. 426p.

Reminiscences of a Methodist minister, giving an account of family life, camp meetings, and schools, as well as events in his career.

Sweet, William Warren. "The Churches as Moral Courts of the Frontier." *Church History*, II (March 1933), 3–21.

"On every frontier from the Alleghenies to the Pacific these were the people who fought the battle for decency and order." Contains several references to Tennessee.

———. "Some Salient Characteristics of Frontier Religion." *Methodist Quarterly Review*, LXXIII (July 1924), 437–52.

A discussion of frontier preaching and the emphasis of various denominations.

Taylor, Auvella Louise. "The Autobiography of Peter Cartwright and the Humor of the Old Southwest." Unpubl. Master's thesis, Vanderbilt Univ., 1961. 51p.

Analyzes the autobiography as containing factual material about Cartwright; historical material on the Methodist Church; exhortatory material stating his views; and anecdotal material. Characterizes him as "the typical backwoods preacher."

Taylor, O.W., ed. *Early Tennessee Baptists 1769–1832*. Nashville: Executive Board of the Tennessee Baptist Convention, 1957. 314p.

Chapters concern the manner of life of early Tennessee Baptists: their home life, and social, civic, and religious life; relation to the Great Revival of 1800; and church procedure and discipline.

Tennessee Historical Records Survey. "Records of Bradley County. Journal of Augustine F. Shannon, 1848–1850." Nashville: Historical Records Survey, 1940. 54p. (Typed copy made by the Works Projects Administration in the Univ. of Tennessee Library, Knoxville.)

The diary of a Methodist circuit rider.

———. *Tennessee Baptist Convention, Ocoee Baptist Association*. Nashville:

Historical Records Survey, 1942. 134p.

Early religious activities in the area and individual churches.

Toomey, Glenn A. *The Romance of a Sesquicentennial Church: The Dumplin Creek Baptist Church of Christ, Jefferson County, Tennessee, Organized 1797.* N.p., 1947. 93p.

A history, giving biographical sketches of ministers, some anecdotes concerning them, rules of decorum, and causes of excommunication of members.

Tryon, Warren S., comp. and ed. *A Mirror for Americans: Life and Manners in the United States 1790–1870 as Recorded by American Travelers.* 3 vols. Chicago: Univ. of Chicago Press, 1952.

Volume 3, Religious Ecstasy on the Frontier, 1804–5, contains an article "On the Jerks," by Lorenzo Dow.

Wagner, Harry C. "Beginnings of the Christian Church in East Tennessee." *East Tennessee Historical Society Publications*, No. 20 (1948), 49–58.

Early groups in Tennessee, their places of meeting and their relationship with other groups.

Wagner, Mary Church. "The Settlement of Zion Community in Maury County, Tennessee, 1806–1860." Unpubl. Master's thesis, Vanderbilt Univ. 1945. 125p.

Settlement of a Presbyterian community, telling of church buildings and church discipline, schools, and the treatment of slaves.

Watson, Andrew Polk. "Primitive Religion Among Negroes in Tennessee."

Unpubl. Master's thesis, Fisk Univ., 1932. 97p.

Religious behavior among Negroes in central Tennessee, described on the basis of early contact of fieldhand slaves with Methodist and Baptist missionaries; "Cornfield Religion." Primarily based on individual interviews.

White, Edwin. "Religious Ideals in the Highlands." *Mountain Life and Work*, XXVII (Fall 1951), 26–31; XXVII (Winter 1952), 18–21.

Religious attitudes and ideals in the Southern Highlands.

Yeatman, Trezevant Player, Jr. "St. Johns—A Plantation Church of the Old South." *Tennessee Historical Quarterly*, X (Dec. 1951), 334–43.

A church built in Maury County for plantation families, including slaves. Brick made by hand from native clay and timber cut from trees in the area. Religious services to 1889. The church's "story is that of plantation society and the religio-social relations that it produced."

Young, Jacob. *Autobiography of a Pioneer; Or, The Nativity, Experience, Travels, and Ministerial Labors of Rev. Jacob Young* . . . Cincinnati: Cranston and Curts [1857]. 528p.

A circuit rider who traveled the Holston Circuit in 1804 and the Nashville Circuit in 1806 tells of the homes where he stayed and the religious gatherings, including an account of "the Jerks."

See also Sections IV and V in which many of the sources give information about local churches and religious observance.

XV. Speech, Proverbs, and Names

Speech

Adams, Homer J. "Speech Patterns." *Tennessee Folklore Society Bulletin*, XLII (June 1976), 70–71.

Lists 26 phrases collected in Georgia, Alabama, Tennessee, and Kentucky.

"Anecdotes Illustrating the Folk Idiom in the American South." *Tennessee Folk-*

lore Society Bulletin, XXVI (March 1960), 8–19.

> Includes 23 anecdotes from Kentucky and Tennessee.

Ball, Donald B. "Notes on the Slang and Folk Speech of Knoxville, Knox County, Tennessee." *Tennessee Folklore Society Bulletin*, XLIV (Sept. 1978), 134–42.

> Lists 70 terms collected from 15 informants during the period December 1974 to November 1975.

Berrey, Lester V. "Southern Mountain Dialect." *American Speech*, XV (Feb. 1940), 45–54.

> Word usage and pronunciation in the Southern Appalachian and Ozark mountains.

Bewley, Irene. "Picturesque Speech." *Tennessee Folklore Society Bulletin*, IX (Sept. 1943), 4.

> Comments on six phrases used in the speech of the hill-folk.

Boswell, George W. "Operation of Popular Etymology in Folksong Diction." *Tennessee Folklore Society Bulletin*, XXXIX (June 1973), 37–58.

> Most of the informants were residents of Middle Tennessee, 1949–54.

Brown, Calvin S., Jr. "Dialectal Survivals in Tennessee." *Modern Language Notes*, IV (Nov. 1889), 410–18.

> Cited are 39 words "to show that some of the colloquial and dialectal expressions of this region have survived from Shakespeare, or, at least, that a resemblance can be traced between them and the language of his day."

——— . "Other Dialectal Forms in Tennessee." *Publications of the Modern Language Association*, VI (July 1891), 171–75.

> "A study of a few of the peculiarities of the language as found in Tennessee, regardless of their origin and history."

——— . "Tennessee." *Dialect Notes*, IV, Part 5, (1916), 345–46.

> Word-list of 15 words with definitions, from Obion County.

Bruce, J. Douglas, et al. "Terms from Tennessee." *Dialect Notes*, IV, Part 1 (1913), 58.

> Lists 13 words and usage.

Carpenter, Charles. "Variation in the Southern Mountain Dialect." *American Speech*, VIII (Feb. 1933), 22–25.

> Illustrations of regional variations in pronunciation and meaning of words.

Cavender, Anthony Patterson. "A Phonemic and Phonetic Analysis of the Folk Speech of Bedford County, Tennessee." Unpubl. Master's thesis, Univ. of Tennessee, Knoxville, 1974. 51p.

> The result of interviews with five elderly rural life-long residents of Middle Tennessee, using the Orton-Wright questionnaire. With some discussion of "migration and linguistic affinity."

Chapman, Maristan. "American Speech as Practised in the Southern Highlands." *Century*, CXVII (March 1929), 617–23.

> Historical and national background of the folkspeech of the region.

Combs, Josiah H. "The Language of the Southern Highlanders." *Publications of the Modern Language Association*, XLVI (Dec. 1931), 1302–22.

> Idioms, pronunciation, and syntax. Region includes Tennessee, but no state classification is given.

——— . "Old, Early and Elizabethan English in the Southern Mountains." *Dialect Notes*, IV, Part 4 (1916), 283–97.

> Word usage of mountaineers of the South from West Virginia to northern Alabama, including Tennessee.

——— . "A Word-List from the South." *Dialect Notes*, V, Part 2 (1919), 31–40.

> Words and dialectic pecularities of Kentucky, Tennessee, Virginia, North Carolina, Arkansas and Oklahoma, listed by state. Includes 17 words from East Tennessee.

——— . "A Word-List from the Southern Highlands." *Publications of the American Dialect Society*, No. 2, (Nov. 1944), 17–23.

Gives pronunciation and definition. Includes Tennessee.

Cox, Ellen Duncan. "A Study of Dialect Peculiarities of Scott County, Tennessee Secondary School Students." Unpubl. Master's thesis. Univ. of Tennessee, Knoxville, 1969. 102p.

Material was gathered from 77 junior and senior high school students through questionnaires and class discussion.

Darnell, H.J., et al. "Terms from Tennessee." *Dialect Notes*, IV, Part I (1913), 58.

Defines 13 terms.

Davis, Alva L., and Raven Ioor McDavid, Jr. " 'Shivaree': An Example of Cultural Diffusion." *American Speech*, XXIV (Dec. 1949), 249–55.

A study of the distribution of the word form "shivaree."

Dennis, Leah A. "A Word-List from Alabama and Some Other Southern States." *Publications of the American Dialect Society*, No. 2 (Nov. 1944), 6–16.

Pronunciation and definition of words. Includes Tennessee.

Dingus, L.R. "Tobacco Words." *Publications of the American Dialect Society*, No. 2 (Nov. 1944), 63–72.

"The geographical area of this list centers around Lexington, Kentucky, reaches over into southern Ohio, eastern Tennessee, and southwestern Virginia."

Drukker, Raymond. "Language By-Ways." *Mountain Life and Work*, XXXVIII (Summer 1962), 50–52.

Pronunciation and usage of a number of phrases in the Appalachian hill country.

Edson, H.A., and Edith M. Fairchild. "Wordlists: Tennessee Mountains." *Dialect Notes*, I, Part VIII (1896), 370–77.

Collections made in Roan Mountain, Tennessee, and Berea, Kentucky.

Farr, T.J. "Folk Speech of Middle Tennessee." *American Speech*, XI (Oct. 1936), 275–76.

There are 63 examples of colloquial and provincial usage from Middle Tennessee, especially the mountain regions.

——— . "The Language of the Tennessee Mountain Regions." *American Speech*, XIV (April 1939), 89–92.

Has 148 words with illustrative sentences.

——— . "More Tennessee Expressions." *American Speech*, XV (Dec. 1940), 446–48.

Some 69 expressions, with illustrative sentences, from the Tennessee mountain regions.

Fink, Paul M. *Bits of Mountain Speech Gathered Between 1910 and 1965 Along the Mountains Bordering North Carolina and Tennessee.* Boone, N.C.: Appalachian Consortium Press, 1974. 31p.

An alphabetical list of words with definition, use in a sentence, and an indication of the part of speech.

Fitzpatrick, Robert J. "Language of the Tobacco Market." *American Speech*, XV (April 1940), 132–35.

Lists 75 terms used by buyers and auctioneers.

Flowers, Paul. "Picturesque Speech." *Tennessee Folklore Society Bulletin*, X (March 1944), 9–10.

On the origin of the term "bo-dollar."

Griffin, William J., ed. "Anecdotes Illustrating the Folk Idiom in the American South." *Tennessee Folklore Society Bulletin*, XXVI (March 1960), 8–19.

Some contributed by Tennesseans.

——— , ed. "Some More Examples of Southern Folk Idiom." *Tennessee Folklore Society Bulletin*, XXVII (June 1961), 35–36.

Anecdotes contributed by various people in Tennessee.

Hall, Joseph S. "Bear-Hunting Stories from the Great Smokies." *Tennessee Folklore Society Bulletin*, XXIII (Sept. 1957), 67–75.

The author's chief interest in the stories

lies in their revelation of the mountain man's colorful personality, and in the picturesque features of dialect.

——— . *The Phonetics of Great Smoky Mountain Speech*. New York: King's Crown Press, 1942. 110p. (American Speech Reprints and Monographs, No. 4.)
"It is the purpose of this study to describe the sounds of one of America's most interesting vernaculars . . . English as it is spoken in the Great Smoky Mountains of Tennessee and North Carolina."

——— . "Recording Speech in the Great Smokies." U.S. National Park Service, Region One, *Regional Review*, III (Oct.-Nov. 1939), 3–8. Rpt. as *Mountain Speech in the Great Smokies*. Washington, D.C.: Government Printing Office, 1941. 12p. (National Park Service Popular Study Series: History, No. 5.)
Discusses recording methods used in a linguistics survey of the native inhabitants of the Great Smoky Mountains region in 1937.

Harder, Kelsie B. "The Baby's 'Dinnel.' " *American Speech*, XXXII (May 1957), 158.
Use of the word in Perry County, Tennessee, "in application to the food a child receives from its mother's breast and the action to receive it."

——— . "Euphemistic Dilemmas in Tennessee." *American Speech*, XXVIII (May 1952), 156–57.
Concerning "goober" and "peanut," and "woodchuck" and "groundhog" in Perry County.

——— . "Hay-making Terms in Perry County." *Tennessee Folklore Society Bulletin*, XXXIII (June 1967), 41–48.
Lists 125 terms with definitions, preceded by a history and description of the haying process.

——— . "The Jake Leg." *Tennessee Folklore Society Bulletin*, XXVII (Sept. 1961), 45–47.
The use of the term in Tennessee's Perry and Gibson counties as differentiated from dictionary and other definitions.

——— . "Let It Go It." *American Speech*, XXXII (Oct. 1957), 240.
A phrase apparently peculiar to Perry County, Tennessee.

——— . "The Mammary Weed." *American Speech*, XXVIII (Oct. 1953), 236–37.
A use of the word "weed" in Perry County, Tennessee.

——— . "Musseling Terms from Tennessee," and "A 'Tub' of Corn." *American Speech*, XXX (Feb. 1955), 74–77.
Terms collected in Perry County from observation and personal acquaintance.

——— . "Pert Nigh Almost; Folk Measurement." *Tennessee Folklore Society Bulletin*, XXIII (March 1957), 6–12.
Folk expressions of measurement, Perry County, Tennessee.

——— . "The Vocabulary of Hog-Killing." *Tennessee Folklore Society Bulletin*, XXV (Dec. 1959), 111–15.
The process of butchering hogs for home meat consumption, and the vocabulary thereof. Terms taken primarily from the speech of Cedar Creek Community, Perry County, Tennessee.

——— . "The Vocabulary of Marble Playing." *Publications of the American Dialect Society*, No. 23 (April 1955), 3–33.
This vocabulary "began as a regional topic, for it grew out of a study of the speech used in a rather isolated area in Perry County, Tennessee, but further research proved the terms used by marble players in this area to be traditional in the English speaking world."

——— . "A Vocabulary of Wagon Parts." *Tennessee Folklore Society Bulletin*, XXVIII (March 1962), 12–20.
Terms used by farmers in Perry County, Tenn., and from the author's knowledge.

Harris, Alberta. "Southern Mountain Dialect." Unpubl. Master's thesis, Louisiana State Univ., 1948. 115p.
Presenting the important characteristics of the dialects of the Southern mountain areas of the United States: southwest Mis-

souri, northwest Arkansas, eastern Kentucky, eastern Tennessee, western North Carolina, and eastern Texas. Phonetic tables give pronunciation in each area.

Hayes, Francis C. "A Word-List from North Carolina." *Publications of the American Dialect Society*, No. 2 (Nov. 1944), 32–37.
Includes some Tennessee usage.

Hinton, Elmer. "Some More Examples of Southern Folk Idiom." *Tennessee Folklore Society Bulletin*, XXVII (June 1961), 35–36.
20 examples of folk speech reprinted from the author's Tennessean column in *The Nashville Tennessean*, March 25, 1960.

Jones, M. Jean. "The Regional English of the Former Inhabitants of Cades Cove in the Great Smoky Mountains." Unpubl. diss. Univ. of Tennessee, Knoxville, 1973. 122p.
A study using the Orton-Wright questionnaire as a workable instrument and suggesting possible changes; also discusses previous studies. An appendix gives a pronouncing index.

Knight, Helen Harris. "Adjectival and Adverbial Comparisons Found in Scott County, Tennessee." 1974. 7p. Student paper in Riedl Collection, Univ. of Tennessee Library, Knoxville.
Has 15 "lists." Results of a questionnaire on phrases heard and phrases used by six informants.

Kroll, Harry Harrison. "A Comparative Study of Upper and Lower Southern Folk Speech." Unpubl. Master's thesis, George Peabody College for Teachers, 1925. 88p.
A dictionary of words used in certain counties in Alabama, Mississippi, Kentucky, and Tennessee heard and recorded by the author.

McBride, John S. "Hill Speech in Southwestern Tennessee." Unpubl. Master's thesis, Columbia University, 1935. 66p.
Word use, with special emphasis on pronunciation, inflection and syntax, in Poca-

hontas Community, Hardeman County. Includes a list of 174 words with definitions.

Maurer, David W. "The Argot of the Moonshiner." *American Speech*, XXIV (Feb. 1949), 3–13.
About 100 entries, with definitions.

Mencken, H.L. *The American Language: An Inquiry Into the Development of English in the United States*. Supplement II. New York: Knopf, 1948. xliii, 890p.
In the Index, Tennessee leads to a number of references discussing the use of words in this area, as well as given names, nicknames and place names.

Miller, Tracey R. "An Investigation of the Regional English of Unicoi County, Tennessee." Unpubl. diss. Univ. of Tennessee, Knoxville, 1973. 176p.
Phonological characteristics of the speech of "elderly, rural, lifelong residents" of the county. Lists 270 terms with brief definitions or explanations.

Neitzel, Stuart. "Tennessee Expressions." *American Speech*, XI (Dec. 1936), 373.
Discusses 5 expressions.

Orton, Harold, and Nathalia Wright, with the assistance of M. Jean Jones. *Questionnaire for the Investigation of American Regional English: Based on the Work Sheets of the Linguistic Atlas of the United States and Canada*. Knoxville: Univ. of Tennessee, Supported by the Better English Fund Established by John C. Hodges, 1972. 139p.
About 1,200 questions for field workers interviewing selected elderly natives to investigate the kind of American English used in certain areas. Lists 80 words replaced by their equivalents.

Owens, Bess Alice. "Folk Speech of the Cumberlands." *American Speech*, VII (Dec. 1931), 89–95.
Recorded in eastern Kentucky, word list with examples of use in the Cumberland Mountains.

"Picturesque Speech." *Tennessee Folklore Society Bulletin*, IX (May 1943), 18–20.

Expressions gathered from replies to questionnaires sent to TFS members in Tennessee.

"Picturesque Speech." *Tennessee Folklore Society Bulletin*, X (June 1944), 10.

Expressions contributed by readers.

Pollard, Mary O. "Terms from the Tennessee Mountains." *Dialect Notes*, IV, Part 3 (1915), 242–43.

Twenty-four expressions used in Gatlinburg.

Reece, James Robert. "Variation in Appalachian English: A Study of the Speech of Elderly Rural Natives of East Tennessee." Unpubl. diss. Univ. of Tennessee, Knoxville, 1977. 398p.

A comprehensive study of speech patterns of 12 persons 65 years or more of age and rural natives of Greene, Hawkins, Unicoi, and Washington counties in upper East Tennessee.

Reinhardt, James M. "Speech and Balladry of the Southern Highlands." *Quarterly Journal of the University of North Dakota*, XVI (Jan. 1926), 139–47.

Discusses the areas of speech which are a product of a past age, giving usages of the Highlander with their background in English literature. Deals also with variations in the English ballad.

Rogers, E.G. "Possible Origins of Some Common Idioms." *Tennessee Folklore Society Bulletin*, XIV (Dec. 1948), 73–78.

"Idiomatic meanings seem to suggest a folk origin": frontier conditions, railroading, navigation, radio, clothing, revival meetings, and sports.

Schulman, Steven A. "Logging Terms from the Cumberland River." *Tennessee Folklore Society Bulletin*, XXXIX (June 1973), 35–36.

Lists 27 terms with explanations, collected while doing research on the Cumberland River logging industry.

Smith, Bruce P. "The Rural/Urban Dichotomy: A Study of Rural and Urban Language Patterns in East Tennessee." 1968. 32p. Student paper, Riedl Collection, Univ. of Tennessee Library, Knoxville.

"Treats a number of sociologically relevant areas using a selected sample of similes and metaphors," from seniors in a Bradley County and a Knox County high school, and an additional sample of adults.

Smith, Rebecca W. "A Tennessean's Pronunciation in 1841." *American Speech*, IX (Dec. 1934), 262–63.

A study of William Donaldson's diary.

Walker, Ralph S. "A Mountaineer Looks at His Own Speech." *Tennessee Folklore Society Bulletin*, V (Feb. 1939), 1–13.

Pronunciation, intonation, and the use of words in the Smoky Mountains, with illustrations of speech transcribed phonetically.

Warren, H.E. "Waste-Basket of Words." *Journal of American Folklore*, II (July-Sept. 1889), 229.

Seven words attributed to Kentucky and Tennessee "noticed in connection with pension claims from the South."

Williams, Cratis D. "Mountain Speech, I: The R in Mountain Speech." *Mountain Life and Work*, XXXVII (Spring 1961), 5–8. "II: AEIOU Vowels and Diphthongs in Mountain Speech." XXXVII (Summer 1961), 8–11. "III: Rhythm and Melody in Mountain Speech." XXXVII (Fall 1961), 7–10. "IV: The Content of Mountain Speech." XXXVII (Winter 1961), 13–17. "V: Verbs in Mountaineer Speech." XXXVIII (Spring 1962), 15–19. "VI: Mountaineers Mind Their Manners." XXXVIII (Summer 1962), 19–25. "VII: Metaphor in Mountain Speech." XXXVIII (Winter 1962), 9–12. "VIII: Metaphor in Mountain Speech." XXXIX (Spring 1963), 50–53. "IX: Metaphor in Mountain Speech." XXXIX (Summer 1963), 51–53. "X: Prepositions in Mountain Speech." XL (Spring 1964), 53–55. "XI: Subtlety in

Mountain Speech." XLIII (Spring 1967), 14–16.

Wilson, George P. "A Word-List from Virginia and North Carolina." *Publications of the American Dialect Society*, No. 2 (Nov. 1944), 38–52.
Dialect words include some from Tennessee.

Wolfram, Walt, and Donna Christian. *Appalachian Speech*. Arlington, Va.: Center for Applied Linguistics, 1976. 190p.
A sociolinguistic study of the Appalachians, based in West Virginia.

Wolfram, Walt. "On the Linguistic Study of Appalachian Speech." *Appalachian Journal*, V (Autumn 1977), 92–102.
Includes a bibliography.

Wood, Gordon R., ed., American Philosophical Society, Committee on Research Report. Philadelphia: *American Philosophical Society Yearbook*, 1961. 602–604.
Report on the work of Gordon R. Wood, University of Chattanooga, describing the results of a postal questionnaire and of the tabulation. "The specific results of this study will be the publication of maps and detailed descriptions which give us a more specific knowledge of vocabulary patterns in the interior South . . . will make available tabular comments on frequency of use of some one thousand words."

Wood, Gordon R. "An Atlas Survey of the Interior South (USA)." *Orbis*, IX (1960), 7–12.
A report on the linguistic survey of 12 southern states directed by the author, the data gathered in Tennessee having been coded and the responses plotted on a series of maps.

———. "Dialect Contours in the Southern States." *American Speech*, XXXVIII (Dec. 1963), 243–56.
"Deals with the presence of Midland and Southern words in those parts of the South which were settled before 1800. . . . to show the diversity of regional vocabularies found in Alabama, Arkansas, Florida, Georgia, Louisiana, Mississippi, Oklahoma and Tennessee."

———. "Heard in the South: The Present Distribution of 'Headcheese.' " *Tennessee Folklore Society Bulletin*, XXVII (Dec. 1961), 69–71.
"One of the many examples showing that the mountain vocabulary has successfully penetrated considerable parts of the rest of the South."

———. "Heard in the South: The Progress of a Word Geography." *Tennessee Folklore Society Bulletin*, XXVI (March 1960), 1–7.
Discussion of the work on word distribution in the South, giving some examples, including word usage in Tennessee.

———. "Heard in the South: Words of Interest to Tennesseans." *Tennessee Folklore Society Bulletin*, XXIII (June 1957), 33–38.
An interest in the location of word usage and the patterns formed as they came together from other sources.

———. "A List of Words from Tennessee." *Publication of the American Dialect Society*, No. 29 (April 1958), 3–18.
A glossary of 142 words, each having a definition, a quotation where necessary or appropriate, and the county reporting the word.

———. "Some Sources of Information on Tennessee Folk Speech." *Tennessee Folklore Society Bulletin*, XXI (March 1955), 20–26.
Various ways and sources of studying folk speech.

———. *Vocabulary Change, A Study of Variation in Regional Words in Eight of the Southern States*. Cabondale: Southern Illinois Univ. Press, 1971. 392p.
Responses of about 1,000 persons to a printed vocabulary questionnaire are analyzed. Tables show the occurrence of certain local words, and maps show a specific geographical distribution.

———. "Word Distribution in the Interior South." *Publication of the American Dialect Society*, No. 35 (April 1961), 1–16.
Maps show the major patterns of word

distribution and likely major linguistic boundaries of selected words, and their frequency of use.

——— . "Word Mapping in the South." *South Atlantic Bulletin*, XXVII (Nov. 1962), 1–4.

A report on a word-usage study of the Southern states, including the regional vocabulary of Tennessee.

Woodbridge, Hensley C. "Tobacco Words." *Kentucky Folklore Record*, V (Oct.-Dec. 1959), 136, 148.

Has 22 tobacco terms remembered from his childhood by William F. Simpson.

"Word Lists: Tennessee Mountains." *Dialect Notes*, I, Part VIII (1895), 368–77.

Compiled in the vicinity of Roan Mountain, Carter County. Combined with a list from Berea, Kentucky. Definitions and usage.

Proverbs and Proverbial Sayings

Blair, Marion E. "The Prevalence of Older English Proverbs in Blount County, Tennessee." *Tennessee Folklore Society Bulletin*, IV (March 1938), 1–24.

A check of the recognition by individuals in Blount County of a selected list of English proverbs.

Boshears, Frances. "Proverbial Comparisons from an East Tennessee County." *Tennessee Folklore Society Bulletin*, XX (June 1954), 27–41.

Some 1,045 comparative phrases collected from Scott County.

Emrich, Duncan. *Folklore on the American Land*. Boston: Little, Brown, 1972. 707p.

Contains 16 examples of proverbs and proverbial speech from Tennessee, collected by Herbert Halpert, with a few songs and quotations.

Hall, Joseph S. *Sayings from Old Smoky: Some Traditional Phrases, Expressions, and Sentences Heard in the Great Smoky Mountains and Nearby Areas: An Introduction to a Southern Mountain Dialect*. Collected and edited by Joseph S. Hall. Asheville: Cataloochee Press, 1972. 149p.

Identifies informants and gives other sources and comparative phrases.

Halpert, Herbert. "More Proverbial Comparisons from West Tennessee." *Tennessee Folklore Society Bulletin*, XVIII (March 1952), 15–21.

Additional items, bringing the list to 1,044.

——— . "A Pattern of Proverbial Exaggeration from West Kentucky." *Midwest Folklore*, I (April 1951), 41–47.

Includes 17 expressions from Tennessee.

——— . "Proverbial Comparisons from West Tennessee." *Tennessee Folklore Society Bulletin*, XVII (Sept. 1951), 49–61.

A list of 753 proverbial exaggerations and comparisons.

——— . "Some Wellerisms from Kentucky and Tennessee." *Journal of American Folklore*, LXIX (April 1956), 115–22.

Contains 62 Wellerisms.

Hilliard, Addie Suggs. "Shakespearian Proverbs in Chester County, Tennessee." *North Carolina Folklore Journal*, XXII (May 1974), 63–74.

Lists 70 proverbs also found in Shakespeare's works.

Rogers, E.G. "Figurative Language the Folk-way." *Tennessee Folklore Society Bulletin*, XVI (Dec. 1950), 71–75.

A list of similes and metaphors classed by subject: food, animals, household articles, people, etc.

——— . "Popular Sayings of Marshall County." *Tennessee Folklore Society Bulletin*, XV (Dec. 1949), 70–75.

Over 100 proverbial sayings relating to animals, propriety of action, fate and fortune, philosophic truth, and literature and the printed legend.

——— . "Some East Tennessee Figurative Exaggerations." *Tennessee Folklore*

Society Bulletin, XIX (June 1953), 36–40.

Lists 90 expressions, the majority from East Tennessee, but some from other Tennessee locations.

Spears, James E. "Proverbs Common to Tennessee: A Note and a Glossary." *Tennessee Folklore Society Bulletin*, XXXVIII (Sept. 1972), 72–76.

Lists 132 proverbs "commonly used or recognized by Tennesseans."

Taylor, Archer, and Bartlett Jerre Whiting. *A Dictionary of American Proverbs and Proverbial Phrases 1820–1880.* Cambridge: Belknap Press of Harvard Univ. Press, 1958. 418p.

"Contains the proverbs and proverbial phrases found in a variety of American authors whose works were published between 1820 and 1880 . . . chosen as representative of various regions and for their popularity." A good reference source.

Taylor, Archer. *The Proverb.* Cambridge: Harvard Univ. Press, 1931. 223p.

"I have endeavored to describe briefly and systematically the way in which proverbs arise, the kinds of proverbs, and the details of proverbial style." Good for background study.

Whiting, B.J. "Proverbs and Proverbial Sayings." In White, Newman Ivey, *The Frank C. Brown Collection of North Carolina Folklore*, Vol. I. Durham: Duke Univ. Press, 1952.

All are reported from North Carolina, but many are familiar to Tennessee.

Personal Names

Grise, George C. "Patterns of Child Naming in Tennessee During the Depression Years." *Southern Folklore Quarterly*, XXIII (Sept. 1959), 150–54.

Based on questionnaires sent to 700 college freshman born between 1935 and 1940.

Harder, Kelsie B. "Rhyming Names in Tennessee." *Southern Folklore Quarterly*, XIX (March 1955), 101–103.

Five rhymes on given names collected in Perry County.

Still, James A. "Christian Names in the Cumberlands." *American Speech*, V (April 1930), 306–307.

Reasons for the selection of certain names for children.

Williams, Homer N. "Your Name, Please." *Tennessee Folklore Society Bulletin*, XV (June 1949), 41–44.

Surnames developed from occupations or titles.

Place Names

Coppock, Paul R. "History in Memphis Street Names." *West Tennessee Historical Society Papers*, XI (1957), 93–111.

Many are personal names of individuals who figured in Memphis history.

Donaldson, R.C. "Document: Key Corner." *West Tennessee Historical Society Papers*, XVII (1963), 126–27.

Origin of the place names Key Corner and Forked Deer River.

Fink, Paul M., and Myron H. Avery. "The Nomenclature of the Great Smoky Mountains." *East Tennessee Historical Society Publications*, No. 9 (1937), 53–64.

"The major portion of the nomenclature of the Great Smoky Mountains either originated or became fixed as a result of Guyot's surveys" in the 1850s.

———. "Smoky Mountains History as Told in Placenames." *East Tennessee Historical Society Publications*, No. 6 (1934), 3–11.

Some of the tradition told by the place names of the Smoky Mountains.

———. "Some East Tennessee Place Names." *Tennessee Folklore Society Bulletin*, VII (Dec. 1941), 40–50.

An interesting discussion of the origin of certain place names.

———. *That's Why They Call It . . . The Names and Lore of the Great Smokies.* Jonesboro, Tenn.: The Author, 1956. 20p.

Development of the nomenclature of the mountains and stories behind the names.

Flowers, Paul. "Place Names in Tennessee." *West Tennessee Historical Society Papers*, XIV (1960), 113–23.

An account of the way geographical locations acquire their names.

Foster, Austin P. *Counties of Tennessee.* Nashville: Tennessee Dept. of Education, Division of History, 1923. 124p.

Important historical events of the county, including the naming of the county and the county seat.

Fullerton, Ralph O. *Place Names of Tennessee.* Nashville: Tennessee Division of Geology, 1974. 421p. (Bulletin 73.)

Lists place names, giving location on map. No account of origin.

Gannett, Henry. *American Names: A Guide to the Origin of Place Names in the United States.* Washington, D.C.: Government Printing Office, 1905; rpt. Public Affairs Press, 1947. 334p.

An alphabetical listing of places throughout the United States.

Glass, P.T. "Sketch of Henry Rutherford." *American Historical Magazine*, V (July 1900), 225–29.

Sketch of an early surveyor. Gives some place names and a general picture of pioneer life.

Harbert, P.M. "Early History of Hardin County." *West Tennessee Historical Society Papers*, I (1947), 38–67.

Useful for place names, personal names, and occupations of early settlers.

Harder, Kelsie B., ed. *Illustrated Dictionary of Place Names, United States and Canada.* New York: Van Nostrand, 1976. 631p.

"An attempt . . . to include a comprehensive selection of the most viable and interesting United States cities and towns."

Howell, Morton B. "First Streets of Nashville." *American Historical Magazine*, VII (April 1902), 179–89.

Tells of the manner in which the city was laid out, with salt licks and salt springs to be kept as public property. Includes surveying terms and place names.

Kay, Donald. "Municipal British-Received Place Names in Tennessee." *Appalachian Journal*, II (Autumn 1974), 78–80.

"Place names of towns, villages, hamlets and cities which occur on roadmaps such as the Rand McNally Road Atlas." Has 95 Tennessee municipal names, with a parallel column of British equivalents.

McAdoo, William Gibbs. *American Geographical Nomenclature . . . Address of Hon. W.G. McAdoo to the Associated Alumni of East Tennessee University at Knoxville, Tennessee, June 20th, 1871.* Milledgeville, Ga.: Federal Union Book and Job Office, 1871. 24p.

Comments on some Tennessee place names.

McWhorter, A.W. "Classical Place Names in Tennessee." *Word Study*, IX (Nov. 1933), 7–8.

Lists 14 names of persons or deities, 8 names of places in classical antiquity, 12 Latin words, all with explanations or definition.

Montgomery, James R. "The Nomenclature of the Upper Tennessee River." *East Tennessee Historical Society Publications*, No. 28 (1956), 46–57.

The various names by which the Tennessee River has been known.

Ordaubadian, Reza. "Rutherford County: A Study in Onamastics." Ph.D. diss. Auburn Univ., 1968. 250p.

Six main classes of place names in Rutherford County, Tennessee.

Phelps, Dawson A., and Edward Hunter Ross. "Names Please: Place-Names along the Natchez Trace." *Journal of Mississippi History*, XIV (Jan.-Oct. 1952), 217–56.

"This is the story of what the place-names . . . mean, of why they were chosen, and of how they can serve as windows through which to glimpse the history of the region."

Quimby, Myron J. *Scratch Ankle, U.S.A., American Place Names and Their Deri-*

vation. New York: A.S. Barnes, 1969. 390.

An entertaining collection of "the histories, legends, and stories behind American communities with unusual names . . . historical in fact, it [the book] is also intended as one of humor." About 15 Tennessee names included.

Shankle, George Earlie. *American Nicknames, Their Origin and Significance*. 2nd ed. New York: H.W. Wilson, 1955. 524p.

Includes Tennessee items.

Shulman, David. "Nicknames of States and their Inhabitants." *American Speech*, XXVII (Oct. 1952), 183–85.

Lists the nicknames given in a number of publications, wtih reference to sources.

Starnes, D.T. "Bull's Gap and Some Other Related Place Names." *Names: Journal of the American Name Society*, XIV (March 1966), 41–42.

Brief history of the origin of names in this general area of Tennessee.

Stewart, George R. *American Place-names*. New York: Oxford Univ. Press, 1970. 550p.

An enlarged edition of *Names on the Land*.

——— . *Names on the Land*. New York: Random House, 1945. 418p.

Story of the naming of American places, including several in Tennessee.

Still, James A. "Place Names in the Cumberland Mountains." *American Speech*, V (Dec. 1930), 113.

Brief list of "names given to creeks, ridges, hollows and villages."

Tennessee Blue Book. Nashville: Secretary of State, State of Tennessee. Annual.

The origin of county names is given.

Williams, Samuel C. "Stephen Holston and the Holston River." *East Tennessee Historical Society Publications*, No. 8 (1936), 26–34.

An account of Holston's activities during the last half of the 18th century, and the naming of the Holston, or Holston's River.

XVI. Folklore—General

Listed here are titles having two or more folklore categories, such as songs and beliefs, beliefs and customs, tales and beliefs.

Bandy, Lewis David. "Folklore of Macon County, Tennessee." Unpubl. Master's thesis, George Peabody College for Teachers, 1940. 173p.

Folk customs gained by interviews or with the help of county school children. Superstitions, witchcraft, marriage customs, social events, games, rimes, speech, medicine, waterwitching.

Brewer, J. Mason. *American Negro Folklore*. Chicago: Quadrangle Books, 1968. 386p.

Tales, religion, songs, superstitions, proverbs, rhymes, riddles, names, children's rhymes, and pastimes.

Burleson, Nell P. "The Evolution of Southern Appalachian Culture as Evidenced in Folklore." Unpubl. Master's thesis, East Tennessee State University, 1963. 59p.

Contains folklore collected in the Fairview Community of Carter County, Tennessee: folk tales, rhymes, riddles, poetry and song, superstitions, beliefs, and cures.

Burton, Thomas G., and Ambrose N. Manning, eds. *A Collection of Folklore by Undergraduate Students of East Tennessee University*. Johnson City, Tenn.: East Tennessee State Univ., Sept. 1966.

80p. (Institute of Regional Studies, Monograph No. 3.)

Ghosts, stories, and legends from various counties; superstitions; folk methods of preserving and processing foods; riddles; and friendship verses.

Chase, Richard, comp. *American Folk Tales and Songs and Other Examples of English-American Tradition as Preserved in the Appalachian Mountains and Elsewhere in the United States.* New York: New American Library, 1956. 240p.

Tales, ballads, songs, games, and country dances. Many are noted as having been heard in Tennessee.

Coffin, Tristram P., and Hennig Cohen, eds. *Folklore in America: Tales, Songs, Superstitions, Proverbs, Riddles, Games, Folk Dramas and Folk Festivals.* Garden City, N.Y.: Doubleday, 1966. 256p.

From Tennessee: a folktale, a folksong, a proverbial rhyme; Beliefs about Children (Farr); To Foil a Witch (Farr); and Riddles from Tennessee (Farr). All reprinted from *Journal of American Folklore.*

DeWitt, John H. "Journal of Governor John Sevier (1790–1815)." *Tennessee Historical Magazine,* V (Oct. 1919), 156–94; VI (April 1920), 18–68.

Brief notations of daily activities, travel, etc., with numerous recipes for home remedies for human and animal ills.

Doran, Edwina B. "Folklore in White County, Tennessee." Unpubl. diss. George Peabody College for Teachers, 1969. 437p.

Contains a wealth of information on place names; legendary and folk tales; speech and vocabulary; proverbs and proverbial phrases; folk medicine; weather signs; planting lore; social activities; school customs; weddings and charivari; funeral and burial customs; calendar customs; supernatural sayings and beliefs; rimes, riddles, and childlore; games; ballads and other songs; recipes.

Eldridge, J.D. *Cracker Barrel Tales.* Livingston, Tenn.: Privately Printed, 1979. Rpt. from "Cracker Barrel News, Coun-

try Store Style" in the *Overton County (Tenn.) News.*

Tales of folk life from poke sallet to water witching.

Fowler, William Ewing. "Stories and Legends of Maury County, Tennessee." Unpubl. Master's thesis, George Peabody College for Teachers, 1937. 221p.

Collected largely by personal interviews with 36 individuals, considerable attention is given to slavery and the Civil War. Earlier chapters include about 60 folk remedies; 92 superstitions; 14 place names; amusements; punishments for crime.

Frazier, Lee. "Some Lore of the Sweetwater Valley." *Tennessee Folklore Society Bulletin,* XIII (Sept. 1947), 55–63.

The words of nine songs sung in the area, and a few miscellaneous items.

Gamble, Margaret Elizabeth. "The Heritage and Folk Music of Cades Cove, Tennessee." Unpubl. Master's thesis, Univ. of Southern California, 1947. 241p. (Copy in the Univ. of Tennessee Library, Knoxville.)

Written largely from visits to Cades Cove and interviews, this thesis includes the words and tunes of about 30 songs as sung by people in the cove, as well as descriptions of the way of living. social gatherings, religion and the churches, foot washings, funerals, singing schools, and Old Harp sings.

Geurin, Wayne. "Some Folkways of a Stewart County Community." *Tennessee Folklore Society Bulletin,* XIX (Sept. 1953), 49–52. A combination of six essays in the Folklore Archive, Murray State College, Kentucky, edited by Herbert Halpert.

The way of life of a hill community in Stewart County, Tenn., its buildings, food, recreation, beliefs in weather signs, medicine, death signs, and death and burial customs.

Greene, Maude. "Folklore of Shelby County, Tennessee." Unpubl. Master's thesis, George Peabody College for Teachers, 1940. 254p.

History of living conditions in the frontier river town; stories of Civil War days; tales and songs of Mississippi River roustabouts; Beale Street and the Negro.

Hurdle, Virginia Jo. "Folklore of a Negro Couple in Henry County." Ed. Herbert Halpert. *Tennessee Folklore Society Bulletin*, XIX (Sept. 1953), 71–78.

Interviews with an elderly Negro couple in Paris, Tennessee, concerning stories of the supernatural and folk medicine.

Lassiter, W.R. "Why I'm an Old Bachelor." *Tennessee Folklore Society Bulletin*, XIII (June 1947), 27–35.

"The reason is simple. I'm afraid of what the modern girls don't know." Wedding customs; gardening; soap making; raising chickens; signs of the weather; remedies; games for children.

Levine, Lawrence W. *Black Culture and Black Consciousness; Afro-American Folk Thought From Slavery to Freedom.* New York: Oxford Univ. Press, 1977. 522p.

"I have attempted to write a history of the thought of a group of people who have been too largely neglected and too consistently misunderstood," using slave tales, gospel song, secular song, black laughter, and heroes.

Lomax, Alan, and Sidney Robertson Cowell. *American Folk Song and Folk Lore; A Regional Bibliography.* New York: Progressive Education Association, 1942. 59 p. (P.E.A. Service Center Pamphlet No. 8.)

A good annotated bibliography.

McDowell, Flora L. *Folk Dances of Tennessee: Folk Customs and Old Party Games of the Caney Fork Valley.* Delaware, Ohio: Cooperative Recreation Service, 1953. 64p.

Tunes, full directions, and diagrams of 28 play-party games and several country dances.

McDowell, Lucien L. "A Background of Folklore." *Tennessee Folklore Society Bulletin*, II (Feb, 1936), 1–8.

A reminiscence of the author's personal background in folklore through his child-

hood and youth in Middle Tennessee hill country. He tells of beliefs and customs, the "Dumb Supper," ghosts, religious songs, love songs, and games played at school and at play parties.

McIlwaine, Shields. *Memphis Down in Dixie.* New York: Dutton, 1948. 400p.

Includes stories about ghosts, steamboating on the Mississippi, rousters' songs, etc.

Mason, Robert. "Folk-Songs and Folk-Tales of Cannon County, Tennessee." Unpubl. Master's thesis, George Peabody College for Teachers, 1939. 241p.

Folk songs and tales collected from the hill people, especially from those living near Short Mountain. No tunes are given.

Mason, Robert Leslie. "The Life of the People of Cannon County, Tennessee." Unpubl. Ph.D. diss. George Peabody College for Teachers. 1946. 251p.

Music, folk songs, dancing, picnics, pie suppers, games, basketry, chair making, soap making, and religion.

Mitchell, George W. "Songs, Games, and Memories of George W. Mitchell." Collected, transcribed, and annotated by Kay L. Cothran. *Tennessee Folklore Society Bulletin*, XXXIV (Sept. 1968), 63–81.

A verbatim account by a 96-year-old man, transcribed from a tape recording. Gives tunes and words of a number of play-party songs and children's games, reminiscences of logrollings and barn raisings, and making soap and hominy.

Parsons, Mildred. "Negro Folklore from Fayette County." *Tennessee Folklore Society Bulletin*, XIX (Sept. 1953), 67–70.

About "haint" stories, plants and animals and funerals.

Payne, Mildred Y., and James E. Spears. *Folk Miscellany of Weakley County, Tennessee: Commemorating the Martin, Tennessee Centennial 1873–1973.* Published under the auspices of and with financial assistance from the Martin, Tennessee Centennial Company, Inc. Jackson: McCowat Press, 1973. 37p.

A compilation of proverbs, superstitions, and folk speech.

Perry, Henry Wacaster. "A Sampling of the Folklore of Carter County, Tennessee." Unpubl. Master's thesis, George Peabody College for Teachers, 1938. 313p.

The sampling was done in the Buck Mountain region of the Unakas and tells of the lay of the land, names and characteristics of the people, and old-time frolics, with their music and games. There are numerous tales, 24 of which concern witches and conjuring. Approximately 150 song-ballads are included, and the chapter on superstitions has 66 general signs, 9 good luck, 40 bad luck, 19 death, 21 weather, 11 moon, 12 planting, 63 remedies, and 10 ways of warding off witches. Also given is a list of barks, roots, and herbs collected and marketed; instructions for moonshining.

Salmon, Lourene Woods. "A Folklife Study of the Big Springs Community." Unpubl. Master's thesis, Middle Tennessee State Univ., 1973. 156p.

A good fieldwork study of the traditional way of life in a community near Murfreesboro, Tennessee. Includes the social customs of "workins"—log rollings, house-raisings; pea shellings, corn huskings; quiltings; dances and games; burial customs; tales; blacksmithing; woodworking and other tools; household utensils; quilts, hand-carved wooden objects; buildings. With clear photographs of the objects.

Sanders, Catherine R. "A Study of the Folklore of Sullivan County." Unpubl.

Master's thesis, East Tennessee State Univ., 1976. 90p.

Contains over 700 items: tales, superstitions, cures and remedies, riddles, rhymes, proverbs, and a few on folklife, collected by a select group of eighth-grade students from 1972 to 1975.

Stephens, J. Harold. *Echoes of a Passing Era (Down Memories Lane).* Fairborn, Ohio: The Author, 1971. 144p.

Beliefs, remedies, anecdotes, etc.

Templeton, Kathy. "Survey of Southern Appalachian Folklore." 1971. 25p. Student paper, Riedl Collection, Univ. of Tennessee Library, Knoxville.

Collection of superstitious beliefs and practices; local customs and games; stories, songs, and sayings taken from literature.

Thomas, Jane H. *Old Days in Nashville, Tennessee.* Nashville: Publishing House, Methodist Episcopal Church, South, Barbee and Smith, Agents, 1897. 190p.

Recollections of life in Nashville in the early 1800s, written by a resident at the age of 95.

White, Edwin E. *Highland Heritage: The Southern Mountains and the Nation.* New York: Friendship Press, 1937. 197p.

An account of the simple life in mountain homes; special occasions such as "dinner on the grounds"; singing groups; church services; funerals; farming, lumbering, mining, and other means of livelihood.

XVII. Superstitions and Beliefs

General

Anderson, Urban. "A Comparative Study of Some of the Older Beliefs and Usages of East Tennessee." *Tennessee Folklore Society Bulletin,* III (Feb. 1937), 1–7.

Limits discussion to "older and rarer" beliefs. Includes superstitions concerning planting and growth of plants (phallic rites), finding water in digging a well, and death.

Bergen, Fanny D., ed. *Current Superstitions: Collected from the Oral Tradition of English Speaking Folk.* Published for the American Folklore Society. Boston: Houghton Mifflin, 1896. 161p. (*Memoirs of the American Folklore Society,* Vol. IV.)

Some 1,475 superstitions, classified from babyhood to weather. The six from Tennessee include birds, cures, moon, plants.

Many others may be recognized as local superstitions.

Broadrick, Estelle D. "Old Folk Sayings and Home-Cures." *Tennessee Folklore Society Bulletin*, XLIV (March 1978), 35–36.

About 15 superstitions.

Burton, Glynn. "Some Folkways of a Lincoln County Community." *Tennessee Folklore Society Bulletin*, XXI (March 1955), 3–8.

"Little sayings we go by" in the vicinity of Camargo community in Tennessee concerning planting signs, weather signs, marriage, death, and cures for diseases.

Caroland, Emma Jean. "Popular Beliefs and Superstitions Known to Students of Clarksville High School." *Tennessee Folklore Society Bulletin*, XXVIII (June 1962), 37–47.

Superstitions concerning luck, planting, weather and remedies known by the students or learned from their parents, relatives, or neighbors.

Carr, Lillian R. "An' Too Skeered to Whistle." *Tennessee Conservationist*, XLI (June 1975), 20–21.

Superstitions about the moon, toads, warts, and a crowing hen.

Carter, Roland D. "Mountain Superstitions." *Tennessee Folklore Society Bulletin*, X (March 1944), 1–6.

Signs, sayings, and folk remedies.

Cole, William E., and Urban Anderson. "Folklore and Folkways in the Blue Ridge and Cumberland Plateau Sections of Tennessee." May 1, 1934. 174p. (A TVA-CWA Project.) Unpubl. typescript in TVA Technical Library, Knoxville, and a copy in Univ. of Tennessee Library, Knoxville.

A rich source of superstitions and beliefs concerning luck; folk medicine; planting and transference of fertility; marriage; children; death and funerals; dreams; witches and conjurers; etc.

Duncan, Hannibal Gerald, and Winnie Leach Duncan. "Superstitions and Say-

ings among the Southern Highlanders." *Journal of American Folklore*, XLII (July-Sept. 1929), 233–37.

Lists 85 superstitions, including folk remedies, weather, luck, friendship and marriage, farming, etc.

Farr, T.J. "Middle Tennessee Folk Beliefs Concerning Love and Marriage." *Southern Folklore Quarterly*, II (Sept. 1938), 165–74.

Lists 190 superstitions prevalent in the Cumberland section of Middle Tennessee.

———. "Survivals of Superstition in Tennessee." *Tennessee Folklore Society Bulletin*, XXI (March 1955), 1–3.

On the value of scholarly collecting.

———. "Tennessee Folk Beliefs Concerning Children." *Journal of American Folklore*, LII (Jan.-March 1939), 112–16.

Lists 105 beliefs concerning babies, including folk remedies.

———. "Tennessee Superstitions and Beliefs." *Tennessee Folklore Society Bulletin*, I (April 1935), 1–16.

Contains 59 folk remedies; 35 bad luck signs; 15 good luck omens; beliefs include 16 on babies, 14 death, 18 lovers and marriage, 12 influences of the moon, 11 plants, trees and seeds, 12 wishes, 10 signs of the Zodiac, 23 weather, and 22 miscellaneous.

Frazier, Neal. "A Collection of Middle Tennessee Superstitions." *Tennessee Folklore Society Bulletin*, II (Oct. 1936), 1–16.

Superstitions cover 50 folk remedies, 16 planting and harvesting, 21 weather, 14 death, 53 luck, 22 love and marriage, as well as a number of smaller categories. Is not a duplicate of Farr's list except for variations sufficient to justify repetition.

Griffin, William J. "Bread and Butter." *Southern Folklore Quarterly*, XXVII (June 1963), 168–70.

The use of the phrase among young people today.

Hand, Wayland D., ed. "Popular Beliefs and Superstitions from North Carolina." In White, Newman Ivey, *The Frank C.*

Brown Collection of North Carolina Folklore. 7 vols. Durham: Duke Univ. Press.

Volume VI covers birth, infancy, childhood; human body, folk medicine; home, domestic pursuits; economic, social relationships; travel, communication; love, courtship, marriage.

Volume VII covers death and funeral customs; witchcraft, ghosts, magical practices; cosmic phenomena; times, numbers, seasons; weather; animals, animal husbandry; fishing and hunting; plants, plant husbandry; miscellaneous.

Harder, Kelsie. "Beliefs and Customs in Perry County, Tennessee." *Tennessee Folklore Society Bulletin,* XXI (March 1955), 9–10.

Of 27 superstitions, almost all are recipes for warding off bad luck.

Hatcher, Mildred. "Superstitions in Middle Tennessee." *Southern Folklore Quarterly,* XIX (Sept. 1955), 150–55.

Good and bad luck, folk remedies, death and miscellaneous superstitions from the vicinity of Clarksville.

Hickerson, Daisy Faulkner. "My Black Mammy Cautions Me." *Tennessee Folklore Society Bulletin,* XV (March 1949), 16–17.

Negro superstitions given in rhyme.

Hilliard, Addie Suggs. "I Remember, I Remember." *Tennessee Folklore Society Bulletin,* XXXII (Dec. 1966), 121–28.

About 150 superstitions from the author's childhood in Chester County, Tennessee, include ailments and remedies, luck, domestic pursuits, death, wishes, sweethearts, weather, and miscellaneous beliefs.

LaBrosse, Diane T. "Superstitions and Folk Beliefs." 5p. and 20 questionnaires with results. Student paper, Riedl Collection, Univ. of Tennessee Library, Knoxville.

Beliefs on weather, good and bad luck, love and marriage, from a test group of University of Tennessee students whose homes are in the Appalachian region.

McGlasson, Cleo. "Superstitions and

Folk Beliefs of Overton County." *Tennessee Folklore Society Bulletin,* VII (Oct. 1941), 13–27.

Ailments and their remedies; good and bad luck, dreams, love and marriage, death, and weather signs.

Miller, Mary E. "A Folklore Survey of Dickson County, Tennessee." *Tennessee Folklore Society Bulletin,* XXIV (June 1958), 57–71.

Superstitions of good and bad luck, love and marriage, weather signs, and medicine.

Morton, Joan. "Dream Interpretation in Southern Appalachia." N.d. 25p. Student paper, Riedl Collection, Univ. of Tennessee Library, Knoxville.

On animals; bad luck; good luck; death; love, marriage, births; good and bad dreams; and dreams that come true.

——— . "Superstitions and Beliefs Concerning Babies in Southern Appalachia." In Faulkner, Charles H., and Carol K. Buckles, eds., *Glimpses of Southern Appalachian Folk Culture: Papers in Memory of Norbert F. Riedl.* [Knoxville]: Tennessee Anthropological Association, 1978. (Miscellaneous Paper, No. 3.)

Traditional beliefs and superstitions concerning the care of infants and children.

Page, Mrs. Marion T. "Superstitions at Home." *Tennessee Folklore Society Bulletin,* XX (Sept. 1954), 53–56.

Superstitions about weather, bad and good luck, death, New Year's Day, miscellaneous.

Puckett, Newbell Niles. *Folk Beliefs of the Southern Negro.* Chapel Hill: Univ. of North Carolina Press, 1926. 644p. Reprinted as *The Magic and Folk Beliefs of the Southern Negro.* New York: Dover, 1969.

A wealth of information. "Some ten thousand beliefs were gathered, most of them coming from Mississippi, Alabama and Georgia . . . though material was obtained from every state of the South, giving an index to the spread of each particular belief."

Redfield, W. Adelbert. "Superstitions and

Folk Beliefs." *Tennessee Folklore Society Bulletin*, III (April 1937), 11–40.

Lists 470 superstitions and beliefs collected by students of Pleasant Hill Academy on the Cumberland Plateau in Tennessee. Includes folk remedies, plant lore, love and marriage, weather, good and bad luck omens, etc.

Roberts, A.H. "We Aren't Magicians, But . . . Verbal Charms Survive in the Machine Age." *Tennessee Folklore Society Bulletin*, XVIII (Sept. 1952), 82–84.

"Magic" words and phrases, their use and their probable origin.

Rogers, E.G. "Family Folk Fronts in Rime and Rhythm." *Tennessee Folklore Society Bulletin*, XI (Feb. 1945), 3–7.

Superstitions told in "a number of efforts in verse which relate to lovers, courtships, marriage, and the general ups and downs of life."

———. "Guideposts to Fortune." *Tennessee Folklore Society Bulletin*, XVI (June 1950), 31–37.

Lists 108 good and bad luck superstitions of Marshall County, Tennessee.

———. "I Wish I May, I Wish I Might." *Tennessee Folklore Society Bulletin*, XIII (June 1947), 36–41.

Suggests 27 ways to make a wish that will come true.

Shelby, Carolyn. "Folklore of Jordan Springs, Tennessee." *Tennessee Folklore Society Bulletin*, XXV (March 1959), 6–17.

Tells of 150 cures and remedies, weather signs, planting signs, love and marriage superstitions, good and bad luck and death signs, and miscellaneous beliefs; a collection based on the memory of former residents of the community which was replaced by the establishment of a military reservation in the area.

Wheeley, Suzanne. "Folk Beliefs." 1970–97. Unpubl. MS. 188 cards. Western Kentucky Univ. Folklore, Folklife, and Oral History Archives.

Many good and bad luck signs, remedies, weather and planting beliefs, etc. Gathered from personal acquaintances of the author,

some of whom were born and raised in Macon County, Tennessee.

Wolf, John Quincy. "Two Unusual Negro Notations Pertaining to Death." *Tennessee Folklore Society Bulletin*, XXXII (June 1966), 56–57.

Expressing fear of the "black bottle."

Animal, Plant, and Weather Lore

Bass, William W. "Dog Days: Some Notes and a Few Superstitions." *Tennessee Folklore Society Bulletin*, XXII (Sept. 1956), 64–68.

A history of "dog days" from its origin in Egypt, through Greek and Roman writers to its influence on our own culture. Includes 15 local superstitions.

Bergen, Fanny D., ed. *Animal and Plant Lore: Collected from the Oral Tradition of English Speaking Folk*. Boston: American Folklore Society, 1899. 180p. (*Memoirs of The American Folklore Society*, Vol. VII.)

The 1,397 entries include 11 from Tennessee, with many others recognizable as local superstitions.

Garriott, Edward B. *Weather Folk-Lore and Local Weather Signs*. Washington, D.C.: Government Printing Office, 1903. 153p. (U.S. Weather Bureau Bulletin 33.)

"The object of this paper is to segregate from the mass of available data the true sayings that are applicable to the United States, and to combine the material thus collected with reports on local weather signs that have been officially and specially prepared by observers of the U.S. Weather Bureau." Reports from Chattanooga, Knoxville, Memphis, and Nashville.

Harder, Kelsie B. "Weather Expressions and Beliefs in Perry County, Tennessee." *Tennessee Folklore Society Bulletin*, XXIII (Sept. 1957), 83–86.

Descriptive terms and weather predictions.

Long, Grady M. "Folk Customs in Southeast Tennessee." *Tennessee*

Folklore Society Bulletin, XXVII (Dec. 1961), 76–84.

Planting by the signs of the Zodiac or the phases of the moon; superstitions concerning death, witches, teeth; home remedies, etc.

Massey, H.V. "Birdlore." *Tennessee Folklore Society Bulletin*, XIV (Sept. 1948), 57–58.

Sayings and superstitions about birds.

O'Dell, Ruth W. "Signs and Superstitions." *Tennessee Folklore Society Bulletin*, X (Dec. 1944), 1–6.

Signs and superstitions relating to planting, butchering, folk remedies and miscellaneous situations.

Rogers, E.G. "Borrowing from the Moon." *Tennessee Folklore Society Bulletin*, XIV (Sept. 1948), 54–56.

Has 45 superstitions of the moon's influence on man's environment: presiding over the natal day, conditioning man's environment, predicting weather, and planting and harvesting.

——— . "Some Animal Superstitions from Marshall County, Tennessee."

Southern Folklore Quarterly, XVIII (Dec. 1954), 233–38.

Lists 155 sayings and beliefs concerning animals, weather, sickness, death, good and back luck, breaking a charm, proverbial sayings, and miscellaneous.

Steffen, Walter A. "Weather Lore of the Southern Appalachians." 1968. 20p. Student paper, Riedl Collection, Univ. of Tennessee Library, Knoxville.

Interviews with farmers of Cocke, Monroe, and Sevier counties in East Tennessee.

Wells, J.C. "Weather and Moon Superstitions in Tennessee." *Journal of American Folklore*, VI (Oct.-Dec. 1893), 298–300.

Influence of the ground hog on the weather, the dark and light of the moon on planting, and other superstitions.

Wiltse, Henry M. "In the Field of Southern Folklore." *Journal of American Folklore*, XIV (July-Sept. 1901), 205–208.

A few superstitions concerning snakes, planting, medicine, and marriage.

XVIII. Medicine and Home Remedies

Anderson, Thomas A. *The Practical Monitor, for the Preservation of Health, and the Prevention of Diseases*. Knoxville: F.S. Heiskell, Printer, 1831. 253p.

A physician's handbook, describing symptoms and treatment, including home remedies.

"Aunt Sarah: Tennessee's Champion Midwife." *Newsweek*, XLVIII (Aug. 20, 1956), 54.

About Sarah England on her retirement. From the age of ten "Tennessee mountain babies were her business."

Bass, William W. "Birthmarks Among the Folk." *Tennessee Folklore Society*

Bulletin, XXV (March 1959), 1–6.

Reports on prenatal marking and beliefs concerning the cause.

Bond, Robert W. "Some Mysteries, Myths, and Methods of the Ancient Art of the Apothecary." *Tennessee Folklore Society Bulletin*, XV (March 1949), 19–23.

Includes some "Tennessee folklore of the apothecary."

Boyd, Mary Ellen. "Southern Appalachian Superstitions and Folklore about Pregnancy, Childbirth, and Death (And Some General Superstitions.)" 1976. 14p.

Student paper, Riedl Collection, Univ. of Tennessee Library, Knoxville.

Lists 125 superstitions from nine East Tennessee informants.

Brantley, Karen. "Home Remedies of Tennessee." 1971. 14p. Student paper, Riedl Collection, Univ. of Tennessee Library, Knoxville.

Lists 96 ailments, from Knox County informants.

Brookman, Rosemary. "Folk Veterinary Medicine in Southern Appalachia." In Faulkner, Charles H., and Carol K. Buckles, eds. *Glimpses of Southern Appalachian Folk Culture: Papers in Memory of Norbert F. Riedl.* [Knoxville]: Tennessee Anthropological Association, 1978. (Miscellaneous Paper No. 3.)

Diseases and treatment of cattle, horses, hogs, and chickens.

———. "Folk Veterinary Medicine in Upper East Tennessee." *Tennessee Folklore Society Bulletin*, XLIII (Sept. 1977), 140–48.

Small rural communities in Washington County.

Cansler, Loman D. "Madstones and Hydrophobia." *Western Folklore*, XXIII (April 1964), 95–105.

"The method of treatment would have been very similar had he gone to a stone in such states as Illinois, Kentucky, Tennessee."

Carr, Lillian R. "Mammy's Home Remedies." *Tennessee Conservationist*, XXXIX (Nov. 1973), 12–13.

Contains about 20 remedies.

Conwell, Edward L. "Tennessee Remedies." *Journal of American Folklore*, XLVI (Jan.-March 1933), 89–90.

Five treatments, including mad stone for hydrophobia, still in use in Middle Tennessee about 1900.

DeWitt, John H. "Journal of Governor John Sevier (1789–1815)." *Tennessee Historical Magazine*, V (Oct. 1919), 156–94; VI (April 1920), 18–68.

Brief notations of daily activities, travel, etc., with numerous recipes for home remedies for human and animal ills.

Garner, Sherry. "Recollections of My Grandmother, Nancy Farris Cain." 1972. 13p. Student paper, Reidl Collection, Univ. of Tennessee Library, Knoxville.

Concerns a West Tennessee woman of Chickasaw ancestry. Tells of her experiences as a midwife, her medical beliefs, warnings of death, etc.

Garrett, Ruby Burris. "Traditional Southern Appalachian Dental Practices." In Faulkner, Charles H., and Carol K. Buckles, eds. *Glimpses of Southern Appalachian Folk Culture: Papers in Memory of Norbert F. Riedl.* [Knoxville]: Tennessee Anthropological Association, 1978. (Miscellaneous Paper No. 3.)

Remedies, superstitions, rhymes, and riddles concerning teeth.

Gattinger, Augustin. *The Medicinal Plants of Tennessee, Exhibiting Their Commercial Value, With an Analytical Key, Descriptions in Aid of Their Recognition, and Notes Relating to Their Distribution, Time and Mode of Collection, and Preparation for the Drug Market.* Arranged and Published Under the Direction of T. F. P. Allison. Nashville: Franc [sic] M. Paul, Printer to the State, 1894. 128p.

A botanical description and listing of medicinal plants designed for the use of pharmacists, to call attention to an important industrial resource previously overlooked. Occasionally gives medicinal uses.

Goodlett, A.G. *The Family Physician, or Every Man's Companion, Being a Compilation from the Most Approved Medical Authors, Adapted to the Southern and Western Climates . . . .* Nashville: Printed at Smith and Nesbit's Steam Press, 1838. 792p.

The author "has taken the liberty of restricting the articles of medicine to those which are less dangerous, and throwing out those which should only be given by medical men of skill and discernment." Includes an account of medicinal plants, herbs, and roots, with directions for use.

Gunn, John C. *Gunn's Domestic Medicine, or Poor Man's Friend: Shewing the Diseases of Men, Women and Children, and Expressly Intended for the Benefit of Families. Containing a Description of the Medicinal Roots and Herbs, and How They Are Used in the Cure of Diseases.* 2nd ed. Madisonville, Tenn.: Printed by J.F. Grant, 1834. 604p. Published in various editions from 1830 to 1872.

    A family medical book incorporating many familiar practices.

―――― . *Gunn's New Domestic Physician: or Home Book of Health, With Directions for Using Medicinal Plants . . . .* Cincinnati: Moore, Wilstach, Keys, and Co., 1860. 1046p.

    Discusses various subjects affecting health. Medical flora listed on pp. 731–886.

Hamer, Philip M., ed. *The Centennial History of the Tennessee State Medical Association 1830–1930.* Nashville: Tennessee State Medical Association, 1930. 580p.

    The first chapter, on the organization of the society, tells of the scarcity of medical attention available to the settlers, of the several occupations in which the available physicians might be engaged, and of the various ways in which medical education might be obtained.

Hand, Wayland D. "Plugging, Nailing, Wedging, and Kindred Folk Medical Practices." In *Folklore and Society, Essays in Honor of Benjamin A. Botkin,* ed. Bruce Jackson. Hatboro, Penn.: Folklore Associates, 1966. 192p.

    An incident in Tennessee of boring a hole in a tree and placing in it a lock of hair as a cure for asthma.

Harder, Kelsie B. "Home Remedies in Perry County, Tennessee." *Tennessee Folklore Society Bulletin,* XXII (Dec. 1956), 97–98.

    Remedies for 17 ailments, dictated by an elderly resident in 1954.

Hilliard, Addie Suggs. "On Swallowing Punkin Seed." *Tennessee Folklore Society Bulletin,* XL (Dec. 1974), 119–121.

    Has 33 items of lore about pregnancy and newborn children, collected in Chester County, Tennessee.

―――― . "What'll We Give to the Baby-O?" *Tennessee Folklore Society Bulletin,* XL (June 1974), 41–46.

    Lists 60 folk remedies for infants and children.

Jordan, Weymouth T. "Plantation Medicine in the Old South." *Alabama Review,* III (April 1950), 83–107.

    Medical care of slaves.

Lacy, Virginia Jayne, and David Edwin Harrell, Jr. "Plantation Home Remedies: Medical Recipes from the Diaries of John Pope." *Tennessee Historical Quartery,* XXII (Sept. 1963), 259–65.

    Concerning the health of human beings and animals: cures for snakebite, hydrophobia, burns, chills, cholera, erysipelas, and more common illnesses.

Law, Harry. "Some Folklore of Macon County, Tennessee." *Tennessee Folklore Society Bulletin,* XVIII (Dec. 1952), 97–100.

    The author recalls home remedies and gives a brief description of social events and other customs.

Lewis, Meriwether. "On the Popular Materia Medica of East Tennessee." *Nashville Journal of Medicine and Surgery,* n.s., XX (Dec. 1877), 272–77.

    Folk remedies, for 26 physical conditions, still being used in 1877.

Long, Grady M. "Folk Medicine in McMinn, Polk, Bradley, and Meigs Counties, Tennessee, 1910–1927." *Tennessee Folklore Society Bulletin,* XXVIII (March 1962), 1–8.

    Tried and true home remedies from plants and trees.

Lumpkin, Ben Gray. "Remedies." Collected by Mrs. R.C. Cooke and Mrs. E.D. Hamner. Submitted by Ben Gray

Lumpkin. *Tennessee Folklore Society Bulletin*, XLII (June 1976), 65–79.

About 75 home, folk, and animal remedies.

Maguire, Edward F. "Frequent Diseases and Intended Remedies on the Frontier (1780–1850)." Unpubl. Master's thesis, St. Louis Univ. 1953. 55p.

"Drawn from a very good cross section of the chronicles, journals and diaries of the Frontier Period. . . . The problem of this paper solely has been to gather together from the available sources and to organize in coherent form the diseases which the settlers and aborigines thought they encountered and the remedies which they thought were efficacious in the curing of these diseases." From Kentucky and the North and West.

Mahoney, James W. *The Cherokee Physician or Indian Guide to Health . . . as Given by Richard Foreman, a Cherokee Doctor.* Chattanooga: Printed at the "Gazette Office," 1846. 416p.

General rules for preserving health without the use of medicines. Contains description of herbs and roots and their use.

Mathes, A.H. *The Botanic Physician, Or Family Medical Adviser . . . .* Madisonville, Tenn.: Published by B. Parker & Co., 1837. 688p.

Cites a number of plants, their use and dosage.

Maxwell, Britt. "Traditional Medical Practices in Rural East Tennessee." 1971. 8p. Student paper, Riedl Collection, Univ. of Tennessee Library, Knoxville.

Informants from Claiborne and Union counties.

Morton, Joan. "Superstitions and Beliefs Concerning Babies in Southern Appalachia." In Faulkner, Charles H., and Carol K. Buckles, eds. *Glimpses of Southern Appalachian Folk Culture: Papers in Memory of Norbert F. Riedl.* [Knoxville]: Tennessee Anthropological Association, 1978. (Miscellaneous Paper No. 3.)

Remedies and superstitions concerning infants.

Norris, Walter C., Jr. "Remedies and Cures from South Allen and North Sumner." 1973–1. Unpublished MS. 269p. (1 item to a page). Western Kentucky Univ. Folklore, Folklife, and Oral History Archives.

Includes some interviews in Sumner County, Tenn.

O'Dell, Ruth W. "Before You Call Your Doctor." *Tennessee Folklore Society Bulletin*, XVII (June 1951), 29–31.

Lists 47 home remedies.

——— . "Dark, Deep Secret of the Black Oak's Heart." *Tennessee Folklore Society Bulletin*, XVI (March 1950), 7–10.

Speculation—may have been a cure for asthma—as to the meaning of locks of human hair found embedded in an oak tree in Cocke County, Tenn.

Parr, Jerry S. "Folk Cures of Middle Tennessee." *Tennessee Folklore Society Bulletin*, XXVIII (March 1962), 8–12.

Remedies used for 25 ailments.

Price, Mary Loretta. "Medicinal Plants of the Southern Highlands." 1968. 21p. Student paper, Riedl Collection, Univ. of Tennessee Library, Knoxville.

Plants listed by family, genus, and species, and their use.

Pruitt, Virginia. "The Bold Hives in Tennessee." *Tennessee Folklore Society Bulletin*, XXX (June 1964), 69–71.

Origins of beliefs about and home remedies for a "disease" afflicting infants.

Reynolds, Hubert. "Grandma's Handbook." *Tennessee Folklore Society Bulletin*, XVI (March 1950), 13–14.

Folk remedies.

Rice, R.E., ed. "The Shadrach Rice Diary." *West Tennessee Historical Society Papers*, XV (1961), 105–16.

Cryptic entries from 1826 to 1862, of life in the village of Orysa, Lauderdale County, Tenn. Includes several recipes for home remedies for rheumatism, bad cough, and dyspepsia.

Roden, Paul. "Ginseng Culture: History, Medicinal Uses, Conversations With Some 'Sangers of East Tennessee.'" 1973. 18p. Student paper, Riedl Collection, Univ. of Tennessee Library, Knoxville.

Rogers, E.G. *Early Folk Medical Practices in Tennessee.* Murfreesboro, Tenn.: Mid-South Publishing Co., 1941. 68p.

The training of early doctors; superstitions and home remedies; midwives and the care of infants; the marking of children; practices of early surgery; madstones; water-witching; the undertaker; etc.

Schaeffer, Elizabeth. *Dandelion, Poke Weed, and Goosefoot, How the Early Settlers Used Plants for Food, Medicine, and In the Home.* Reading, Mass.: Addison-Wesley, 1972. 94p. (Young Scott Books.)

"Describes the various plants used by the early settlers as food and medicine and includes recipes as well as instructions for starting a garden.

Shelton's American Medicine: Or Improvement in Uniting His New Steam System and the Old Practice of Medicine. The Valuable Practice and Preparations of Dr. Isaac Wright of Tennessee Are Fully Developed in This Work. Madisonville, Tenn.: Printed at the Office of Henderson & Johnston, Wm. Harvey, Printer, 1834. 400p.

Includes remedies from plants and roots.

Snead, R. "Quackery in East Tennessee."

Nashville Journal of Medicine and Surgery, XVI (1859), 485–87.

A letter in reply to one from an Indiana physician, giving "a brief history of the pretenders in the practice of medicine in my region of the country"—so-called "injun doctors" and those who read a little, or claim to be students of certain doctors.

Vogel, Virgil J. *American Indian Medicine.* Norman: Univ. of Oklahoma Press, 1970. 583p.

Considers the influence of Indian medicine on folk medicine. Has several references to Cades Cove in the Smoky Mountains.

Watkins, Violet Jane. "Pioneer Medicine in the Tennessee-Kentucky Frontier Region." Unpubl. Master's thesis, Vanderbilt Univ., 1941. 80p.

Health on the frontier; home medicine; frontier doctors; medical training; and the advance of medicine.

Wright, Isaac. *Wright's Family Medicine, or System of Domestic Practice, Containing the Improvements Suggested by an Experience of Forty Years.* Madisonville, Tenn. Printed at the Office of Henderson, Johnston, & Co., 1833. 276p.

Discusses the understanding and treatment of various diseases and health problems.

Yoakley, Ina C. "Wild Plant Industry of the Southern Appalachians." *Economic Geography,* VIII (July 1932), 311–17.

The gathering of medicinal wild plants, with a brief paragraph on medicinal uses still prevalent in isolated communities.

XIX. Customs

Ball, Donald B. "Observations On the Form and Function of Middle Tennessee Gravehouses." *Tennessee Anthropologist,* II (Spring 1977), 29–62.

"An intensive survey of three contiguous Middle Tennessee counties (Cannon, Coffee, and Rutherford) has documented a total

of sixteen extant gravehouses in nine cemeteries plus the former location of several others."

——— . "Social Activities Associated with Two Rural Cemeteries in Coffee County, Tennessee." *Tennessee Folklore*

Society Bulletin, XLI (Sept. 1975), 93–98.

Grave decoration and home-coming celebrations in Robinson and Shady Grove cemeteries.

———. "Wooden Gravemarkers: Neglected Items of Material Culture." *Tennessee Folklore Society Bulletin*, XLIII (Dec. 1977), 167–85.

Locates and describes extant markers in Tennessee.

Bettis, Myra, Michael Blackwell, Robert Hoffman, Patty Sonka, and Loretta Swingle. "The Care of the East Tennessee Dead." In Faulkner, Charles H., and Carol K. Buckles, eds., *Glimpses of Southern Appalachian Folk Culture: Papers in Memory of Norbert F. Riedl.* [Knoxville]: Tennessee Anthropological Association, 1978. (Miscellaneous Paper No. 3.)

"Deals with the preparation of the body, burial, and cemetery customs of the East Tennessee Region."

Borah, Leo A. "Home Folk Around Historic Cumberland Gap." *National Geographic*, LXXXIV (Dec. 1943), 741–68.

The old customs seen in a modern time, descriptions accompanied by pictures of a country store, cutting sorghum cane, stirring off molasses, sacking meal at the mill, 'tater digging, games, "shoes in a circle," singing games, a church service and foot-washing ceremony.

Boshears, Frances. "The Shivaree." *Tennessee Folklore Society Bulletin*, XIX (Sept. 1953), 65–67.

Personal recollections of serenades of newly-married couples in Scott and Morgan counties, Tennessee.

Brewster, Paul G., ed. "Beliefs and Customs." In White, Newman Ivey, *The Frank C. Brown Collection of North Carolina Folklore*, Vol. I. Durham, N.C.: Duke Univ. Press, 1952.

Childhood; courtship and marriage; holidays and "get-togethers"; household superstitions; plants and animals; death and burial; quilt patterns; dyeing; cooking and preserving; beverage-making—all beliefs and customs found in North Carolina but with frequent notes concerning Tennessee.

Butler, Francelia, ed. "Appalachia: Where Yesterday is Today.—A Recognition of the Cultural Wealth of the Area by Students at The University of Tennessee." 1965. Unpaged. Copy in Univ. of Tennessee Library, Special Collections, Knoxville.

An unpublished collection of customs old and new.

Calloway, James E. "A Past Institution: The Mill Rock." *Kentucky Folklore Record*, XIV (July-Sept. 1968), 61–68.

The use of a highly polished rock tied into a sack of grain for the identification of the owner.

Chambers, W.R. "Some Reminiscences of an Old Lawyer." *Tennessee Historical Magazine*, Ser. 2, II (Oct. 1931), 67–70.

"Largely local to Wilson County," Tennessee, it has several stories about hunters and hunting.

Clark, Joseph D. "Easter Eggs and Peckers: Three Reminiscences." *Appalachian Journal*, I (Spring 1973), 119–24.

Gives the preparation for the celebration at the Boone's Creek Christian Church near Johnson City, Tenn., and the celebration itself. Also tells of box suppers.

Clark, Thomas D. "The American Backwoodsman in Popular Portraiture." *Indiana Magazine of History*, XLII (March 1946), 1–28.

The personal characteristics and habits of the backwoodsman on the frontier.

Cobb, James E. "Cockfighting in East Tennessee." In Faulkner, Charles H., and Carol K. Buckles, eds., *Glimpses of Southern Appalachian Folk Culture: Papers in Memory of Norbert F. Riedl.* [Knoxville]: Tennessee Anthropological Association, 1978. (Miscellaneous Paper No. 3.)

"Techniques of breeding, raising, training and fighting gamecocks are discussed."

Congleton, Betty Carolyn. "The Southern Poor Whites 1800–1860, With Particular Reference to Kentucky and Tennessee." Unpubl. Master's thesis, Univ. of Kentucky, 1948. 124p.

Useful for descriptions of community diversions such as marksmanship contests, "driving the nail," "snuffing the candle," "barking off the squirrel," "shooting for the beef." Covers hunting raccoons, bear, deer, fox, etc.

Conn, Philip W. "Traditional Courtship and Marriage Customs of the Appalachian South." In Faulkner, Charles H., and Carol K. Buckles, eds., *Glimpses of Southern Appalachian Folk Culture; Papers in Memory of Norbert F. Riedl.* [Knoxville]: Tennessee Anthropological Association, 1978. (Miscellaneous Paper No. 3.)

Customs and superstitions concerning courtship, marriage, and the setting up of housekeeping.

Cowan, Samuel Kinkade. *Sergeant York and his People.* New York: Grosset and Dunlap, 1922. 292p.

Gives detailed accounts of turkey shoots and beef shoots, corn-huskings, and gatherings at the country store.

"Death and Burial in the Mountains: The Preparation and Burial of the Dead." *Appalachian Heritage*, II (Winter 1974), 57–63.

Customs in the Southern Highlands.

Donaubauer, Elton Henry. "Some Annual Tennessee Celebrations." Unpubl. Master's thesis, George Peabody College for Teachers, 1951. 111p.

"The more interesting features and highlights of fifteen celebrations annually held in fourteen Tennessee towns and cities." Of special interest to this bibliography is the Irish Nomads' Reunion, Nashville.

Greene, Maude. "The Background of the Beale Street Blues." *Tennessee Folklore Society Bulletin* , VII (March 1941), 1–10.

Customs and folk-beliefs among the Negroes of Beale Street, Memphis.

Gunter, Charles R., Jr. "Cockfighting in East Tennessee and Western North Carolina." *Tennessee Folklore Society Bulletin*, XLIV (Dec. 1978), 160–69.

"The conditioning of the game fowl, especially what is often referred to as 'the keep'; the mechanics of the fights or derbies; the legal aspects of cockfighting; and the point of view of the cockfighters."

Hamilton, Gary. "Grave Huts: A Preliminary Report on Their Occurrence in the Southeastern States." 1972. 9p. Student paper, Riedl Collection, Univ. of Tennessee Library, Knoxville.

Grave houses, with photographs.

Harder, Kelsie B. "Just an April Fool." *Tennessee Folklore Society Bulletin*, XXVII (March 1961), 5–7.

April Fool traditions in Perry County, Tennessee.

Harrison, Bill, and Charles Wolfe. "Shooting the Anvil." *Tennessee Folklore Society Bulletin*, XLIII (March 1977), 1–13.

Purpose is two-fold: "To create a loud, satisfying boom, and to propel the top anvil as high into the air as possible." to celebrate traditional holidays and frontier occasions.

Haun, Mildred. "The Traditions of Cocke County." *Tennessee Folklore Society Bulletin*, XXXIII (Sept. 1967), 72–79.

Relates customs of home life and community gatherings such as logrollings, quilting parties, helping in times of illness and death, corn huskings, all-day singings, and singing schools. Taken from the preface to the author's thesis at Vanderbilt Univ., 1937.

Hilliard, Addie Suggs. "An Elizabethan Note." *Kentucky Folklore Record*, XI (1965), 26–27.

The practice handed down from Elizabethan times of perfuming household linens with dried flowers or fruits stuck with cloves.

Humphrey, Valerie L. "The Burial Customs of Fentress County, Tennessee." 1973. 10p. Student paper, Riedl Collection. Univ. of Tennessee Library, Knoxville.

Preparation for burial, and funeral and burial customs.

Jackson, Ewing. "God's Country." *Tennessee Folklore Society Bulletin*, XIX (Sept. 1953), 58–64.
 Description of a community in Henry County, Tennessee. Holiday customs, graveyard cleaning, dinner-on-the-ground.

Kane, Harnett T. *The Southern Christmas Book: The Full Story from Earliest Times to Present: People, Customs, Conviviality, Carols, Cooking.* New York: David McKay, 1958. 337p.
 Mountain Christmas of the South includes Tennessee. Some mention of the Memphis area.

Law, Anne F. "Tales of a Tobacco-chewer." *Kentucky Folklore Record*, VII (1961), 45–53.
 Anecdotes of chewing and spitting contests in Kentucky and Tennessee.

Lofton, Terry. "The Southern Appalachian Way of Dying." 1968. 20p. Student paper, Riedl Collection, Univ. of Tennessee Library, Knoxville.
 Customs prior to death; preparation for burial; the wake; funeral; mourning.

Lyon, Bob. "Death and Burial Customs in the Southern Appalachians." 1974. 16p. Student paper, Riedl Collection, Univ. of Tennessee Library, Knoxville.
 Signs, superstitions, and customs.

Maddux, Bob Lee. *Hill Topping.* N. p.: Hunter's Horn, 1951. 29p.
 Narratives of fox hunting, the hunters, and their dogs, taken from letters written by the author to *The Hunter's Horn.*

———. "A One Man Race." In *Stories of the Chase*. Sand Springs, Okla.: Hunter's Horn, 1942. 31p.
 A fox hunt in Smith County, Tenn.: the long wait, the sound of the horns, thoughts about other hunters, and their philosophy and sayings.

Moore, Dougal. "Customs of Scottish Origins in Southern Appalachia: Superstitions and Calendar Customs." 1974. 17p. Student paper, Riedl Collection, Univ. of Tennessee Library, Knoxville.
 Interviews with residents of Anderson County, Tenn., who were of Scottish descent.

"Peters Hollow Traditional Egg Fight." *Tennessee Folklore Society Bulletin*, XXXV (June 1969).
 Cover photograph.

Riedl, Norbert F., and Carol K. Buckles. "House Customs and Beliefs in East Tennessee." *Tennessee Folklore Society Bulletin*, XLI (June 1975), 47–56.
 Superstitions and customs concerning the building of a house, entering and leaving a house, life crises (birth, marriage and death), and house cleaning. About 80 items were collected from 11 informants.

Robertson, James I., Jr. "Frolics, Fights and Firewater in Frontier Tennessee." *Tennessee Historical Quarterly*, XVII (June 1958), 97–111.
 Conversation and practical jokes, hospitality, camp meetings, horseracing, hard cider and corn whiskey, and fistfighting.

Seeger, Ruth Crawford. *American Folk Songs for Christmas*. Garden City, N.Y.: Doubleday, 1953. 80p.
 Introduction tells of folk customs. Only one song is noted as of Tennessee, but many are familiar.

"Stir-Off Time in Tennessee: Fun Starts in Hills as Molasses Boils." *Life*, XXIX (Nov. 13, 1950), 156–60.
 Descriptive article accompanies photographs of participants in stir-off parties near Cumberland Gap.

Tutwiler, Mary Anderson. "Mountain People." *Tennessee Folklore Society Bulletin*, XXVI (Dec. 1960), 87–91.
 Anecdotes of customs and speech of mountain people known by the author in the Lookout Mountain area.

Whitaker, Walter C. *The Southern Highlands and Highlanders*. Hartford, Conn.: Church Missions Publishing Co., 1916. 147p.
 Tells of social conditions and events, religious gatherings, and funerals.

Yeager, Allison. "Historic Egg Fight."

Tennessee Folklore Society Bulletin, XXXV (June 1969), 41–43.

An account of the "more-than-a-century-old contest between the hardy Anglo-Saxon peoples of Iron Mountain and Peters Hollow" in East Tennessee at Eastertime.

———. "History of the Tennessee Egg Fight." *Tennessee Folklore Society Bulletin*, XXXVIII (March 1972), 6–10.

An attempt to trace the origin of an Easter egg fight (Peters Hollow) to other countries.

Young, Chester Raymond. "The Observance of Old Christmas in Southern Appalachia." In Williamson, J.W., ed., *An Appalachian Symposium: Essays in Honor of Cratis D. Williams*. Boone, N.C.: Appalachian State Univ. Press, 1977.

See Index for other references.

XX. Music, Song, and Dance

Ballads and Folk Songs

Allen, William Francis, Charles Pickard Ware, and Lucy McKim Garrison. *Slave Songs of the United States*. New York: A.Simpson & Co., 1867. 115p. Rpt. Freeport, N.Y.: Books for Libraries Press, 1971.

Contains a few songs from inland slave states, including Tennessee.

Anderson, Geneva. "Additional English and Scottish Ballads Found in East Tennessee." *Tennessee Folklore Society Bulletin*, VIII (Sept. 1942), 59–78.

Words of 14 ballads of pre-nuptial affairs, marriage, and sacred legend.

———. "A Collection of Ballads and Songs from East Tennessee." Unpubl. Master's thesis, Univ. of North Carolina, 1932. 317p.

Words of 196 songs and ballads, arranged by types, including nursery and game songs.

———. "A Collection of Ballads and Songs from East Tennessee." *Tennessee Folklore Society Bulletin*, II (Oct. 1936), 1–15.

Discussion of eight English and Scottish ballads. Full texts not given.

Belden, H.M., ed. "Ballads and Songs Collected by the Missouri Folk-Lore Society." *University of Missouri Studies*, XV (Jan. 1, 1940). 530p.

A voluminous collection giving words and a few tunes, gathered by students at the University of Missouri. Headnotes show the appearance of each item in other collections, with many in Tennessee.

———, and Arthur Palmer Hudson, eds. "Folk Ballads from North Carolina." In White, Newman Ivey, *The Frank C. Brown Collection of North Carolina Folklore*, Vol. II. Durham: Duke Univ. Press, 1952.

Includes 314 ballads, "The Older Ballads—Mostly British" and "Native American Ballads"; gives text and variations, history and locations. Many in Tennessee.

———, eds. "Folk Songs from North Carolina." In White, Newman Ivey, *The Frank C. Brown Collection of North Carolina Folklore*, Vol. III. Durham: Duke Univ. Press, 1952.

Some 658 folk songs as distinguished from ballads, arranged by type such as courting songs, drink and gambling songs, play-party and dance songs, lullabies and nursery rhymes, religious songs. Many noted as occurring in Tennessee.

Boswell, George W. "An Analysis of Text-controlled Tune Variations in 'The Boston Burglar.' " *Tennessee Folklore*

Society Bulletin, XIX (March 1953), 5–10.

A discussion of the ballad as heard in Franklin County, Tenn.

—— . "Five Choice Tennessee Folk Songs." *Tennessee Folklore Society Bulletin*, XVI (June 1950), 25–30.

Gives the words and tune, name of the singer, and county in which the song was heard.

—— . "Five More Choice Tennessee Folksongs." *Tennessee Folklore Society Bulletin*, XVI (Sept. 1950), 46–53.

Gives the words, tune, name of the singer, and county in which the song was heard.

—— . "Otherwise Unknown or Rare Ballads from the Tennessee Archives." *Tennessee Folklore Society Bulletin*, XLIV (Dec. 1978), 170–78.

Words of five ballads, with tunes for four.

—— . "Progress Report: Collection of Tennessee Folksongs in Recent Years." *Tennessee Folklore Society Bulletin*, XXV (June 1959), 31–79.

An analysis of the author's collection, 770 variants of 440 folksongs collected in Tennessee and southern Kentucky.

—— . "Seven Comic Tennessee Folksongs." *Tennessee Folklore Society Bulletin*, XXIV (March 1958), 72–83.

Words and tunes of humorous songs.

—— . "Some Characteristics of Folksongs in Middle Tennessee." *Tennessee Folklore Society Bulletin*, XV (Dec. 1949), 63–69.

Songs analyzed as to meter, rhythm, and tune, with a map indicating the location in Middle Tennessee where each song was learned by the author.

—— . *Tennessee Folk Songs*, collected by George Boswell, arranged by Charles F. Bryan. Printed for use in Tennessee Public Schools with permission of the authors. Nashville: State Department of Education, c1950. 7p.

Six songs, with music.

—— . "Third Edition: Five Tennessee Folksongs." *Tennessee Folklore Society Bulletin*, XVII (Dec. 1951), 85–92b.

A continuation of "Five Choice Tennessee Folk Songs" and "Five More Tennessee Folksongs," listed above.

—— . "Three Tennessee Folksongs." *Tennessee Folklore Society Bulletin*, XLIII (Dec. 1977), 188–201.

Words and music of "Little Pig," "Green Coffee Grows on White Oak Tops," and "Cumberland Gap."

—— . "Usage in the Southern Ballad and Folk Song." *Tennessee Folklore Society Bulletin*, XV (June 1949), 32–40.

An investigation of word usage characteristic of the poetry of Southern folksongs.

Bronson, Bertrand Harris. *Traditional Tunes of the Child Ballads, With Their Texts, According to the Extant Records of Great Britain and America*. 4 vols. Princeton, N.J.: Princeton Univ. Press, 1959–72.

Words and tunes, including many variants from Tennessee.

Burt, Olive Woolley. *American Murder Ballads and Their Stories*. New York: Oxford Univ. Press, 1958. 272p.

Includes ballads from Tennessee.

Burton, Thomas G., and Ambrose N. Manning, eds. *The East Tennessee State University Collection of Folklore: Folksongs*. Johnson City: East Tennessee State Univ. Institute of Regional Studies. Nov. 1967. 114p. 2nd ed., 1970. (Monograph No. 4.)

Gives the tune and words of a number of folksongs, principally ballads, traditional in East Tennessee.

Cambiaire, Celestin Pierre. *East Tennessee and West Virginia Mountain Ballads*. London: Mitre Press, n.d. 179p.

A collection of ballads and songs, without tunes, with a lengthy introduction on pioneer people and their ways. The Melungeons are included.

Campbell, Marie. "Play Party Tunes and

Fritter-Minded Ballads." *Tennessee Folklore Society Bulletin*, V (April 1939), 17–48.

Words of 36 ballads sung at play parties, weddings, and other mountain frolics, as distinguished from sad ballads.

Campbell, Olive Dame, and Cecil J. Sharp. *English Folk Songs from the Southern Appalachians, Comprising 122 Songs and Ballads, and 323 Tunes.* New York: Putnam's, 1917. 341p.

In the introduction Cecil Sharp gives his impression of the personal characteristics of the mountain people and their singing.

——— . "Songs and Ballads of the Southern Mountains." *The Survey*, XXXIII (Jan. 2, 1915), 371–74.

Relates the changes that have taken place in ballads due to their having been passed on from generation to generation, and also due to a change in environment.

Carter, Isabel Gordon. "Some Songs and Ballads from Tennessee and North Carolina." *Journal of American Folklore*, XLVI (Jan.-March 1933), 22–50.

Words of 30 songs and ballads.

Coffin, Tristram Potter. *The British Traditional Ballad in North America.* Revised edition with a Supplement by Roger DeV. Renwick. Austin: Univ. of Texas Press, 1977. 297p. (American Folklore Society, Bibliographical and Special Series.)

A bibliographical guide to story variation in the tradional ballad of America.

——— . "Six Unusual Texts from Mildred Haun's Cocke County Ballads and Songs." *Southern Folklore Quarterly*, XXIX (June 1965), 179–87.

East Tennessee variants of Child ballads.

Combs, Josiah H. *Folk-Songs of the Southern United States* [Folk-Songs du Midi des Etats-Unis]. Ed. D.K. Wilgus. Austin: Published for American Folklore Society by Univ. of Texas Press, 1967. 254p.

A translation of Combs' doctoral dissertation, 1925. Discussion of the ancestry of

the highlanders, songs of British origin, native American songs, and the Highlander's music, with text of a number of songs.

Crabtree, Lillian Gladys. "Songs and Ballads Sung in Overton County, Tennessee—A Collection." Unpubl. Master's thesis, George Peabody College for Teachers, 1936. 316p.

Words of 323 songs and ballads gathered from people in Overton County and from files of the Tennessee Folklore Society at Cookeville, Tennessee. Classified as dealing with family life, war and war influence, crime, religion, death, humor and nonsense, etc.

Duncan, Ruby. "Ballads and Folk Songs Collected in Northern Hamilton County." Unpubl. Master's thesis, Univ. of Tennessee, Knoxville, 1939. 388p.

Words of many ballads and songs, playparty games, and children's singing games and songs, with introductory notes.

Gamble, Margaret Elizabeth. "The Heritage and Folk Music of Cades Cove, Tennessee." Unpubl. Master's thesis, Univ. of Southern California, 1947. 241p. (Copy in the Univ. of Tennessee Library, Knoxville.)

Includes the words and tunes of about 30 songs as sung by people in the cove. *See also* the note under Folklore—General.

Gower, Herschel. "The Great West As Seen In the Ballads of Cocke County." *Tennessee Folklore Society Bulletin*, XX (March 1954), 14–21.

A discussion of the Cocke County (Tenn.) western songs collected by Mildred Haun.

Haun, Mildred. "Cocke County Ballads and Songs, Collected and Edited by Mildred Haun." Unpubl. Master's thesis, Vanderbilt Univ., 1937. 448p.

Includes 206 ballads and songs, many of which were sung by the author's mother, who had learned them from her mother and grandmother. Includes nonsense songs and game and dance songs. An introductory essay gives the folk background of the songs and is interesting for its treatment of speech, beliefs, remedies, and social gatherings.

Henry, Mellinger E. "Ballads and Songs of the Southern Highlands." *Journal of American Folklore*, XLII (July-Sept. 1929), 254–300.

The words of 23 songs, with some tunes.

——— . *Folk-Songs from the Southern Highlands*. New York: Augustin, 1938. 460p.

The words, with an occasional air, of 180 songs, with variants.

——— . "More Songs from the Southern Highlands." *Journal of American Folklore*, XLIV (Jan.-March 1931), 61–115.

Words of 35 songs.

——— . "Still More Ballads and Folksongs from the Southern Highlands." *Journal of American Folklore*, XLV (Jan.-March 1932), 1–176.

Includes 93 songs, many from Tennessee, giving the words and occasional tunes, with name, place, and date of the contributor and references to comparative sources.

Horne, Dorothy D. "An Inquiry into the Musical Backgrounds of Folk Songs of the Southern Mountains." *Tennessee Folklore Society Bulletin*, IV (Nov. 1938), 70–81.

Discussion of about 15 songs sung mostly by people of Maryville, Tenn.

Howse, Ruth Whitener. "Folk Music of West Tennessee." *Tennessee Folklore Society Bulletin*, XIII (Dec. 1947), 76–88.

Includes the words of several ballads such as "Davy Crockett" and "Casey Jones," and Negro roustabout songs, as well as a crude folk musical map of West Tennessee.

Hudson, Arthur Palmer. "Folk-Songs of the Southern Whites." In Couch, W.T., *Culture in the South*. Chapel Hill: Univ. of North Carolina Press, 1935.

English and Scottish popular ballads; native American ballads; outlaws, feudalists, and vagrants; nursery and nonsense songs; game songs; religious folk-songs—all discussed as "a part of the racial memory."

Johnson, Guy B. "Negro Folk Songs." In

Couch, W.T., *Culture in the South*. Chapel Hill: Univ. of North Carolina Press, 1935.

Characteristics of Negro folk songs as shown in spirituals, the blues, "bad man stuff," work songs, and narrative ballads.

Kirkland, Edwin C. "A Checklist of the Titles of Tennessee Folksongs." *Journal of American Folklore*, LIX (Oct.-Dec. 1946), 423–76.

An attempt to include all published folksongs that have been found in Tennessee.

——— , and Mary N. Kirkland. "Popular Ballads Recorded in Knoxville, Tennessee." *Southern Folklore Quarterly*, II (June 1938), 65–80.

Thirteen popular ballads selected from the authors' extensive collection.

——— . "Welsh Folksongs." *Tennessee Folklore Society Bulletin*, IX (Dec. 1943), 1–7.

Six Welsh songs and rhymes, with tunes, collected from a resident of East Tennessee.

Laws, G. Malcolm, Jr. *American Balladry from British Broadsides: A Guide for Students and Collectors of Traditional Song*. Philadelphia: American Folklore Society, 1957. 315p. (Publications of the American Folklore Society, Bibliographical and Special Series, Vol. VIII.)

Includes a number of references to Tennessee in the discussion of "British Broadside Ballads Current in American Tradition: A Bibliographical Syllabus."

——— . *Native American Balladry: A Descriptive Study and a Bibliographical Syllabus*. Rev. ed. Philadelphia: American Folklore Society, 1964. 298p.

Deals largely with ballads which have originated in this country and in the Maritime Provinces of Canada. Includes a bibliography.

Lomax, Alan. *The Folk Songs of North America in the English Language*. Garden City, N.Y.: Doubleday, 1960. 623p.

Music and words, with descriptive notes.

——— and Sidney Robertson Cowell.

American Folk Songs and Folk Lore: A Regional Bibliography. New York: Progressive Education Assoc., 1942. 59p. (P.E.A. Service Center Pamphlet No.8)

A good annotated bibliography.

Lomax, John A., and Alan Lomax. *American Ballads and Folk Songs.* New York: Macmillan, 1934. 625p.

An extensive collection, including work songs, playparty songs, etc.

——— and ———, eds. *Folk Song U*S*A*: The 111Best American Ballads,* Collected, adapted, and arranged by John A. Lomax and Alan Lomax. New York: Duell, Sloan and Pearce, 1947. 407p. Rpt. as *Best Loved American Folk Songs:* New York: Grosset and Dunlap. 1947. 407p.

Words and tunes with piano accompaniment, and introductory chapters giving pioneer stories and backgrounds.

———. *Our Singing Country: A Second Volume of American Ballads and Folk Songs.* New York: Macmillan, 1941. 416p.

Four songs from Tennessee: two religious songs, one social song, and one Negro gang song.

McDowell, Mrs. L.L. (Flora Lassiter) *Tennessee Folk Songs.* Delaware, Ohio: Cooperative Recreation Service, 1939. 6p.

Words and music of five Tennessee ballads.

McDowell, Lucien L., and Flora Lassiter McDowell. *Memory Melodies: A Collection of Folk Songs from Middle Tennessee.* Smithville, Tenn.: n.p., 1947. 128p.

Words and tunes of traditional songs, most of which were remembered by the authors from their childhood and youth.

Mason, Robert Leslie. "Ten Old English Ballads in Middle Tennessee." *Southern Folklore Quarterly,* XI (June 1947), 119–37.

Traditional ballads sung in Cannon County.

Miles, Emma Bell. "Some Real American Music." *Harper's Monthly Magazine,* CIX (June 1904), 118–23.

Words and tunes illustrative of the mountaineers' characteristics of humor and religious emotion. Includes ballads and dance tunes. Also reprinted as Chapter VIII in her *Spirit of the Mountain* (see Section IV, General Sources).

Niles, John Jacob. *The Ballad Book of John Jacob Niles.* Boston: Houghton Mifflin, 1961. 369p.

A collection of balladry and folklore, giving words and tunes, some history of the ballad, and stories told by the people who sang them. About 10 items were located in Tennessee.

———. *Ten Christmas Carols from the Southern Appalachian Mountains.* Collected and Simply Arranged With Accompaniment for Piano. New York: G. Schirmer, 1935. 22p.

Two songs were recorded in Tennessee.

Odum, Anna Kranz. "Some Negro Folk-Songs from Tennessee." *Journal of American Folklore,* XXVII (July-Sept. 1914), 255–65.

Words of 25 songs, sung by the children of one rural family in Sumner County.

Odum, Howard W. "Folk-Song and Folk-Poetry as Found in the Secular Songs of the Southern Negroes." *Journal of American Folklore,* XXIV (July-Sept. 1911), 255–94; (Oct.-Dec. 1911), 351–96.

Collected from Mississippi, Georgia, and North Carolina, but many were heard in Tennessee.'

——— and Guy B. Johnson. *The Negro and His Songs: A Study of Typical Negro Songs in the South.* Chapel Hill: Univ. of North Carolina Press, 1925. 306p.

A discussion of religious and secular Negro songs, with something of their setting. Includes songs collected in Tennessee by Anna Kranz Odum.

Page, Marion Taylor. "Child Ballads from Montgomery County." *Tennessee*

Folklore Society Bulletin, XXXVII (March 1971), 9–14.
> Words and tunes of four ballads.

Perrow, E.C. "Songs and Rhymes from the South." *Journal of American Folklore*, XXV (April-June 1912), 137–55; XXVI (April-June 1913), 123–73; XXVIII (Jan.-March 1915), 129–90.
> Songs of outlaws; songs in which animals figure; game songs and nursery rhymes; religious songs and parodies; railroad songs; drinking and gambling; songs of the plantation; and songs of love. Many from Tennessee, and a brief account of speech, customs, and personal characteristics.

Richardson, Ethel Park, comp. *American Mountain Songs*. Ed. and Arranged by Sigmund Spaeth. N.p. Greenberg, 1927. 120p.
> Words and music of about 60 songs "gathered in the mountainous districts of Tennessee, the Carolinas, North Georgia, Kentucky, Virginia and Missouri."

Schinhan, Jan Philip. "The Music of the Ballads." In White, Newman Ivey, *The Frank C. Brown Collection of North Carolina Folklore*, Vol. IV. Durham: Duke Univ. Press, 1952.
> Contains the music for ballads in Volume II (*see* Belden, Henry M.).

———, ed. "The Music of the Folk Songs." In White, Newman Ivey, *The Frank C. Brown Collection of North Carolina Folklore*, Vol. V. Durham: Duke Univ. Press, 1952.
> Contains the music for folk songs in Volume II (*see* Belden, Henry M.). Also includes additional songs such as children's games and rhymes; courtship and marriage games; dancing games.

Seeger, Ruth Crawford. *American Folk Songs for Children in Home, School and Nursery School, a Book for Children, Parents and Teachers*. Garden City, N.Y.: Doubleday, 1948. 190p.
> Words and music. Three songs noted from Tennessee.

———. *Animal Folk Songs for Children:*

Traditional American Songs. Garden City, N.Y.: Doubleday, 1950. 80p.
> Words and music. Includes some songs from Tennessee.

Sharp, Cecil James, and Maud Karpeles. *Eighty English Folk Songs from the Southern Appalachians*. Cambridge, Mass.: MIT Press, 1968. 109p.
> Ballads and narrative songs, jigs and game songs, nonsense and children's songs, with words and tunes. Notes give reference to contributions from Tennessee.

———. *English Folk-Songs from the Southern Appalachians*. Ed. Maud Karpeles. 2 vols. London: Oxford Univ. Press, 1932.
> Important collection of ballads, songs, hymns, nursery songs, jigs, and play-party games; includes many sung by Tennesseans.

Van Wey, Adelaide, and Donald Lee Moore. *Smoky Mountain Ballads*. New York: Omega Music Edition, 1949. 15p.
> Words and music of 10 songs, with guitar, banjo, ukelele, and zither symbols.

West, Roy Andre. "The Songs of the Mountaineers." Unpubl. Master's thesis, George Peabody College for Teachers, 1922. 118p.
> Gives a brief description of the way of life in the Appalachian highlands, and the words of about 80 ballads, sacred songs, folk songs, etc.

White, Newman Ivey. *American Negro Folk-Songs*. Cambridge, Mass.: Harvard Univ. Press, 1928. 501p.
> History and characteristics of religious songs, work songs, social songs, songs about animals, and others, collected by the author mostly in Alabama and North Carolina but with a number of references to Tennessee.

Dances and Singing Games

American Folk Dances. Delaware, Ohio: Cooperative Recreation Service, 1939. 48p.
> Square dances of the Great Smoky Mountains.

Burnett, Edmund Cody. "The Hog Drivers' Play-Song and Some of Its Relatives." *Agricultural History*, XIII (July 1949), 161–68.

Gives the words and the tune of "The Hog Drivers' Play-Song" and words of two other songs, with a description of the circumstances under which they were played and of the church's reaction to them.

Cothran, Kay L. "Songs, Games, and Memories of Mr. George W. Mitchell." *Tennessee Folklore Society Bulletin*, XXXIV (Sept. 1968), 63–81.

Recollections of a 96-year-old man about play-party games, giving words and tunes, barn-raisings, log-rollings, etc.

Duncan, Ruby. "The Play-Party in Hamilton County." *Tennessee Folklore Society Bulletin*, VI (March 1940), 1–15.

Words and directions for playing 16 games. No tunes given.

Edwards, Lawrence. "Square Dancing at Speedwell." *The Appalachian South*, I (Spring and Summer 1966), 20–21.

A story of a party of some years ago, with a description of the dancers, fiddlers, and callers.

Emery, Lynne Fauley. *Black Dance in the United States from 1619 to 1970.* Palo Alto, Calif.: National Press Books, 1972. 370p.

"Dance on the plantations" discusses types of dances: special occasions, Christmas dances, corn-shucking and quilting dances, and sacred dances. The only specific reference to Tennessee is the origin of "The Black Bottom."

Ford, Ira W. *Traditional Music of America.* New York: Dutton, 1940. 480p.

"Gives a picture of America's early social and work activities expressed in some of its unwritten traditional music and history." Few geographical origins are given, but it is useful for fiddle tunes, square dance calls, and words of game songs.

Gannaway, Mary Ann. "The Singing Games of the Cumberland Mountains in Tennessee." Unpubl. Master's thesis,

George Peabody College for Teachers, 1935. 131p.

Words and tunes for 38 games, with directions for playing.

Hall, Joseph S. "Some Party-Games of the Great Smoky Mountains." *Journal of American Folklore*, LIV (Jan.-June 1941), 68–71.

Five group games from Cosby Creek, Cocke County, Tennessee.

Hendrix, D.B. *Smoky Mountain Square Dances.* Ann Arbor: Edwards Brothers, 1941. 38p.

Information on square dance calls and figures, with diagrams.

McDowell, Flora L. *Folk Dances of Tennessee: Folk Customs and Old Party Games of the Caney Fork Valley.* Delaware, Ohio: Cooperative Recreation Service, 1953. 64p.

Tunes, full directions, and diagrams of 28 play-party games and several country dances.

McDowell, Lucien L. "Finding Folk Dances in Tennessee." *Tennessee Folklore Society Bulletin*, IV (Dec. 1938), 1–99.

Concerning the collection and preservation of words, tunes, and dance figures of play-party games, which are distinctive American folk dances.

————, and Flora Lassiter McDowell. *Folk Dances of Tennessee: Old Play Party Games of the Caney Fork Valley.* Ann Arbor: Edwards Brothers, 1938. 78p.

From the memory of the authors and their friends—tunes, directions, and diagrams for 28 play-party games and some country dances.

————. "The Play-Party and Song." *Tennessee Folklore Society Bulletin*, XI (May 1945), 3–8.

Words and tunes.

McLendon, Altha Lea. "A Finding List of Play-Party Games." *Southern Folklore Quarterly*, VIII (Sept. 1944), 201–34.

"Attempts to make available . . . a complete reference to versions and variants of traditional American play-party games published in state and regional collections and in professional education books."

O'Dell, Ruth W. "Tennessee Play-Parties." *Tennessee Folklore Society Bulletin*, XVIII (Sept. 1952), 68–70.

Two types of singing games described: circle games and two lines facing each other.

Price, M. Katherine. *The Source Book of Play Party Games*. Minneapolis: Burgess Publishing Co., 1949. 170p.

About 100 games with tunes and directions. Many are familiar in Tennessee.

Rohrbough, Lynn, ed. *American Folk Dances* combined with *Square Dances of the Great Smoky Mountains*, by Frank H. Smith. Delaware, Ohio: Cooperative Recreation Service, 1939. 48p.

Directions and tunes for dances.

———, ed. *Play Party Games*. Delaware, Ohio: Cooperative Recreation Service, 1930. 32p.

Words, tune, action given.

———, ed. *Southern Singing Games*. Delaware, Ohio: Cooperative Recreation Service, 1938. 31p.

Includes nine games from Tennessee. Words, tune, and action given.

Ryan, Grace L. *Dances of Our Pioneers*. New York: A.S. Barnes, 1939. 196p.

Collected in the Middle West, Rocky Mountains, and eastern Appalachians. Includes a good definition of terms, music or suggested tunes, and calls.

Sanders, J. Olcutt. "Finding List of Southeastern Square Dance Figures." *Southern Folklore Quarterly*, VI (Dec. 1942), 263–75.

The list gives the title, references to similar figures, publications in which the figure appears, brief descriptive note, and the Southeastern state in which the figure is found.

Smith, Frank H., and Rolf E. Hovey. *The Appalachian Square Dance*. Berea, Ky.: Berea College, 1955. 86p.

Instructions, with good illustrations and 20 tunes.

———. "Dances and Singing Games." In Ford, Thomas R., ed., *The Southern Appalachian Region*. Lexington: Univ. of Kentucky Press, 1962.

Emphasis is on efforts to preserve "a valuable part of our cultural heritage."

———. *Square Dances of the Great Smoky Mountains*. Delaware, Ohio: Cooperative Recreation Service, 1939. 29p.

Has 25 dances with instructions, calls, and some tunes.

Williams, Charles H. *Cotton Needs Pickin': Characteristic Negro Folk Dances*. Norfolk, Va.: Guide Publishing Co., 1928. 24p.

"The publication of this group of eight dances is an attempt to use the Negro songs and dance steps for educational purposes in the schools." Gives music, words, costumes, instructions, and photographs.

Religious Songs

Barton, William E. *Old Plantation Hymns: A Collection of Hitherto Unpublished Melodies of the Slave and the Freedman, With Historical and Descriptive Notes*. 1899; rpt. Boston: Lamson, Wolffe and Co., 1972. 45p.

Words and tunes of Negro songs collected by the author from 1880 to 1887.

Caldwell, William. *Union Harmony: Or Family Musician. Being a Choice Selection of Tunes, Selected From the Works of the Most Eminent Authors Ancient and Modern Together With a Large Number of Original Tunes, Composed and Harmonized By the Author To Which is Prefixed a Comprehensive View of the Rudiments of Music, Abridged and Adapted to the Capacity of the Young*. Maryville, Tenn.: F.A. Parham, 1834. 151p.

Words and music.

Cobb, Buell E., Jr., "The Sacred Harp: An Overview of a Tradition." Unpubl. Master's thesis, Auburn Univ., 1969. 184p.

Discusses the background of the movement, local variations in territorial conventions, the song book (*The Sacred Harp*) and the singing. Centered in Alabama and Georgia, but some mention is given to Tennessee.

Davidson, Donald. "White Spirituals: The Choral Music of the South." *The American Scholar*, IV (Autumn 1935), 460–73.

Discusses "shape note" singers and their songs.

Davidson, Samuel C. *Camp Meeting Songster: Or a Collection of Hymns and Spiritual Songs, With a Few Pieces Never Before Published, Designed, Principally, For Camp Meetings.* Knoxville: F.S. Heiskell, 1832. 120p.

Words of 97 songs and hymns.

Henderson, Connie. "They Called Him 'Singin Billy.' " *Mountain Life and Work*, XXXVIII (Fall 1962), 49–52.

Concerns William Walker, promoter of singing schools in Southern states and author of *Southern Harmony*, a songbook with shaped notes.

Horne, Dorothy D. "Folk-Hymn Texts in Three 'Old Harp' Books." *Tennessee Folklore Society Bulletin*, XXII (Dec. 1956), 91–97.

Hymns from Swan's *New Harp of Columbia*, Walker's *Southern Harmony and Musical Companion*, and *The Original Sacred Harp*, "selected because they are still in use and thus represent a living example of the continuance of a very old tradition."

———. "Quartal Harmony in the Pentatonic Folk Hymns of the Sacred Harps." *Journal of American Folklore*, LXXI (Oct.-Dec. 1958), 564–81.

A study using Swan's *The New Harp of Columbia*, Walker's *Southern Harmony and Musical Companion*, and White's *The Original Sacred Harp*.

———. "Shape-Note Hymnals and the

Art Music of Early America." *Southern Folklore Quarterly*, V (Dec. 1941), 251–56.

Characteristics of a primitive art which became a definite style and survives in the shape-note singing of the South.

———. *Sing to Me of Heaven: A Study of Folk and Early American Materials in Three Old Harp Books.* Gainesville: Univ. of Florida Press, 1970. 212p.

Words, music, and folklore analysis of songs in *The Southern Harmony, The Original Sacred Harp* and *The New Harp of Columbia*. Includes a description of an Old Harp Singers' gathering.

Jackson, George Pullen. *Another Sheaf of White Spirituals, Collected, Edited, and Illustrated by George Pullen Jackson.* Gainsville: Univ. of Florida Press, 1952. 253p.

Words, music, and commentary on religious folksongs. Many were sung, recorded, or published in Tennessee.

———. "Buckwheat Notes." *The Musical Quarterly*, XIX (Oct. 1933), 393–400.

"It is the purpose of the author to tell . . . of a little-known but far-reaching and successful rural American attempt at simplifying the problems of reading music." A history of shape-notations and "the sort of songs to which this peculiar notation has clung." Religious choral pieces.

———. *Spiritual Folk-Songs of Early America; Two Hundred and Fifty Tunes and Texts With an Introduction and Notes, Collected and Edited by George Pullen Jackson.* New York: J.J. Augustin, 1937; rpt. Dover, 1964. 254p.

Religious ballads, hymns, and spiritual songs, stressing especially the tunes.

———. *The Story of the Sacred Harp, 1844–1944.* Nashville: Vanderbilt Univ. Press, 1944. 46p. Reprinted in the 1968 publication of *The Sacred Harp* by B.F. White and E.J. King.

A description and history of the types of song, and the singers using the *Sacred Harp* songbook.

———. *White and Negro Spirituals,*

Their Life Span and Kinship: Tracing 200 Years of Untrammeled Song Making and Singing Among Our Country Folk, With 116 Songs as Sung By Both Races. New York: J.J. Augustin, 1943. 349p.

Many songs are noted as having been sung in Tennessee.

———. *White Spirituals in the Southern Uplands; The Story of the Fasola Folk, Their Songs, Singings, and "Buckwheat Notes."* Chapel Hill: Univ. of North Carolina Press, 1933. 444p.

"How and where I found them, (aged handbooks of spiritual folk-song,) what strange sorts of songs they contained, whence the unique notation in which the songs are recorded, who made, collected, and sang them, how, when, and where they came into being, and how and where their singing persists at present. . . . have provided matter for discussion." Many references to Tennessee, including the "Old Harp Singers" of eastern Tennessee.

Jackson, John B. *The Knoxville Harmony of Music Made Easy* . . . Pumpkintown, East Tennessee: Johnston & Edwards, 1840. 200p.

Words and tunes for hymns and spiritual songs. "Intended for the use of such schools and churches as are in the habit of using what are called the shaped notes, or four singing syllables."

Johnson, Andrew W. *The American Harmony.* Nashville: W.H. Dunn, 1829. 64p.

"Containing a plain and easy introduction to the grounds of music, in as short a manner as would be expedient." Mostly religious songs in shaped notes.

———, *Western Psalmodist* . . . Nashville: The Author. Printed at the Nashville Union Office, 1853. 127p.

Shaped-note songs "well adapted to Christian Churches, Singing Schools, Private Societies."

McDowell, Lucien L. *Songs of the Old Camp Ground: Genuine Religious Folk Songs of the Tennessee Hill Country.* Ann Arbor: Edwards Brothers, 1937. 85p.

"Every song herein written is from the lips of those who sang them in my presence just as I have them written, and they had never a book to find them in."

Read, Daniel. *The Columbian Harmonist . . . Number 2.* New Haven: Printed For & Sold By the Editor, n.d. (1795?) 71p. Additional music, 16p.

A collection of sacred songs with music and words, terms of scale, tones, time, etc.

Swan, M.L. *The New Harp of Columbia.* Nashville: Publication House of the M.E. Church, South, 1919. 226p. Facsimile edition with new Introduction, Knoxville: Univ. of Tennessee Press, 1978. (Tennesseana Editions.)

Introduction to the New Edition contains "The New Harp of Columbia and Its Music in the Singing-School Tradition" by Dorothy D. Horn, and "East Tennessee Harp Singing" by Ron Peterson and Candra Phillips.

Swan, W.H., and M.L. Swan. *Harp of Columbia.* Knoxville: The Authors, 1848. 224p.

Shaped-note songs sung by Harp Singers in East Tennessee.

White, B.F., and E.J. King, comps. *The Sacred Harp.* Facsim. of the 3d ed., 1859, including as a historical introduction: *The Story of The Sacred Harp,* by George Pullen Jackson. Nashville, Broadman Press, 1968. 432p.

Gives words and shaped-note tunes of Psalms and hymns, odes and anthems.

Wilson, Leon. "The White Spirituals." *Mountain Life and Work,* XIX (Summer 1943), 12–14.

Cites opportunities for hearing "singings" in 1943 and makes reference to old song books used.

Work Songs

Adams, James Taylor, comp. *Death in the Dark; A Collection of Factual Ballads of American Mine Disasters, With Historical Notes.* Big Laurel, Va.: Adams-Mullins Press, 1941. 119p.

Includes Fraterville Mine at Coal Creek, Tennessee, and Cross Mountain Mine at Coal Creek, 1911.

Burman, Ben Lucien. "Mississippi Roustabout." *Harper's Monthly*, CLXXX (1940), 635–43.

Good verbal picture of the Negro roustabout in the heyday of riverboats, giving songs, "hoodoo," superstitions, etc.

Green, Archie. *Only a Miner: Studies in Recorded Coal-Mining Songs*. Urbana: Univ. of Illinois Press, 1972. 504p.

Gives considerable attention to the insurrection at the Coal Creek mine in Anderson County, Tenn., caused by the convict-lease system, and to the ballads titled "Coal Creek Troubles," "Coal Creek War," and "Coal Creek Rebellion."

———. "Recorded American Coal Mining Songs." Ph.D. diss. Philadelphia: Univ. of Pennsylvania, 1969. 522p.

"A statement on sound recordings as cultural documents and communicative devices. It is restricted to eight studies of coal mining songs issued in discs in the United States between 1925–1969." *Dissertation Abstracts*, 1970, 30:4894A-95A. Includes "Coal Creek Troubles" in Coal Creek, Tennessee, and "Roll Down the Line," originally sung by Negro convicts in mines at Tracy City, Tenn.

Korson, George. *Coal Dust on the Fiddle: Songs and Stories of the Bituminous Industry*. Philadelphia: Univ. of Pennsylvania Press, 1943. 460p.

An account of the way of living in mining camps; food and the company store; folk medicine and folklore; and songs and ballads, including those about the Fraterville explosion, the Cross Mountain explosion, and the Coal Creek rebellion in Tennessee.

Manning, Ambrose. "Railroad Work Songs." *Tennessee Folklore Society Bulletin*, XXXII (June 1966), 41–47.

A search for railroad workers who knew and could chant work songs. Words of the songs are given.

Odum, Howard W., and Guy B. Johnson. *Negro Workaday Songs*. Chapel Hill:

Univ. of North Carolina Press, 1926. 278p.

"represents the group of songs current in certain areas in North Carolina, South Carolina, Tennessee and Georgia, during the years 1924–25. . . . all sung or repeated by actual Negro workers or singers." This study by sociologists aims to give "glimpses of common backgrounds of Negro life and experience in Southern communities." Few designations of specific Tennessee materials.

Scarborough, Dorothy. *On the Trail of Negro Folk-Songs*. Cambridge, Mass.: Harvard Univ. Press, 1925; rpt. Hatboro, Penn.: Folklore Associates, 1963. 295p.

A chapter on songs about animals and a chapter on work-songs each contain one contribution of John Trotwood Moore, with several other brief references to Tennessee.

Seeger, Pete. "The Coal Creek Rebellion." *Sing Out*, V (Summer 1955), 19–21.

Words and tune of " 'Buddy Won't You Roll Down the Line,' a miner's version of a song made up by Negro convicts working in the mines." Includes an account of the Coal Creek rebellion in Tennessee.

Syford, Ethel C. "A Tennessee Mountain Work Song." *Journal of American Folklore*, LVIII (April-June 1945), 157.

The words of a song beginning "Oh, My Paw He's Lost His Shoe," sung by a hired man in the 1920s.

Wheeler, Mary. *Steam-Boatin' Days: Folk Songs of the River Packet Era*. Baton Rouge: Louisiana State Univ. Press, 1944. 121p.

An interesting story of the roustabouts and their songs, and the packet boats on the Ohio, Mississippi, and Tennessee rivers. Gives words and tunes of songs as sung by Negroes who had worked on the river; also includes superstitions, herb cures, and other folk material.

Wood, C.L. "Early Days." *Tennessee Folklore Society Bulletin*, X (Sept. 1944), 5–6.

Drovers' games and songs while driving stock from Kentucky and Tennessee to Southern markets.

Musical Instruments

Brown, David J. "J.W. and Don Galla-
gher, Master Guitar Craftsmen." *Tennessee Folklore Society Bulletin*, XLIV
(March 1978), 13–24.
  An interview with two present-day guitar
craftsmen, giving details about construction.

Bryan, Charles Faulkner. "American
Folk Instruments." I. "The Appalachian
Mountain Dulcimer." *Tennessee Folklore Society Bulletin*, XVIII (March 1952),
1–5; II. "The Hammered Dulcimer."
XVIII (June 1952), 43–47; III. "Improvised
Instruments." XVIII (Sept. 1952), 65–67.
  I. Sketches of shapes and types of instruments, and suggestions concerning tuning and materials. II. Sketches of shapes,
strings, tuning pin, tuning wrench, etc. III.
Various means of improvising instruments
with materials at hand. Photographs of dulcimers, Jews-harp, cane-flute, and turtle
banjo, from the author's collection.

————. "The Appalachian Mountain
Dulcimer Enigma." *Tennessee Folklore
Society Bulletin*, XX (Dec. 1954), 86–90.
  A report of an unsuccessful search in
museums in the United States and Europe
for the ancestor or the history of the
plucked dulcimer.

Burman-Hall, Linda C. "Southern Amer-
ican Fiddle Styles." *Ethnomusicology*,
XIX (Jan. 1975), 47–65.
  Includes the Southern Appalachian style.

Force, Robert, and Albert d'Ossché. *In
Search of the Wild Dulcimer*. New York:
Vintage Books, 1974. 109p.
  "Complete instruction on how to play
this traditional Appalachian instrument
and how to adapt it to contemporary
music."

George, Frank. "5-String Banjo." *Appalachian South*, II (Spring and Summer
1967), 52–53.
  Brief history and description of banjos
and banjo-guitars, including those made
from gourds.

Greene, Bruce. "Traditional Fiddle

Music." 1972–413. Unpublished MS.
10p. Western Kentucky Univ. Folklore,
Folklife, and Oral History Archives.
  A description of technique; a list of 54
old-time tunes; breakdowns, reels, horn-
pipes, marches, and waltzes. An interview
with an old-time fiddler.

Hulan, Richard H. "Music in Tennessee." *Antiques*, C (Sept. 1971), 418–19.
  Instruments and songs found in Tennessee, with pictures of dulcimers.

Irwin, John Rice. *Musical Instruments of
the Southern Appalachians: A History of
the Author's Collection Housed in the
Museum of Appalachia, Norris, Tennessee*. Norris: Museum of Appalachia
Press, 1979. 95p.
  Photographs of almost 100 instruments,
with a brief history and description. Chapters on the fiddle, mountain banjo, mouth
bow, Appalachian dulcimer, and miscellaneous instruments, including guitar,
mandolin, Jews harp, harmonica, etc.

**"Mountain Music and Hand-made In-
struments."** In Eaton, Allen H., *Handicrafts of the Southern Highlands*. New
York: Russell Sage Foundation, 1937.
370p.
  Dulcimers, fiddles, and gourd instruments.

Putnam, John. "The Plucked Dulcimer."
Mountain Life and Work, XXXIV, No. 4
(1958), 7–13.
  Short biographies with photographs of
makers of dulcimers, and drawings of various shaped instruments.

————. *The Plucked Dulcimer and How
to Play It*. Berea: Council of Southern
Mountains, 1964. 29p.
  Illustrated instructions for various ways
to tune and play. Several folk tunes are giv-
en.

Pyle, Paul W. *To Build a Dulcimer, a
Simplified Economical Demonstration
in the Constructing, Tuning and Playing
of the Dulcimer*. Tullahoma, Tenn.: Paul
Pyle Studio, 1972. 15p.
  Includes the words of a few songs, with
instructions for playing them.

Ritchie, Jean. *The Dulcimer Book.* New York: Oak Publications, 1963. 45p.

History of the Appalachian mountain dulcimer, how to tune and play, with 16 songs.

"Robert Mize, Dulcimer Maker." *Foxfire,* VIII (Fall 1974), 230–40.

Photographs and directions for making a dulcimer, by Robert Mize of Blountville.

Rosenbaum, Art. *Old-time Mountain Banjo: Method of playing the old-time five-string mountain banjo based on the styles of traditional banjo-pickers.* New York: Oak Publications, 1968. 88p.

Tunes, with detailed instructions.

Seeger, Charles. "The Appalachian Dulcimer." *Journal of American Folklore,* LXXI (1958), 40–51.

History, with photographs of the instruments.

Seeger, Pete. *How to Play the 5-String Banjo: A Manual For Beginners.* 3rd ed. Beacon, N.Y.: The Author, 1961. 72p.

A brief history of the instrument, with words and tunes and instructions for playing.

Vogedes, Glenn A. "The Dulcimer of Southern Appalachia." 1971–26. Unpublished MSS. 22p. Western Kentucky Univ. Folklore, Folklife, and Oral History Archives.

The instrument as constructed and used in Southern Appalachia, with photographs and sketches. Includes interviews with Tennessee craftsmen.

Surveys and Performers

Artis, Bob. *Bluegrass: From the Lonesome Wail of a Mountain Love Song to the Hammering Drive of the Scruggs-style Banjo–The Story of an American Musical Tradition.* New York: Hawthorne Books, 1975. 182p.

A history of Bluegrass and the singers.

Blaustein, Richard Jason. "Traditional Music and Social Change: The Old Time Fiddlers Association Movement in the United States." Ph.D. diss. Indiana Univ., 1975. 182p.

Chapter I, Historical Overview of Fiddling Traditions in North America, discusses music and dance in the frontier areas as well as other sections of the country, and "the fiddler's position in the social life of rural North America."

Burton, Thomas G., ed. *Tom Ashley, Sam McGee, Bukka White: Tennessee Traditional Singers.* Knoxville: Univ. of Tennessee Press, 1981. 240p.

Includes musical notations and discographies, in addition to careers of the singers. The three sections are written by Ambrose N. Manning and Minnie M. Miller, Charles K. Wolfe, and F. Jack Hurley and David Evans.

Cohen, Anne, and Norm Cohen. "Folk and Hillbilly Music: Further Thoughts on Their Relation." *JEMF Quarterly,* XIII (Summer 1977), 50–55.

Fox, Mrs. Jesse W. "Beale Street and the Blues." *West Tennessee Historical Society Papers,* XIII (1959), 128–47.

Gives the folk history of Beale Street, as well as of W.C. Handy and the Blues.

Greene, Robert B. "Henry L. Bandy: The Old-Time Fiddler." *Kentucky Folklore Record,* XVIII (Oct.-Dec. 1972), 99–102.

A biographical sketch of the blacksmith and fiddler who broadcast in Grand Ole Opry from the late 1920s.

Haden, Walter D., ed. *Fiddlin' Sid's Memoirs: The Autobiography of Sidney J. Harkreader.* Los Angeles: John Edwards Memorial Foundation, 1976. 37p. (JEMF Special Series, No. 9.)

An interesting account of his life on a farm in Wilson County, Tennessee, and of the development of his career as an early country music fiddler and "one of the first performers on the Grand Ole Opry in Nashville."

King, Carl Darlington. "Charles Faulkner Bryan: Tennessee Educator and Musician." Unpubl. diss. Univ. of Tennessee, Knoxville, c1965. 284p.

An appreciative biography of Bryan as a teacher, musician, and composer of works based on folk themes. Includes a bibliography of his works.

Malone, Bill C. *Country Music U.S.A.: A Fifty-Year History*. Austin: Univ. of Texas Press, 1968. 422p. (Published for The American Folklore Society.)

Chapter I, The Folk Background—Before the Coming of Commercialism, discusses folk music of the rural South, including songs, musical instruments, fiddle dance tunes, etc.

Miller, Minnie M. "Tom Clarence Ashley, An Appalachian Folk Musician." Unpubl. Master's thesis, East Tennessee State Univ., 1973. 64p.

The life of a Mountain City, Tenn., entertainer, guitarist, banjopicker, singer, 1895–1967.

Rinzler, Ralph, and Norm Cohen. *Uncle Dave Macon: A Bio-Discography*. Los Angeles: John Edwards Memorial Foundation, Inc., 1970. 51p. (JEMF Special Series, No.3.)

Published on the "100th anniversary of the birth of David Harrison (Uncle Dave) Macon, first featured star of Grand Ole Opry, and one of the most beloved figures of the early decades of country music." Macon was a native of Warren County, Tenn.

Rosenberg, Neil V. *Bill Monroe and His Blue Grass Boys: An Illustrated Discography*. Nashville: Country Music Foundation Press, 1974. 122p.

A biography of Monroe, his professional career, and a discography of his works. Illustrated with numerous photographs.

Smith, Jon G. " 'She Kept On A-Goin': Ethel Park Richardson." *JEMF Quarterly*, XIII (Autumn 1977), 105–17.

Written by Mrs. Richardson's grandson, who calls her "a plucky old woman from Tennessee" who made a career of collecting mountain folksongs and presenting them to urban American audiences. (See her book *American Mountain Songs* under Ballads and Folk Songs).

Whisnant, David E. "Thicker Than Fiddlers in Hell: Issues and Resources in Appalachian Music." *Appalachian Journal* V, (Autumn 1977), 103–15.

A survey of what has been done and what needs to be done in the study of Appalachian music.

Wilbur, Cousin (Willie Egbert Wesbrooks), with Barbara M. McLean and Sandra S. Grafton. *Everybody's Cousin*. New York: Manor Books, 1979. 203p.

Reminiscences of a country music performer and comedian from West Tennessee. Photographs.

Wilgus, D.K. *Anglo-American Folksong Scholarship Since 1898*. New Brunswick, N.J.: Rutgers Univ. Press, 1959. 466p.

A critical history of folksong study which "has developed from an antiquarian, esthetic, and literary pastime toward a disciplined study of a segment of traditional culture."

————, and Lynwood Montell. "Clure and Joe Williams: Legend and Blues Ballad." *Journal of American Folklore*, LXXXI (Oct.-Dec. 1968), 295–315.

"Deals with the value of a local ballad in a study of folk culture" and with the Williams family in south-central Kentucky and north-central Tennessee. A Blues ballad, telling of the exploits of McClure Williams and others who were raftsmen on the Cumberland River.

————, and John Greenway, eds. "Hillbilly Issue." *Journal of American Folklore*, LXXVIII (July-Sept. 1965), 195–287.

Six articles by Wilgus, Archie Green, Norman Cohen, L.M. Smith, and Ed Kahn on the study of hillbilly music and its recordings.

Wolfe, Charles K. "Early Country Music in Knoxville." *Old Time Music*, No. 12 (Spring 1974), 19–31.

————, *The Grand Ole Opry: The Early Years, 1925–1935*. London: Old Time Music, 1975. 128p. (Old Time Music Booklet 2.)

"An attempt to document, as accurately as possible, the historical story of the Opry during its first ten years. . . . the 'old time music' age of the Opry."

———, *Tennessee Strings: The Story of Country Music in Tennessee*. Knoxville: Univ. of Tennessee Press, 1977. 118p. (Tennessee Three Star Books.)

Tells the story from the "Folk Background" to the "Nashville Skyline."

Work, John Wesley. *Folk Song of the American Negro*. Nashville: n.p., 1915;

rpt. New York: Negro Universities Press, 1969. 131p.

A history of American Negro songs, their characteristics, number, and classification; what the songs mean to the Negro; the performance of the Fisk Jubilee Singers. Chapter VI tells of the "birth and growth of certain songs," some of which originated in Tennessee.

XXI. Games and Toys

Games

Bass, William A. "A Recollected Idyll." *Tennessee Folklore Society Bulletin*, XXVIII (Dec. 1962), 85–88.

Reminiscences of games and adventures devised in the author's childhood in Warren County, Tennessee.

Blevins, Carolyn, Vivian Davis, Ann Shephard, and Cindy Walker. "The Games People Play—and Have Played—in Southern Appalachia." 1972. 35p. Student paper, Riedl Collection, Univ. of Tennessee Library, Knoxville.

From 53 Tennessee informants.

Brewster, Paul G. *American Nonsinging Games*. Norman: Univ. of Oklahoma Press, 1953. 218p.

Several games reported from Tennessee, and many others are familiar to the region.

———, ed. "Children's Games and Rhymes." In White, Newman Ivey, *The Frank C. Brown Collection of North Carolina Folklore*. Durham: Duke Univ. Press, 1952. Vol. I.

Games are grouped into 18 divisions, using the most distinctive features as a basis for inclusion in a given group. Rhymes are likewise classed in 16 groups. All are North Caroliniana, but reference is given to many parallels and variants in Tennessee.

Freedle, Martha. "Children's Games and

Amusements in Sumner County in 'The Good Old Days.' " *Tennessee Folklore Society Bulletin*, XXVII (June 1961), 23–31.

Describes "amusements involving homemade toys and resources at hand; amusements centered around community resources; games played at school; nighttime games and amusements enjoyed with family and friends."

Horne, Dorothy D. "Chick-A-Ma-Craney Crow." *Tennessee Folklore Society Bulletin*, XI (May 1945), 9–11.

Recollections of several individuals about a children's game, written in response to an inquiry by columnist Paul Flowers in the *Memphis Commercial Appeal*.

Jurgens, Katherine Williams. "Games Played in the Rural Schools of Scott County, Tennessee." Unpubl. Master's thesis, George Peabody College for Teachers, 1937. 180p.

Directions are given for playing 91 games "either not found in the game books examined or, if found, not identical with games by the same name played in Scott County." Not intended as a folk culture study but useful.

Justus, May. *The Complete Peddler's Pack: Games, Songs, Rhymes, and Riddles from Mountain Folklore*. Knoxville: Univ. of Tennessee Press, 1967. 100p. Revised edition of *Peddler's Pack*, 1957.

Nonsense rhymes, riddles, tongue-twisters, counting-out rhymes, songs and singing games, play-party games, and signs and predictions.

Kappes, Eveline Elizabeth. "A Study of the Play Activities of Three Sections of the Great Smoky Mountains National Park." Unpubl. Master's thesis, Univ. of Michigan, 1938. 71p. (Copy on film in Univ. of Tennessee Library, Knoxville).

The three sections are Cades Cove, Wears Valley, and Gatlinburg, Tennessee.

Lassiter, Robert. "The Games We Played." *Tennessee Folklore Society Bulletin*, XII (March 1946), 17–22.

Games played at school.

McDowell, Flora L. "Games of Long Ago." *Tennessee Folklore Society Bulletin*, X (Sept. 1944), 1–4.

Children's games, including riddles and counting-out rhymes.

Tharp, Mel. "Grab." *Tennessee Folklore Society Bulletin*, XLIII (June 1977), 89–90.

A traditional game.

Toys

Comstock, Henry B. "Folk Toys Are Back Again." *Popular Science*, CLXXVI (March 1960), 144–47.

Whimmydiddle, cornstalk fiddle, bullroarer, fly killer, and flipperdinger are the folk toys. Illustrations and instructions for making are included.

Creekmore, Betsey B. *Traditional American Crafts*. N.p., Hearthside Press, 1968. 191p.

Handmade toys: wooden dolls, shuck dolls, rag dolls, apple dolls.

"Dried Apple Dolls from the Tennessee Mountains: Faces of Character Dolls Sculptured from Fruit." *The Mentor*, XV (July 1927), 54–55.

Portraiture presented in dried fruit sculpture by Isabel Million.

Eaton, Allen H. *Handicrafts of the Southern Highlands*. New York: Russell Sage Foundation, 1937; rpt. Dover, 1973. 370p.

Chapter on dolls, toys, and miniature furniture.

Fawcett, Clara H. "Wooden Dolls For the Young Collector." *Hobbies*, LXVI (April 1961), 36–37.

A brief article on Helen Bullard and her dolls, with 3 photographs.

Foley, Daniel J. *Toys Through the Ages; Dan Foley's Story of Playthings, Filled With History, Folklore, Romance & Nostalgia. A Book for All Ages.* Philadelphia: Chilton Books, 1962. 145p.

Chapter 12, Toys in the New World, tells of the "play pretties" of the Southern Highlands: gee haw whimmydiddle, fly killer, howler, flipperdinger, clubs, slingshots, airguns, bows and arrows, corncob and cornhusk dolls, whistles, balls, etc.

King, H. David. "Folk Toys, Or What's a Gee Haw Whimmydiddle, Anyhow?" N.d. 9p. Student paper, Riedl Collection, Univ. of Tennessee Library, Knoxville.

A description of the toy, how it is made, and its probable original use.

McConnell, John C. "The Dumbull or Scrauncher." *Tennessee Folklore Society Bulletin*, XXV (Sept. 1959), 89.

A widely distributed noisemaker.

Mills, Winifred H., and Louise M. Dunn. *The Story of Old Dolls and How To Make Them*. New York: Doubleday, 1940. 234p.

Mentions cornhusk dolls in Tennessee.

Pettit, Florence. *How to Make Whirligigs and Whimmy Diddles and Other American Folkcraft Objects*. New York: Thomas Y. Crowell Co., 1972. 349p.

Includes corn shuck dolls. Gives detailed instructions for tools and materials.

Schnacke, Dick. *American Folk Toys: 85 American Folk Toys and How To Make Them*. New York: Putnam's, 1973. 219p.

Toys popular in the Middle and Southern Appalachian region. Includes crow calls and turkey calls. Contains instructions, diagrams, and materials needed.

XXII. Riddles and Rhymes

Riddles

Carter, Isabel Gordon. "Mountain White Riddles." *Journal of American Folklore,* XLVII (Jan.-March 1934), 76–80.

Riddles collected in eastern Tennessee and western North Carolina.

Farr, T.J. "Riddles and Superstitions of Middle Tennessee." *Journal of American Folklore,* XLVIII (Oct.-Dec. 1935), 318–36.

Contains 110 riddles, 59 folk remedies, 35 bad luck omens, 15 good luck omens, 16 babies, 14 death, 17 love and marriage, 23 weather, 12 influence of the moon, 10 signs of the Zodiac, 11 plants and seed, 12 wishes, and others. Almost entirely a duplicate of Farr's "Riddles of Middle Tennessee" and "Tennessee Superstitions and Beliefs," in *Tennessee Folklore Society Bulletin,* Volume I.

———. "Riddles of Middle Tennessee." *Tennessee Folklore Society Bulletin,* I (Oct. 1935), 1–14.

Has 110 folk riddles.

Halpert, Herbert. "East Tennessee Question-And-Answer Tales; A Folk Riddle Collection of Frances Boshears, Stearns, Kentucky." *Tennessee Folklore Society Bulletin,* XVIII (Dec. 1952), 101–103.

Eight riddle questions used in Scott County, Tennessee.

———. "Riddles from West Tennessee." *Tennessee Folklore Society Bulletin,* XVIII (June 1952), 29–42.

Has 60 riddles, limited to "true riddles" as defined by Professor Archer Taylor. The majority of riddles are from Henry County.

Justus, May. *The Complete Peddler's Pack: Games, Songs, Rhymes, and Riddles from Mountain Folklore.* Knoxville: Univ. of Tennessee Press, 1967. 100p. Revised edition of *Peddler's Pack,* 1957.

Nonsense rhymes, riddles, tongue-twisters, counting-out rhymes, songs and sing-

ing games, play-party games, and signs and predictions.

Redfield, W.A. "A Collection of Middle Tennessee Riddles." *Southern Folklore Quarterly,* II (Sept. 1937), 35–50.

Has 144 riddles collected from students of Pleasant Hill Academy, Cumberland Plateau.

Taylor, Archer. *English Riddles from Oral Tradition.* Berkeley: Univ. of California Press, 1951. 959p.

Has a number of riddles from Tennessee sources.

———, "Riddles." In White, Newman Ivey, *The Frank C. Brown Collection of North Carolina Folklore,* Vol. I. Durham: Duke Univ. Press, 1952.

Many references to Tennessee in footnotes.

Rhymes

Bolton, Henry Carrington. *The Counting-Out Rhymes of Children: Their Antiquity, Origin and Wide Distribution. A Study in Folk-Lore.* New York: D. Appleton & Co., 1888; rpt. Singing Tree Press, Book Tower, 1969. 121p.

Ten references to Tennessee.

Brewton, John E. "Folk Rimes of Southern Children." *Tennessee Folklore Society Bulletin,* XXVI (Dec. 1960), 92–99.

"Consideration is given to those rimes, chants, and jingles which have been transmitted by children to children rather than by adults to children."

Flowers, Paul. "Rhymes, Songs and Ditties." *Tennessee Folklore Society Bulletin,* X (Sept. 1944), 7–9.

Familiar "old bits of nonsense" sent by readers to his column the "Greenhouse," *Memphis Commercial Appeal.*

Harder, Kelsie B. "Jingle Lore of Pigtales,

Pals and Puppy Love." *Tennessee Folklore Society Bulletin*, XXII (March 1956), 1–9.

A discussion of album rhymes and friendship verses.

Justus, May. *The Complete Peddler's Pack: Games, Songs, Rhymes, and Riddles from Mountain Folklore.* (See entry under Riddles.)

King, Myrna. "Skip-Rope Rhymes in Bell Buckle, Tennessee." *Tennessee Folklore Society Bulletin*, XXXVIII (March 1972), 11–19.

Has 67 rhymes collected from students and others at Bell Buckle School.

Nulton, Lucy. "Jump Rope Rhymes as Folk Literature." *Journal of American Folklore*, LX (Jan.-March 1948), 53–67.

Narrative, dramatic conversations, and humor. One recorded in Tennessee.

Olson, Margaret. "Rhymes of Childhood." In Faulkner, Charles H., and Carol K. Buckles, eds., *Glimpses of Southern Appalachian Folk Culture: Papers in Memory of Norbert F. Riedl.* [Knoxville]: Tennessee Anthropological Association, 1978. (Miscellaneous Paper No. 3.)

Jump rope rhymes are emphasized, with the exclusion of rhymes used to accompany games.

Talley, Thomas W. *Negro Folk Rhymes Wise and Otherwise: With a Study.* New York: Macmillan, 1922; rpt. Port Washington, N.Y.: Kennikat Press, 1968. 347p.

Love songs, dance songs, animal and nature lore, nursery rhymes, charms and superstitions, play songs, and others. With a treatise on the use, origin, and evolution of the Negro rhyme. Has Tennessee field calls and responses.

XXIII. Folk Narratives

Legends of the Supernatural

Agee, Hugh. "Ghost Lore From Sevier County, Tennessee." *Tennessee Folklore Society Bulletin*, XXXIX (March 1973), 8–10.

Four incidents, told by a native of Sevierville.

Anderson, Geneva. "Tennessee Tall Tales." *Tennessee Folklore Society Bulletin* (Oct. 1939), 51–65.

Tall tales of hunting, witchcraft, and haunted houses, as told by individuals in East Tennessee who heard them from fathers and grandfathers.

Auer, Maria. "The Uncanny in East Tennessee." *Tennessee Folklore Society Bulletin*, XXIX (Sept. 1963), 60–63.

Ghost stories.

Bandy, Lewis David. "Witchcraft and Divination in Macon County." *Tennessee Folklore Society Bulletin*, IX (May 1943), 1–13.

Stories showing old beliefs in witches and spirits, including one on water-witching, as told to the author.

Barr, Gladys. "Witchcraft in Tennessee." *Tennessee Valley Historical Review*, II (Fall 1973), 24–29.

Two trials, folk beliefs, and the Bell Witch.

Baughman, Ernest W. *Type and Motif-Index of the Folktales of England and North America.* The Hague: Mouton and Co., 1966. 606p. (Indiana University Folklore Series No. 20.)

This standard American folktale index includes a good bibliography. It has many references to Tennessee.

Bell, Charles Bailey. *The Bell Witch: A*

Mysterious Spirit. Nashville: The Author, 1934. 228p. (Bound with Miller, Harriet Parks, *The Bell Witch of Middle Tennessee*. Clarksville, Tenn.: Leaf-Chronicle Publishing Co., 1930. 72p.)

An account of the presence and activities of the Witch, which members of the Bell family preferred to call a Spirit, in Robertson County, Tennessee, from 1816 to 1820, and its return in 1828.

Bolté, Mary. *Dark and Bloodied Ground*. Photographs by Mary Eastman. Riverside, Conn.: Chatham Press, 1973. 128p.

Stories and legends of evil and the supernatural include "John Brown's Tavern" at Moccasin Bend, "The Bell Witch"; and "The Reelfoot Legend."

Clinard, Pam, and Laura Drew. "Bell Witch," 1972–161. Unpublished MSS. 32, 18p. Western Kentucky Univ. Folklore, Folklife, and Oral History Archives.

A collection from printed sources and accounts by informant interviews.

Crawley, Clyde, Jr. "Tales of Ghosts and the Supernatural from East Tennessee," 1974–84. Unpublished MSS. 29p. Western Kentucky Univ. Folklore, Folklife, and Oral History Archives.

Seven stories from Bradley County, Tennessee.

Edwards, Lawrence. "The Old Scratch and the Mean Woman." *Tennessee Folklore Society Bulletin*, XVII (Dec. 1951), 72–76.

A ghost story heard when the author was a boy.

"The Famous Bell Witch." *Tennessee Conservationist*, XXV (June 1959), 11, 21.

A brief account of the Bell Witch.

Gower, Herschel. "Mildred Haun: The Persistence of the Supernatural." *Louisana Studies*, VII (Spring 1968), 65–71.

"Mildred Haun's stories in *The Hawk's Done Gone* are strong evidence to support the persistence of the supernatural among the folk."

Hall, Joseph S. "Witchlore and Ghostlore in the Great Smokies." *Tennessee Folklore Society Bulletin*, XXXVI (March, June 1970), 1–6; 31–36.

The identification of witches, counter measures, and other superstitions concerning witches and ghosts.

Hargrave, Harry A. "Demonic Visits of the Bell Witch." *North Carolina Folklore Journal*, XXIII (May 1975), 47–55.

"My retelling of a few of the many episodes is with some hope of bringing into order the events that have often been recorded."

Haun, Mildred. *The Hawk's Done Gone, and Other Stories*. Ed. Herschel Gower. Nashville: Vanderbilt Univ. Press, 1968. 356p. (First published in 1940 by Bobbs-Merrill, Indianapolis.)

A collection of fictional stories full of folk material, such as old proverbs, beliefs in the supernatural, and speech. Includes several stories on the Melungeons.

Hudson, Arthur Palmer, and Pete Kyle McCarter. "The Bell Witch of Tennessee and Mississippi: A Folk Legend." *Journal of American Folklore*, XLVII (Jan.-March 1934), 45–63.

This version of the legend has been recovered exclusively from oral traditions in Mississippi. Footnotes give comparison with Ingram and Miller accounts.

Hurdle, Virginia Jo. "Folklore of a Negro Couple in Henry County." Ed. Herbert Halpert. *Tennessee Folklore Society Bulletin*, XIX (Sept. 1953), 71–78.

Interviews with an elderly Negro couple in Paris, Tennessee, concerning stories of the supernatural and folk medicine.

Ingram, M.V. *An Authenticated History of the Famous Bell Witch*. Clarksville, Tenn.: The Author, 1894. Rpt. Nashville: Rare Book Reprints, 1961. 316p.

The story of the Bell Witch, including the account by Richard Williams Bell, who "it seems was the only one who kept a diary of what transpired, which he put in shape in 1846."

Johnson, Kathy McH. "The Legend of

the Bell Witch." *North Carolina Folklore Journal*, XXII (Aug. 1976), 43–48.

Lists "motifs, some of which can be found in *Thompson's Motif-Index of Folk-Literature*, illustrated in the Bell Witch legends."

Karl, Debbie. "Folktale: The Bell Witch: Witch or Ghost," 1970–40. Unpublished MSS. 23p. Western Kentucky Univ. Folklore, Folklife, and Oral History Archives.

Based on accounts in Ingram's *Authenticated History of the Bell Witch*, with eight stories told to the author by several informers.

Lett, Anna. "Some West Tennessee Superstitions about Conjurers, Witches, Ghosts and the Devil." *Tennessee Folklore Society Bulletin*, XXXVI (June 1970), 37–45.

Over 100 superstitions, many of them countermeasures to break a spell.

Lumpkin, Ben Gray. "Stories from Montgomery County." *Tennessee Folklore Society Bulletin*, XLI (Sept. 1975), 126–27.

Several brief stories of ghosts, recalled by Mrs. Marion Henry Hamner and by Dr. Robin Ferguson.

Marlowe, Mikii. "The Supernatural in Summerfield." *Tennessee Folklore Society Bulletin*, XXVII (Sept. 1961), 52–55.

Three stories of witchcraft and the supernatural, told in Grundy County, Tenn.

Miller, Harriet Parks. *The Bell Witch of Middle Tennessee*. Clarksville, Tenn.: Leaf-Chronicle Publishing Co., 1930. 72p. (Bound with Bell, Charles Bailey, *The Bell Witch: A Mysterious Spirit*. Nashville: The Author, 1934. 228p.)

The story of the Bell Witch, incorporating the accounts of various individuals, "data secured from reliable people, some of whom visited the Bell home."

Miller, Olive Beaupré. *Heroes, Outlaws & Funny Fellows of American Popular Tales*. New York: Doubleday, 1940. 332p.

Includes "The Bell Witch: A Folk Tale of North Carolina, Tennessee and Mississippi."

O'Dell, Ruth W. "An East Tennessee Ghost Tale." *Tennessee Folklore Society Bulletin*, XX (June 1954), 42–43.

"The Long Dog" appeared after a murder by the John A. Murrell gang.

——— . "The Moonshine Still Ghost." *Tennessee Folklore Society Bulletin*, XX (Sept. 1954), 57.

A ghost story from Cocke County, Tenn.

——— . "The Warping Log Chains." *Tennessee Folklore Society Bulletin*, XX (March 1954), 13–14.

A ghost story from East Tennessee.

Petrocelli, Joseph. "The Bell Witch," 1970–42. Unpublished MSS. 48p. Western Kentucky Univ. Folklore, Folklife, and Oral History Archives.

Stories and comments about the Bell Witch by residents of Adams, Tennessee, and neighboring areas.

Reynolds, James. *Ghosts in American Houses*. New York: Farrar, Straus and Cudahy, 1955. 229p.

"The Longest Boy in Tennessee, Memphis, 1845," pp. 219–29, gives an account of Raike Gaston and mentions his appearances as an apparition leaving a crudely drawn rake head as his sign.

Salmon, Lourene. "The Tale of the Mysterious Barrel and Other 'Haint' Tales Collected in Big Springs." *Tennessee Folklore Society Bulletin*, XXXVII (Sept. 1971), 59–72.

Mysterious happenings in Rutherford County, Tenn.

Spears, James E. "Five Original Negro Vignettes." *Tennessee Folklore Society Bulletin*, XXXVII (June 1971), 40–45.

Stories about strange happenings.

Thornell, Fran. " 'The Handerchief Story' and 'The Haunted House': Two Middle Tennessee Ghost Stories." *Tennessee*

Folklore Society Bulletin, XIX (June 1978), 71–75.
> Stories from Smith and Stewart counties.

Trewhitt, Frank G. "Ghost Tales from Bradley County." *Tennessee Folklore Society Bulletin*, XXIX (March 1963), 10–12.
> Several stories of mysterious events.

Welsh, Jack. "The Bell Witch." *Kentucky Folklore Record*, XIX (Oct.-Dec. 1973), 112–16.
> An interview with two members of the Bell family concerning the Witch.

Wiltse, Henry M. "In the Southern Field of Folk-Lore." *Journal of American Folklore*, XIII (July-Sept. 1900), 209–12.
> Three tales of witchcraft from Scott County, Tenn., and the Cumberland Mountains.

Other Legends

Auer, Maria. "Big Nat Stories from East Tennessee." *Tennessee Folklore Society Bulletin*, XXIX (March 1963), 12–14.
> Big Nat Wagner of Johnson City.

Boynton, Percy H. "Popular Story and Song." *Literature and American Life*. New York: Ginn and Co., 1936. Pp. 601–624.
> A summary of tall tales about real and legendary figures, and songs that came out of the southwest frontier.

Howse, Ruth Whitener. "Mills Darden: The Giant of Tennessee, World's Largest

Man." *Tennessee Folklore Society Bulletin*, XVII (Dec. 1951), 82–83.

Lloyd, A. Dennis. "The Legend of Granny White." *Tennessee Historical Quarterly*, XXVII (Fall 1968), 257–61.
> "Fact and fiction have become so thoroughly mixed . . . that one doubts his ability to determine who she actually was and what circumstances surrounded her influence on Middle Tennessee." This is the woman for whom Granny White Pike was named.

Turner, Robert Randolph. "Tennessee Legends: An Analysis in Terms of Motifs, Structure, and Style." Ph.D. diss. George Peabody College for Teachers, 1970. 494p.
> A study of 13 theses written at Peabody, containing Tennessee legends, from which the author has framed the following categories: ghost tales; personal legends; place legends; historical legends; witch stories; joke, jest, and lie, a final catch-all.

See also other legends in the following sections:
Section IV, General Sources
Walker, *Tennessee Tales*.
Section XVI, Folklore—General
A Collection of Folklore . . . ; Doran, "Folklore in White County, Tennessee"; Fowler, "Stories and Legends of Maury County, Tennessee."
Section XXIV, Humor and Folk Tales
Dorson, ed., *Davy Crockett, American Comic Legend*; Dorson, "Davy Crockett and the Heroic Age"; Dorson, "Sources of Davy Crockett, American Comic Legend"; Mason, *Folk Tales of Cannon County*.

XXIV. Humor and Folk Tales

Anderson, Geneva. "Tennessee Tall Tales." *Tennessee Folklore Society Bulletin*, V (Oct. 1939), 51–65.
> Tall tales of hunting, witchcraft, and

haunted houses as told by individuals in East Tennessee who heard them from fathers and grandfathers.

Anderson, John Q., comp. *With the Bark*

On; Popular Humor of the Old South.
Nashville: Vanderbilt Univ. Press, 1967.
337p.

A collection of humorous stories taken
from newspapers and magazines from 1835
to 1860. Several stories from Tennessee.
Grouped by subjects: The River; The Back-
country; Varmints and Hunters; Fun and
Frolic; The Professions; Jokes and Jokers;
Masculine Amusements; Politicians, Ac-
tors, Yokels in the City.

Aswell, James R., et al. *God Bless the
Devil! Liars' Bench Tales.* Chapel Hill:
Univ. of North Carolina Press, 1940.
254p.

Has 26 stories collected by members of
the Tennessee Writers' Project, including 7
Negro stories and 4 Melungeon tales.

Baughman, Ernest W. *Type and Motif-
Index of the Folktales of England and
North America.* The Hague: Mouton and
Co., 1966. 606p. (Indiana University
Folklore Series, No. 20.)

This standard American folktale index
includes a good bibliography. It has many
references to Tennessee material.

Blair, Walter. *Horse Sense in American
Humor: From Benjamin Franklin to
Ogden Nash.* Chicago: Univ. of Chicago
Press, 1942. 341p.

Chapter II, David Crockett: Horse Sense
on the Frontier, pictures Crockett as seen
in contemporary newspaper accounts, and
in his own words.

——— . *Native American Humor, 1800–
1900.* New York: American Book Co.,
1937; rpt. San Francisco: Chandler Publishing Co., 1960. 573p.

"Definitely, much of this literature had
its origin in the Greatest American folk
art . . . the art of oral story-telling." Includes humor of Davy Crockett and George
Washington Harris.

——— . *Tall Tale America: A Legendary
History of Our Humerous Heroes.* New
York: Coward McCann, 1944. 262p.

Tall tales about the Crocketts, including
Davy Crockett, Tennessee Settler; Davy
Crockett, Soldier, Congressman and Comet
Licker.

——— . "Traditions in Southern Humor." *American Quarterly,* V (Summer
1953), 132–42.

The influence of tall tales and folk tradition on Southern humor between 1830 and
1867.

Boatright, Mody C. *Folk Laughter on the
American Frontier.* New York: Macmillan, 1949. 182p.

Contains Davy Crockett stories and a
few other references to Tennessee.

Botkin, B.A., ed. *A Treasury of American
Folklore: Stories, Ballads, and Traditions
of the People.* New York: Crown, 1944.
932p.

Sketches, tall tales, and ballads, including John Henry, Casey Jones, Davy Crockett, and Robert Love Taylor's stories, and
the Bell Witch.

Carter, Isabel Gordon. "Mountain White
Folk-lore: Tales from the Southern Blue
Ridge." *Journal of American Folklore,*
XXXVIII (July-Sept. 1925), 340–74.

Eight East Tennessee tales.

Crockett, David. *A Narrative of the Life
of David Crockett of the State of Tennessee.* Facsimile edition with Annotations and an Introduction by James A.
Shackford and Stanley J. Folmsbee.
Knoxville: Univ. of Tennessee Press,
1973. 211p. (Tennesseana Editions.)

"Here in the *Narrative* may be discovered the factual roots of the real David
Crockett, the frontier humorist and teller
of tall tales, the naive yet wily mountaineer who feigned more ignorance than could
be found in his makeup, the politician, the
Indian fighter, and the rough-and-ready
hero." An early example of American
humor, proverbial expressions, tall tales.

Day, Donald. "The Life and Works of
George Washington Harris." Unpubl.
diss. Univ. of Chicago, 1942. 124p.

Helpful both for the discussion of the Sut
Lovingood writings and for Harris's description of life in Knoxville and East Tennessee during the 1820–40 era.

Dorson, Richard M., ed. *Davy Crockett,
American Comic Legend.* New York:

Printed at the Spiral Press for Rockland Editions, 1939. 171p.

Tall tales and legends from the Crockett almanacs.

———. "Davy Crockett and the Heroic Age." *Southern Folklore Quarterly*, VI (June 1942), 95–102.

Elements of the Davy Crockett legends common to old world heroic narratives.

———. "The Sources of Davy Crockett, American Comic Legend." *Midwest Folklore*, VIII (Fall 1958), 143–49.

Lists the Crockett stories in *Davy Crockett's Almanacks*, 1835–56.

Edwards, Lawrence. *Gravel in My Shoe: Tales and Talk of Mine Own People in the Cumberland Wonderland Before the Invasion of Messrs. Ford and MacAdam Brought the Triumph of Machine Over Man.* Montevallo, Ala.: Times Printing Co., 1963. 181p.

A series of sketches about the author's native Claiborne County, Tennessee: The People; Ghost Tales; Tall Tales; The Boys; Scrap Lumber.

———. *Tall Tales of Uncle Miles*. N.p., n.d. 19p.

Stories told at the country store.

Garland, Ruth W. "Tales Told in Lincoln County, Tennessee." *Tennessee Folklore Society Bulletin*, XXI (March 1955), 11–13.

Five brief tales.

"Go Ahead!" Davy Crockett's Almanack of Wild Sports of the West, and Life in The Backwoods Calculated for All the States in the Union. 1835. Nashville: Snag and Sawyer, 1834. 47p.

Contains the usual calendar, but most of the contents are tall tales and block prints.

Gordon, Robert. "Hunting Lies and Fishy Stories from Bedford County." *Tennessee Folklore Society Bulletin*, XLIII (March 1977), 23–26.

Five tales.

Hall, Wade. *The Smiling Phoenix:*

Southern Humor from 1865 to 1914. Gainesville: Univ. of Florida Press, 1965. 375p.

Amusing sketches of pioneer and backwoods life. Anecdotes from Srygley, Crockett, John Trotwood Moore, and Robert L. Taylor.

Halpert, Herbert. "The Folktale in Tennessee." *Tennessee Folklore Society Bulletin*, XXII (June 1956), 36–39.

A discussion of published Tennessee folktales, a few private collections, and an appeal for more scholarly interest.

Harris, George Washington. *High Times and Hard Times: Sketches and Tales by George Washington Harris.* Ed. M. Thomas Inge. Nashville: Vanderbilt Univ. Press, 1967. 348p.

"The purpose of this volume is to make available to both the scholar and the general reader, in an authoritative but readable text, Harris's uncollected writings." Contains 48 stories, one poem, and a good bibliography.

———. *Sut Lovingood: Yarns Spun by a "Nat'ral Born Durn'd Fool."* New York: Fitzgerald Publishing Corp., 1867. 200p.

One of the most original of the humorists of the Old Southwest.

———. *Sut Lovingood's Yarns*. Edited for the Modern Reader by M. Thomas Inge. New Haven: College and Univ. Press, 1966. 336p.

"This edition contains the best of the Sut Lovingood sketches written by Harris between 1854 and 1869, the year of his death." Has a useful introduction by the editor.

Inge, M. Thomas, ed. *The Frontier Humorists: Critical Reviews.* Hamden, Conn.: Archon Books, Shoe String Press, 1975. 331p.

A collection of articles on tall tales and humor of the Old Southwest, by and about various authors. Includes material on George Washington Harris and David Crockett, with a bibliography by Charles E. Davis and Martha B. Hudson.

Jagendorf, M.A. *Folk Stories of the*

South. New York: Vanguard Press, 1972. 355p.

Eleven tales from Tennessee.

Jones, Dazzie Lee. "Some Folktales from Negro College Students." *Tennessee Folklore Society Bulletin,* XXIV (Sept. 1958), 102–11.

Ten stories from Alabama, Mississippi, Tennessee, and Virginia, told by college students of urban tradition.

Jordan, Philip D. "Humor of the Backwoods, 1820–1840." *Mississippi Valley Historical Review,* XXV (June 1938), 25–38.

"A native wit was apparent and its backwoods element perhaps was at its best during the two decades under discussion." David Crockett and Andrew Jackson are the principal Tennessee subjects.

Knight, Donald Robert. "Religion as a Subject of Southwestern Humor." Unpubl. Master's thesis, Univ. of Tennessee, 1967. 73p.

The chapters titled Circuit Rider, Burlesque Sermon, and Denominational Joke all include Sut Lovingood stories.

Mason, Robert L. *Folk Tales of Cannon County.* Woodbury, Tenn.: Cannon County Historical Society, 1977. 62p. (Cannon County Historical Society, Publication No. 1.)

Tales and legends.

Mathes, Hodge. *Tall Tales from Old Smoky.* Kingsport, Tenn.: Southern Publishers, 1952. 241p.

Stories written about mountain people.

Meine, Franklin J., ed. *The Crockett Almanacks, Nashville Series, 1835–1838.* Edited, with an Introduction by Franklin J. Meine and with a Note on Their Humor by Harry J. Owens. Chicago: Caxton Club, 1955. 150p.

A reprint of "Go Ahead! Davy Crockett's Almanack, of Wild Sports of the West, and Life in the Backwoods. Calculated for all the States in the Union."

——— . *Tall Tales of the Southwest: An Anthology of Southern and Southwestern Humor, 1830–1860.* New York: Knopf, 1930. 456p.

The collection contains one story attributed to David Crockett and five stories by George W. Harris. A good introduction to Southern humorists.

Pearce, James. T. "Folk Tales of the Southern Poor-White, 1820–1860." *Journal of American Folklore,* LXIII (Oct.-Dec. 1950), 398–412.

Discussion of various folk tales and folk heroes as indicative of the thought processes of the poor whites. References to the Bell Witch story and to Davy Crockett tales.

Penrod, James. "Folk Humor in Sut Lovingood's Yarns." *Tennessee Folklore Society Bulletin,* XVI (Dec. 1950), 76–84.

"Concerned with an analysis of . . . sketches of folk customs, tall talk, rambling narration and comic sayings, reflecting mountaineer attitudes."

——— . "The Folk Mind in Early Southwestern Humor." *Tennessee Folklore Society Bulletin,* XVIII (June 1952), 49–54.

Folk superstitions and the frontiersman's view of culture as shown by yarnspinners in the generation before the Civil War. Includes Sut Lovingood.

——— . "Teachers and Preachers in the Old Southwestern Yarns." *Tennessee Folklore Society Bulletin,* XVIII (Dec. 1952), 91–96.

Includes Sut Lovingood's depiction of preachers.

——— . "Two Types of Incongruity in Old Southwestern Humor." *Kentucky Folklore Record,* IV (1958), 163–73.

Includes Sut Lovingood yarns.

Plater, Ormonde. "Narrative Folklore in the Works of George Washington Harris." Unpubl. diss. Tulane Univ., 1969. 338p.

"The purpose of this study is to identify tale types and motifs in Harris's works, and to show how Harris uses folklore to express his view of mankind and the quality of Sut

Lovingood's imagination." Diss. Abs. 4461-A, 1970.

―――― . "Tall Tales and Tall Talk in the Sut Lovingood Stories: An Oral Tradition Influences a Literary Technique." Unpubl. Master's thesis, Tulane Univ., 1965. 125p.

An analysis of the stories with reference to folk elements and customs, dialect and attitudes of the East Tennessee mountaineer.

Rhea, Carolina McQueen. "Sketches and Legends of Upper East Tennessee." Unpubl. Master's thesis, George Peabody College for Teachers, 1932. 325p.

A variety of stories told by elderly citizens about individuals who were early settlers; some hunting stories, ghost stories, Negro stories, and places.

Rickels, Milton. *George Washington Harris.* New York: Twayne Publishers, 1965. 159p.

Biographical and critical information, with a selective bibliography.

Roberts, Leonard. "Folktales Told in Tennessee: I, Jack and the Beanstalk." *Tennessee Folklore Society Bulletin,* XXI (June 1955), 33–35.

A version told by a 97-year-old man in Oneida.

Rodes, Sara. "Folktales Told in Tennessee: II, Bluebonnet." *Tennessee Folklore Society Bulletin,* XXI (June 1955), 35–37.

A well-known story as told by a grandmother in Putnam County.

Rogers, E.G. "More Tall Tales from Tennessee." *Southern Folklore Quarterly,* XXV (Sept. 1961), 178–83.

Eleven stories gathered by students. The majority of stories are from the TVA region and the Valley of East Tennessee.

―――― . "Tall Tales from Tennessee." *Southern Folklore Quarterly,* XIX (Dec. 1955), 237–42.

Nine tales from East Tennessee "typical of the area."

Rourke, Constance. *American Humor: A Study of the National Character.* New York: Harcourt, Brace, 1931. 324p.

Shows the effect of backwoods tales, the Crockett almanacs, the folk theater, etc., on American literature. Has a good bibliography.

Stephens, J. Harold. *Echoes from the Hills: (Tall Tales from Tennessee).* Hattiesburg, Miss.: The Author, 1966. 75p.

A collection of humorous anecdotes, having few tall tales.

Tandy, Jennette. *Crackerbox Philosophers in American Humor and Satire.* New York: Columbia Univ. Press, 1925. 181p.

Chapter IV treats the Development of Southern Humorists. "The first Southern humorist was an out-and-out frontiersman," David Crockett. Harris's Sut Lovingood is also included.

Taylor, Robert Love. *Lectures and Best Literary Productions of Bob Taylor.* Nashville: Bob Taylor Publishing Co., 1912. 354p.

Full of humorous anecdotes.

Tharp, Mel. "A Social Study of Mountain Folk Humor." *Tennessee Folklore Society Bulletin,* XLIII (Dec. 1977), 186–187.

Four anecdotes.

Vincent, Bert. *Bert Vincent's Strolling, Being Sort of a Sideglance at the Little Odds and Ends of Life in These Parts.* Knoxville: W. L. Warters Co., 1940. 47p.

―――― . *The Best Stories of Bert Vincent.* Ed. Willard Yarbrough. [Maryville]: Printed by Marion R. Mangrum, Brazos Press, 1968. 208p.

―――― . *Here in Tennessee.* Knoxville: n.p., 1945.

―――― . *More of the Best Stories of Bert Vincent.* Published by Marion R. Mangrum, [Maryville]: Brazos Press, 1970. 207p.

————— . *Us Mountain Folks*. Second revised print of *Bert Vincent's Strolling*.
Knoxville: W. L. Warters Co., 1940. 60p.

Mountain stories "to picture some of the
life, and folklore, and traditions of a people
who have lived here hundreds of years before tourists discovered the area's beauty,
and the TVA came." All of the Bert Vincent
volumes are full of stories and legends,
superstitions, and hants, from Vincent's
strolling column in the *Knoxville News-
Sentinel*.

Williams, Cratis. "Sut Lovingood as a
Southern Mountaineer." *Appalachian
State Teachers College Faculty Publica-
tions*, XLIV (April 1966), 1–4.

Described as epitomizing the Southern
mountaineer, with "few counterparts in
mountain fiction." "One of the more en-
during mountain character types, feud
leaders and moonshiners not withstand-
ing."

Author Index

Govan, Gilbert E., 29
Gower, Herschel, 96, 112
Grafton, Sandra S., 107
Grant, Madison, 4
Gray, John W., 17
Gray, Lewis Cecil, 42
Green, Archie, 104
Green, William M., 65
Greene, Bruce, 105
Greene, Howard, 17
Greene, Maude, 80, 92
Greene, Robert B., 106
Greenway, John, 107
Greve, Jeanette S., 29
Griffin, William J., 71, 83
Grise, George C., 77
Grossman, Charles S., 37
Guild, Josephus C., 17
Guilland, Harold F., 47, 49
Gunn, John C., 88
Gunter, Charles R., Jr., 92

Häcker, J.G., 7
Haden, Walter D., 106
Hahn, Phyllis Elizabeth, 6
Hale, Will T., 18, 26, 31
Hall, Frederick, 18
Hall, James, 62
Hall, Joseph S., 18, 71, 76, 100, 112
Hall, Russell, 18
Hall, Wade, 116
Hallum, John, 61
Halpert, Herbert, 76, 80, 81, 110, 112, 116
Hamer, Philip M., 26, 88
Hamilton, Gary, 92
Hand, Wayland D., 83, 88
Harbert, P.M., 34, 78
Harder, Kelsie B., 72, 77, 78, 84, 85, 88, 92, 110
Hargrave, Harry A., 112
Harlow, Alvin F., 57, 60
Harney, Andy Leon, 49
Harper, Herbert L., 41
Harrell, David Edwin, Jr., 88
Harris, Alberta, 72
Harris, George Washington, 116
Harrison, Bill, 92
Harrison, C. William, 62
Hart, John Frazer, 39, 40
Harvey, Frank, 2
Hatcher, J. Wesley, 18
Hatcher, Mildred, 42, 60, 84
Haun, Mildred, 92, 96, 112
Hawkins, Donald, 18
Hayes, Francis C., 73
Haywood, Charles, 2
Haywood, John, 61
Henderson, C.C., 31
Henderson, Connie, 102
Hendrix, D.B., 100

Henry, H.M., 62
Henry, Mellinger Edward, 2, 97
Herndon, Marion, 59
Hersh, Alan, 51
Hesseltine, W.B., 4
Hickerson, Daisy Faulkner, 84
Hicks, Nannie Lee, 37
Highsaw, Mary Wagner, 7
Hilliard, Addie Suggs, 76, 84, 88, 92
Hilliard, Sam Bowers, 54
Hills, J.L., 54
Hinton, Elmer, 73
Hoagland, H.E., 57
Hodges, Sidney Cecil, 45
Hoffman, Robert, 91
Holland, James Wendell, 57
Holmes, Jack D.L., 58
Holt, Albert C., 18
Hooker, Elizabeth R., 65
Horne, Dorothy D., 97, 102, 108
Horwitz, Elinor Lander, 45
Hovey, Rolf E., 101
Howard, H.R., 62
Howell, Morton B., 78
Howse, Ruth Whitener, 65, 97, 114
Hubbard, Freeman H., 57
Hudson, Arthur Palmer, 94, 97, 112
Hudson, J. Paul, 37
Huff, Vicki, 48
Hulan, Richard H., 37, 48, 105
Humphrey, Valerie L., 92
Humphreys, Cecil C., 34
Hunn, M., 18
Hunt, Raymond F., Jr., 51
Hurdle, Virginia Jo, 81, 112
Hutson, Andrew C., Jr., 49

Imes, William Lloyd, 62
Imlay, Gilbert, 18, 27
Ingram, M.V., 112
Inge, M. Thomas, 116
Irwin, John Rice, 18, 105
Ivey, Saundra Keyes, 9

Jackson, Bruce, 88
Jackson, Ewing, 93
Jackson, Frances Helen, 6, 43
Jackson, George Pullen, 102
Jackson, John B., 103
Jaffe, Harry Joe, 2
Jagendorf, M.A., 116
Johnson, Andrew W., 103
Johnson, Charles A., 66
Johnson, Clifton H., 66
Johnson, Guy B., 97, 98, 104
Johnson, Kathy McH., 112
Johnson, Leland R., 35
Johnson, Mary Elizabeth, 18
Jones, Alice Marie, 66
Jones, Dazzie Lee, 117

Subject Index

Tennessee Folk Culture was composed on the Mergenthaler Variable Input Phototypesetter in Trump Medieval type by Computer Composition, Inc., printed offset by Thomson-Shore, Inc., and bound by John H. Dekker & Sons. The book was designed by Jim Billingsley. The paper on which the book is printed bears the watermark of S.D. Warren and is designed for an effective life of at least three hundred years.

THE UNIVERSITY OF TENNESSEE PRESS : KNOXVILLE